THE
UNIFYING
FACTOR

THE UNIFYING FACTOR

A REVIEW OF KABBALAH

Nekhama Schoenburg

JASON ARONSON INC.
Northvale, New Jersey
London

This book was set in 12 pt. Granjon by Alpha Graphics in Pittsfield, New Hampshire.

Library of Congress Cataloging-in-Publication Data
Schoenburg, Nekhama, 1966–
    The unifying factor : a review of Kabbalah / by Nekhama
Schoenburg.
        p. cm.
    Includes bibliographical references and index.
    ISBN 1-56821-562-2 (alk. paper)
    1. Cabala—History. I. Title.
BM526.S335   1996
296.1'6—dc20   95-9630
                                                        CIP

Manufactured in the United States of America. Jason Aronson Inc. offers books and cassettes. For information and catalog write to Jason Aronson Inc., 230 Livingston Street, Northvale, New Jersey 07647.

For Mom and Dad

Contents

Preface

PHYSICS AND METAPHYSICS

Metaphysics is the missing piece to our existential puzzle and the source of answers to our questions of the sciences—natural, astrophysical, social, physical. As this book will try to elucidate, this piece comprises the bulk of reality. It is this piece that directed the big bang, motivated the building of the pyramids, and even guides human behavior to this day. And it is because this piece has not been incorporated into the various formal disciplines that progress and human understanding in general have reached their limit and still cannot explain all of existence.

I assess that people have steered away from metaphysics for one of three reasons: (1) fear of the unknown; (2) a sense of being overwhelmed by the very existence of the supernatural or by the diversity in explaining such concepts of eternity and all-pervasiveness—the many religions, doctrines, and cults that exist all seem to conflict in the way they explain our existential questions; and, finally, (3) there are those who assert that the pursuit of understanding the supernatural or metaphysics is sacrilegious or, more specifically, antithetical to Judeo-Christian doctrine.

This book purports to dispel, or at least assuage, the first two concerns by providing a *road map* and *globe* to indicate exactly where each doctrine and principle fits and how they function vis-à-vis the picture at large. This grand, cosmic picture enables us to see where we fit in the grand scheme of things, just as it defines the various forces that dictate the laws of physics and metaphysics. What this book also strives to do is to correct the misunderstanding of the third category, by illustrating how the essence of Judaism and many of the principles and practices of Christianity are based on the science of Kabbalah.

In addition, I hope to impress upon the adherents of "scientism"[1] that metaphysics is not to be regarded as light entertainment. The forces discussed and tapped in metaphysics are real and powerful. Because of this, I have tried to keep discussions and explanations straightforward, with a bottom-line tone, as opposed to the typical mode of metaphysical discussion, being tabloidlike ghost stories. Moreover, I hope to provide the reader with some basics of how to begin to flow with, rather than against, the metaphysical forces that will be defined.

KABBALAH

The unification theory that modern science purports yet to discover was actually revealed with the Torah on Mount Sinai over 3,000 years ago. It is called Kabbalah. The metaphysical principles that Kabbalah lays out clearly demonstrate how theories like relativity and quantum mechanics are really one and the same. Thus, among other things, I will refer directly to Dr. Stephen Hawking's writings in *A Brief History of Time* and to the fundamental questions he poses regarding Creation, by applying kabbalistic concepts.

Kabbalists have been expressing "unification theories" throughout the ages, incorporating all natural phenomena. However, there have been several problems that have kept Kabbalah from the masses. For one thing, kabbalistic writings have been written in kabbalistic jargon without a key for the layman. Secondly, documented Kabbalah is tremendously voluminous. To get a picture of what Kabbalah is all about in its entirety, one would need to peruse many books, listen to dozens of lectures, and hear scores of tapes. Each book or lecture deals with only one aspect or a few particular teachings. To date, no one has consolidated and

---

1. Carl N. Klahr defines scientism in his essay "Science versus Scientism," as the "conviction . . . that the only valid answers to almost all questions of fact or philosophy must come from extrapolations of science. No other basis for human civilization but the derivations of science are recognized" (*Challenge*, p. 289).

summarized into one readable volume all of this information. Moreover, rabbis at different times have discouraged and even forbidden the study of Kabbalah. Yet, even where Kabbalah has been studied, it has still been restricted to its small circles of study. This volume attempts to overcome these various obstacles and provide an outline and overview of metaphysics for anybody and everybody.

The fundamental framework of my dissertation is the understanding of Kabbalah as taught by Rabbi Dr. Philip Berg, Dean of the Research Centre of Kabbalah. My first years of study of Kabbalah were through Rabbi Berg's teachings, in Israel and North America. And I definitely owe much gratitude to this master kabbalist, Rabbi Berg. But, while continuing these studies after a number of years and working to internalize and practice kabbalistic principles and tools, I have also assumed a self-study of Kabbalah through the writings of other kabbalists of our time.

UNITY

If there is one point I believe to be especially crucial, it is humankind's need to understand, on a metaphysical level, why fragmentation—of any kind—is destructive and even deadly. In an age of specialization, which is one form of fragmentation, and of political wake-up calls, I believe unity is truly the ultimate of all wake-up calls. And I intend to explain this in depth.

Thus, the theme of this book is unity. And one of its main goals is to alert and convince humankind as to the need to bring harmony to all conflicting things in our world, be it of nations and people or ideas and theories or forces and theories of all natures, physical and metaphysical. In line with this goal, I have tried to demonstrate unity's feasibility by illustrating metaphysical principles and insights from a small collage of diverse sources, from classical literature to the writing of various spiritual doctrines to the natural sciences. The picture at large offers a unification of physical theories, for example, of general relativity and quantum mechanics. It also reconciles perceived conflicts, say, between the theories of evolution and the Big Bang and the Bible's account of the seven–day creation of the world.

While Kabbalah is methodical and precise, any attempt to

map out a step-by-step comprehensive study program is "compli-cated" by the fact that everything in the universe, and hence in Kabbalah, is unified and thus all interconnected and interdependent. I have tried to include the essential concepts, to explain what Kabbalah really is. Yet for the sake of brevity and simplicity, some secondary points and concepts have been excluded. Even with those I do touch on, it is important to note that I have by no means exhausted any topic discussed on Kabbalah. For further reference, I have listed additional sources that are on a beginner's level and easily accessible. Kabbalah is an entire mode of thinking—a total way of life that inevitably involves a lifetime of study. I hope this book will whet the reader's appetite enough to pursue a deeper study of Kabbalah.

Introduction

WHY KABBALAH

Life seems to have become increasingly complex and difficult. Despite all the faith and funds we invest in science, medicine, and even government, things just don't seem to get any better for the individual, society as a whole, or even the planet. While we may be living longer and more luxurious lives in the Western world, new forms of crime, new kinds of disease, and new natural disasters continue to plague us and take us by surprise. Our various security systems and calculations seem to be to no avail. Is there really any such thing as certainty in our life? In this world?

Most of us would like to believe that there is such a thing as God; but even He doesn't seem to fit into the modern scheme of things. And *God* by whose definition? There are so many spiritual doctrines out there promising to have all the answers, from existential questions to health issues. How does one judge or evaluate all these answers and systems?

The good news is that there is such a thing as certainty and a solution to every ailment that ever plagued this planet and ever will. It is not a new product on the market. In fact, it is so ancient that its subject even predates time itself. It is like an old, well-established product that gets dusty on the shelf but makes a comeback as its magical powers are rediscovered. In his book *Zen and the Art of Motorcycle Maintenance*, Robert Pirsig encapsulates this point perfectly, when he writes, "The truth knocks on the door and you say, 'Go away, I'm looking for the truth,' and so it goes away. Puzzling" (p. 13). That is basically what we have been telling our source of all solutions.

But this is not a sales pitch. The answer referred to here does not cost anything. It does not ask anyone to wear certain clothes, leave our families or our jobs, subscribe to any group, or require any hi-tech contraptions. It does not even matter with which religion or spiritual doctrine we are affiliated. What it does do is provide an overview of everything that exists in our universe so that we can understand and then choose what is best for us. It merely *requests* that we raise our consciousness to the level of the picture at large, to see the world we live in from a new perspective. It also asks us to be willing to accept the possibility that there may be room for improvement in the way we look at the world and how we interact in it.

With a view from above, we can see where all the various spiritual doctrines fit—what each is designed to do and thus what each can and cannot do: What exactly is the power of the Star of David? Or of the pyramids and mummies? With a view from above we can reconcile the apparent conflict between science and religion regarding the creation of the world and claims to its future. With a view from above, each and everyone of us can see where we individually fit into the grand scheme of things, so we can discover our purpose in life.

The funny thing is that all the clues and signs as to how to solve all our problems are all around us; we just need to learn how to read those signs. Rabbi Dr. Philip S. Berg[1] uses the neatest metaphor to illustrate this. For most of us, life is like driving down a highway at night without our lights on. The signs are everywhere as we drive along, but since we haven't activated our lights to reveal those signs, it is as if they do not exist. But to be sure, our direction signs are right there; they simply are not revealed. This book purports to fulfill a number of objectives, one of which is to show how we can activate the light within us so that we can steer ourselves on the right road to reach our destination.

Already from the title, one may be a bit apprehensive, since, after all, Kabbalah is "something Jewish." How can something Jewish solve all or even some of our problems and improve the quality of our lives? How does this assertion accord with the fact that—de-

---

1. From his recorded special lecture on "How to Bring Moshiach to Our Lives."

spite their Kabbalah—the Jews have been hated since the inception of Judaism, they have been enslaved twice, and they have had to endure pogroms, persecution, the Inquisition, and the Holocaust while active anti-Semitism continues to this very day? Who is anybody trying to fool?! But it is through Kabbalah that we will receive our answers.

In her book on modern witchcraft, Robin Skelton says, "A strong belief in anything is productive of psychic energy. What we believe has reality for us; we are what we believe we are" (p. 23).[2]

Since this book will address something that is anything but time or space bound, the above is particularly important to address and argue against, since it points to the very point that Kabbalah has to offer. Kabbalah would say that, first of all, the word *belief* is a term of art that needs to be defined. To attach any old meaning to the word does not give it any real, metaphysical connections.

There have been Jews who for centuries have had what they defined and thought to be a strong belief. Jews have gone to miserable deaths with a belief in God's existence in their hearts. Has that helped them? Apparently not.

According to Kabbalah, self-defined belief is not sufficient. In chapter 5, we will define what the word "belief" means, as its definition relates to a very specific means of bridging the spiritual world with the physical. To draw the protective, healing, all-powerful energy of God (however one wishes to define God), one needs to make the right connections, as it were. In more mechanical terms, that means that to reap any benefits, one needs to know how to (a) activate spiritual energy, (b) establish the proper wiring, and (c) make the connection or communication.

It is precisely because of these requisites that this volume is laid out the way it is. In Part I, we will discuss Creation to know from where all existence derives. In Section II, we will discuss the means to activate the energy of God. In Section III, we will touch on the various means of wiring to God. And in Section IV, we will apply the tools we acquire in the first three sections to discuss specific topics particularly relevant to our modern, Western society.

Before that, though, we will define what Kabbalah is, where it comes from, and who, by Jewish Law, can study it. And in the

---

2. Robin Skelton. *The Practice of Witchcraft Today.*

process, we will define many vague terms used loosely, such as "belief." To establish just how Kabbalah works, we will also try to raise comparisons to other spiritual doctrines, such as Wiccan or witchcraft, Oriental doctrines, Christianity, and even satanism, to show that even beliefs and practices that appear to be similar to the naked eye are actually, and from their essence, polar opposites. When it comes down to it, the internal essence—the metaphysical composition—of all things is what defines and makes all the difference.

Just for the record, Judaism is a spiritual doctrine. What Moses introduced at Mount Sinai was never intended to be solely an institutionalized religion. Nothing in Judaism merely symbolizes or memorializes; it is and exists for specific spiritual–metaphysical objectives. Unfortunately many, if not most of the children of Israel have forgotten what the gift of God *really* was and thus have rendered it an artistic fixture at best. It is hoped that this gift will be dusted off so that we can relearn its power, which, in the process, will answer all of our questions about the world we live in.

However, two points need clarification before we go any further. The first is that metaphysical energy is real. People engage in occult or supernatural means of drawing energy, even quite innocently. They are, nevertheless, drawing energy all the same, and when they do, they are not exempt from the consequences of their actions. Ignorance of the law will not immune the violator from prosecution on the physical or metaphysical levels.

Bob Larson, the nationally known radio host of *Talk-Back*, notes in his book *Satanism: The Seduction of America's Youth* that young listeners, as others, think psychic or occult practice is fun and harmless: "That unsuspecting evaluation is the enchantment by which many teens are trapped" (p. 36). In fact, Larson's book shows just how prevalent satanism is in our youth culture (p. 31).

Larson demonstrates his point through three mediums in our society: various fantasy games, heavy metal rock groups and Halloween. With regard to the first example, Larson reveals:

The National Coalition on Television Violence says [Dungeons & Dragons] is linked to more than fifty teenage deaths. One attorney, representing the family of a young suicide victim who was involved in D&D, declared, "It is a game that

tells kids how to perfect the art of premeditated murder"
(p. 49).[3]

Larson goes on to show how "[s]ome aspects of D&D are directly linked with Satanism" (p. 50).

Heavy-metal rock music, so prevalent in Western society, is loaded with lyrics regarding satanic practice, and many such rock groups hold satanic rite-like concerts in the U.S. and Europe. Even Halloween, a major pagan holiday to occultists from witches to satanists, is engaged in by America at large for fun.

But the truth is, when one presses a key on a computer keyboard, a certain sequence of events begins to unfold, whether the user knew what he was doing or not and whether it was by accident or for fun. Metaphysics works very much the same way. For example, Larson warns us to pay attention to the game instructions of D&D [Dungeons & Dragons] that say that "'There is no assurance that conjuring an imagined entity will prevent a real spirit from responding!'" (*Satanism*, p. 54).

Dusty Sklar and Joseph Carr are two of a number of writers who have exposed the Nazis', particularly Adolf Hitler's, involvement in the occult. Carr explicitly states:

Nazism was no mere political movement of racist gangsters and misfits, as is commonly believed, but rather, it was an *occultic religion* in which Adolf Hitler was the Messiah, Heinrich Himmler the High Priest, and the blood-drenched men of the SS Death's Head Formation the clergy (*The Twisted Cross*, p. 13, sic).

We will discuss the satanic practices of the Nazi reign more in chapter 8. However, the point relevant to our present discussion is what Sklar points out, which is, "We are learning now, from contemporary cults in America, that the process of turning human beings into robots can actually begin quite innocently" (*Gods and Beasts*, p. 103).

To be sure, there is real energy in Metaphysics—energy that can heal and bring fulfillment and energy that can destroy and kill.

---

3. Larson takes this from John Weldon and James Bjornstad's "Fantasy Games People Play," *Contemporary Christian Magazine*, December 1984.

In chapter 8, we will define what exactly *Satan* is and thus demystify this term, which in our lack of understanding has left us in spooked awe at best. To rephrase Sklar and Carr's titles, it is time to reveal the beast and explain exactly why it is twisted.

The second point that warrants clarification is that Kabbalah is *not* one of the occult practices of what is called the New Age movement. This point will be explained further in this book.

THE SOURCE OF ALL KNOWLEDGE

In his book *Cults That Kill*, Larry Kahaner quotes Detective Cleo Wilson, a Denver police officer working on occult related crimes, as saying, "One thing I've always noticed is that people who have knowledge intimidate those who don't. Instead of learning about it, they become intimidated by it" (p. 37).

To be sure, where there are no rules, utter chaos and pandemonium rein. Where rules abound, but no one understands them, those people suffer without knowing why. Moveover, where basic terms or concepts of these laws are not defined, anyone can call a rose not a rose, but a grapefruit if they like and worsen and perpetuate the "why's" and "why me's" in this world. Knowledge should not intimidate, nor should it be vague.

The unknown mystifies and scares us because we do not know how to deal with it. But once it becomes known and defined, we can know, at least, how to deal with it. As Rabbi Matityahu Glazerson expresses, "Truth is the medium which induces harmony" (*From Hinduism to Judaism,* p. 47). Knowledge should be understandable and clear. Such buzzwords as "holy" and "sin" and "good" and "evil" and "Satan" and "the afterlife" need to be defined. And what exactly the power of the number 13 or 7 or the ado about Atlantis or of the pyramids should also be concretely defined.

All of these will be explained and understood from this book; we will see where they all fit. In short, it is high time that the power of the unknown be known.

Everything there is, was, or ever will be to know about the universe is contained in the Bible.[4] Yes, the Bible. The Bible is the

---

4. The Bible refers to The Old Testament, specifically to the Five Books of Moses: Genesis, Exodus, Leviticus, Numbers, and Deuteronomy.

guidebook to the universe that codifies all the natural cosmic laws that govern us, from the laws of nature and physics to the laws of human nature and metaphysics.

Most spiritual doctrines will explain, as does Kabbalah, that everything on this physical plane consists of two elements: a body and a soul. If one observes, say, the atom, the fundamental building block of physical matter, one will be dumbfounded by the fact that most of the atom's mass consists of empty space. In chapter 5, we will define what this empty space is, as we will discuss the atom's structure and how it parallels the structure of everything in our universe, from the human body to the solar system.

For now, however, we will simply note that only about 1 percent of the atom is actually of physical substance; whereas about 99 percent of the atom is comprised of a metaphysical "substance." Thus, in general, Kabbalah defines *reality* as the totality of all that we can perceive through our five senses and all that we cannot. Reality, therefore, includes such things or phenomena as the sound waves dogs hear but humans do not, the infrared waves bees see but humans do not, and everything else that exists in our universe, whether we can sense it or not or whether or not we even know of its existence.

The soul, the metaphysical component, is what Kabbalah defines as the true essence of all people and things. The soul is the primary determining factor. Even medicine and science admit that when the soul leaves the body, all of our hi-tech means cannot substitute for the soul. Nor, as Mary Shelley has expressed, can the soul be duplicated by mortal efforts.[5] The nonphysical, intangible aspect is thus also referred to as the 99 percent of that being. But on this plane, the soul must be contained in a physical body to survive. Conversely, in order for the internal essence, the soul, to be revealed on this plane, it needs a body. The body would be the 1 percent that the atom reveals as physical substance. We will expand on this in chapter 5.

The appearance of the body does not necessarily reveal the soul; but through the actions, behavior, and speech of an individual or thing, the nature of the soul can be detected. The body is what our five senses can perceive. In chapter 5, we will discuss why all spiritual energies in our physical realm are concealed with a body of some sort.

---

5. Reference to Mary Shelley's *Frankenstein*.

The Bible, or Torah,[6] which is our sourcebook, was given in its entirety to Moses on Mount Sinai. What that implies is that while Moses received the physical, tangible (body) aspect of Torah, he also received its spiritual, intangible aspect (soul) as well. It is therefore said that Moses received both the written and the oral Torah or "Law." And Kabbalah is part of the Oral Law; Kabbalah is considered the "soul of the soul of Torah." (Parenthetically, we will briefly note the four levels of the study of Torah in chapter 6.)

Since Kabbalah is part of the inner essence of the Law, it, with the Written Law, was handed down from God to Moses (13th century B.C.E., per the *Yudaica Lexicon*), then to Joshua, and then to the seventy elders. This wisdom remained in oral form until 70 C.E., when Rabbi Shimon Bar Yokhai revealed all of the wisdom of Kabbalah for his student and scribe, Rabbi Abba, to transcribe. The written product was the *Zohar*, which to date is the central text of Kabbalah. Kabbalah's lineage will be further discussed in chapter 2. But what is important to emphasize here is Kabbalah's initial reception on Mount Sinai.[7]

HOW TO READ THE SOURCE

As we have said, the Bible, which is our sourcebook, is tremendously powerful, but one must know how to read and use it. Two points, then, need to be taken into consideration: (1) the terminol-

---

6. "Torah" basically refers to the Bible (The Old Testament) and to the body of Jewish Law that has stemmed from the Bible and has accumulated since its receipt on Mount Sinai over three thousand years ago. Rabbi Gershom in his book *Beyond the Ashes* summarizes the vast body of Jewish Law along more conventional lines as follows: "the Talmud . . . spans over seven centuries, from approximately 200 B.C.E. to 500 C.E. (the time of the Greco–Roman Empire)" (p. 50). "The Talmud contains two basic kinds of writings: (1) *halachah* or material on Jewish law and ritual, and (2) *aggadah* or nonlegal material" (p. 5). "Collectively this vast body of knowledge—Bible, Talmud, *halachah*, *aggadah*, mysticism, parables, stories, rituals, ethical literature, etc.—is referred to as *Torah*" (p. 52).

7. The "revelation" was a revelation of cosmic law to an entire nation. The same information or know-how was known to Adam (over 5,750 years ago) and was revealed, individually, to Abraham (almost 4,000 years ago).

ogy and jargon employed; and (2) its original language, being Hebrew. Even simple mistranslations from the original Hebrew have led to monstrous misunderstandings. One example of such a mistranslation is from verses 28, 29, and 35 of Exodus chapter 34 (i.e., Exodus 34:28,29,35), in which after descending from Mount Sinai, Moses does not realize that the skin of his face shone so much so that the Israelites were afraid to approach him. The phrase in Hebrew is *Karan Or Panav*, while *Karan* (shone) is the word that has been mistranslated throughout the ages.

Karan is the past tense of the verb to shine. *Keren*, however, of the same three root letters in Hebrew (*K-R-N*), is a noun that can be translated as either a ray of light or as a horn, depending on the context. Either way, the word in the chapter, all three times, is *Karan*, being the verb. This has not stopped translators from getting away with stating that Moses came down with horns. To show just how far a mistranslation can be carried and believed, one only needs to go to the Piazza della Republica in Rome to witness a giant-size statue of Moses with horns atop his head!

But more important than merely translating the Bible correctly for those who do not know Hebrew is the necessity of deciphering the coded message. The Bible was intentionally encoded—which is why it is considered the cosmic *code* to our universe. The reasons why it is encoded will be discussed in chapter 4. For now, suffice to say that on its literal (physical) level, the Bible offers us little cosmic knowledge.

BODY VERSUS SOUL OF THE TORAH

The Torah, or the physical Bible that God gave Moses on Mount Sinai, must contain both a body and a soul. The body—the book itself—is what we can read with our eyes and touch with our hands. But according to Kabbalah, the essence of Torah, its soul—like all souls—is concealed. Its body serves merely as a vehicle for its soul.

The body of the Torah can be likened to Grimm brothers' fairy tales. Bruno Bettelheim, in his book *The Uses of Enchantment: The Meaning and Importance of Fairy Tales*, demonstrates that the figures in the fairy tales we read to our children are actually dramatized and personified psychological processes and phenomena that occur, particularly in children, as they mature to adulthood.

In Bettelheim's words, "In the tales' content, inner psychological phenomena are given body in symbolic form" (p. 36). Such abstract processes and phenomena are personified or encoded so that the child may perceive the basic direction of the process. Bettelheim even asserts, "In a fairy tale, internal processes are externalized and become comprehensible as represented by the figures of the story and its events" (p. 25).

The Bible acts in a similar way. Concepts that are not of the physical realm—energies, natural forces, etcetera—are given corporeal embodiment: That is, they are made physical within the body aspect of the Torah. One example of this is when God tells the Jews of the exodus, coming toward the Land of Israel:

1. When the Lord thy God shall bring thee into the land whither thou goest to possess it, and cast out many nations before thee, the Hittites, and the Girgashites, and the Emorites, and the Canaanites, and the Perizzites, and the Hivites, and the Jebusites, seven nations, greater in number and mightier than thou;
2. And when the Lord thy God shall deliver them before thee, and thou dost smite them: thou shalt utterly destroy them; thou shalt not make any covenant with them, nor show mercy unto them (Deuteronomy 7:1–2).

That the Jews should "smite" and "utterly destroy" another person, let alone a nation or *seven*, contradicts the Commandment "Thou Shalt Not Kill." Parenthetically, in chapter 4, we will see why the word "commandment" is a mistranslation, and we will define what it really means. Moreover, a more accurate translation of the above-referenced principle *Lo Tirtzakh* is really "[You] will not *murder*" and not the mistranslated imperative, "Thou shalt not kill."

The "seven nations" refer to the seven forms of negativity the Jews of the desert needed to remove from *within* themselves in preparation of entering the Holy Land. [In chapter 5, we will also define the age-old mysteriousness of the number 7]. Thus, using the allusion to *Grimm's Fairy Tales*, the seven nations would be like the externalized wicked witch who, in "Hansel and Gretel," is the "personification of the destructive aspects of orality" (Bettelheim, p. 162) or the big bad wolf who, in "The Three Little Pigs," is an "externalization, a projection of the child's badness— and the story tells how this can be dealt with constructively" (ibid.,

p. 44). In the fairy tale, the negativity must be destroyed for goodness to rein again in the kingdom.

So, did the people, places, and events in the Bible really happen? Yes. The events tell of how certain energies became revealed to us in our world: how they were actualized from their potential state in the spiritual realm. Real, living human beings needed to exercise free will for such energies to be revealed. But the physical aspect of these people, places, and events are only the effect—the final expressions of the metaphysical causes that brought them about and made them significant to us today.

Were there seven nations in the Land of Israel? Yes. But they were not physically killed when the Israelites purified themselves from within and were ready to enter the Land of Israel. These nations simply left. No confrontation. No bloodshed.

All references to killing of other human beings in the Torah should be understood in this context. The same holds true for the four types of "death sentences" exacted for specific transgressions in the Torah "portion" or section of *Shoftim* (Judges). Rabbi Berg explains that the Talmud specifically says that real death was never enforced because the "death sentence" is pronounced on negative energy intelligence and not on human beings or physical bodies. The reference is also to the human means of getting rid of metaphysical negativity surrounding the individual from his own or from others' negative activity.[8] Even the concept of "an eye for an eye" refers to a particular exchange of metaphysical energy, which will be discussed in chapter 4, and not to a real, physical catfight.

Rabbi Shimon Bar Yohai, the author of the *Zohar*, said that if one reads the Bible like a storybook, he loses almost all the value of this great spiritual work and that better stories could be created by great minds of the day.[9] This is why, as Rabbi Berg expresses,

---

8. From Rabbi Dr. Philip S. Berg's recorded explanation of *Shoftim.*

9. It is in this context that "The *Zohar* declares, 'Woe unto those who see in the *Torah* nothing but simple narratives and ordinary words.' The truth of the matter is that every word of the Bible contains a sublime coded mystery which, when deciphered, reveals a wealth of elevated meaning. The narratives of the Torah are but the outer garments in which the real meaning is clothed. And woe unto him who mistakes the outer garment for the Bible itself. This was precisely the idea to which King David addressed himself when he declared, 'Open mine eyes that I might behold wondrous things from thy *Torah*'" (from Rabbi Berg's *The Zohar: Parashat Pinhas,* vol. í, p. xxxii).

to most people, about ninety percent of the Bible appears to be totally irrelevant to our present life and thus appears useless. Instead,
as he explains, the Bible

> is a coded, completely obtuse, compendium of all of our ex-
> periences—*our* experiences. Not the experiences of Abraham,
> Isaac, and Jacob. Not the experiences of the Jews leaving
> Egypt from bondage. But, each and every single verse refers
> to our own single lives (Rabbi Berg's recorded lecture, "How
> to Bring Moshiach to Our Lives").

In short, the Bible is a cosmic code or the code of cosmic law.

Every chapter, every verse, every word constitute for us the
switches that aid us in revealing the Light in our life. Not even a
single word in the whole Torah is redundant. Where the Bible tells
of physical figures (people), events, or dialogue, the physicality
implies that a hidden, spiritual message needs to be revealed.

ILLUSION

One of the ways to understand how the spiritual value of the Bible
can be directly applied to our present life is by understanding a basic
metaphysical concept of illusion. Most spiritual doctrines in one
way or another speak of the physical world as the world of *illusion*.[10] Illusion here does not mean a hallucination. A brick wall is
not a hallucination (and that can easily be demonstrated empiri-
cally!); but it is considered an illusion in the grand scheme of things
because its physical substance has no existence in the spiritual
world. The spiritual world, as we will learn, is of a constant, eternal energy, thus anything of a temporal or mutable nature—for
example, time, space, and motion—is rendered an illusion.

Moreover, as we will also expand on later, Kabbalah gives us
the means to transcend the influence of the physical and with this,
actually defy such illusions or their influences. While the body of
the Torah may seem to speak of time- and space-specific issues and
tales (regarding oxen, tents, and various individuals who have long
since died), the soul of Torah, its internal essence and function,

---

10. Richard Bach vivifies this principle in his novel *Illusions*.

transcends the limitation of time, space, and motion. And as we will discover throughout this book, even the tales speak of universal issues that directly relate to and influence us today.

HALAKHAH VERSUS KABBALAH

While the body of the Bible may be likened to *Grimm's Fairy Tales*, the soul of the Torah may be likened to man-made law. Law can basically be divided into two aspects: adjective law and substantive law. Both are equally important in determining whether or not your case will hold weight in court.

Adjective law may be defined as the laws that define the rules of evidence and procedure. Everything about how one's document to a court needs to look (paper size, margin size, fonts, and so on), who can submit the document (party, minor), where one can submit it (to which court, in which jurisdiction) and the time frames that need to be adhered to (deadlines for pleadings, motions, appeals), are all defined. One may have the most brilliant motion, pleading, brief, or memorandum, but if one submits it to the wrong court or passes the deadline, all his hard work is rendered futile.

Substantive law, on the other hand, deals with the content of the document. It defines what a crime or tort is, what needs to be demonstrated to win a case, and what the law regarding the pertinent issue has to say. Substantive law deals with the substance, the internal essence, of the document, whereas adjective law deals with the externalities of the document.

Halakhah may be likened to adjective law. It defines who and how one needs to do whatever one needs to do, where, when, and under what circumstances. *Halakhah* deals with the procedure. The word *Halakhah*, in fact, stems from the Hebrew root *Halakh*, meaning [to] go. *Halakhah* thus explains how things are to go, that is, their procedure. The procedure provided by *Halakhah* is as important as fine-tuning a musical instrument or a radio dial to just the exact frequency to draw the radio waves clearly and without static. The procedure tells us the hows of hooking us up to get the maximum effect. Kabbalah, then, defines the why.

In chapter 3, we will explain why, for example, on the physical plane, certain elements under certain circumstances should not be combined. In this context we will be able to understand why Torah forbids, say, the mixing of milk and meat. Or why men and women sit separately during prayer. *Halakhah* on this issue defines the who, what, where, when, and how, whereas Kabbalah provides the metaphysical reasons *why*.

SITREI TORAH VERSUS TA'AMEI TORAH

Within Kabbalah there are two aspects of study: *Sitrei* Torah and *Ta'amei* Torah. For the layman to delve into *Sitrei* Torah would be like deep-sea diving without undertaking the necessary preparation process of decompression to withstand the intense forces of the deep. Without the proper preparation, the body would "explode."

The levels of energy dealt with in *Sitrei* Torah are so strong that, like deep-sea diving, one must first fulfill various prerequisites, the particulars of which are irrelevant here, since this is not the aspect of Kabbalah that will be discussed. Suffice to say that what most people say, if they know anything about Kabbalah, is that it is forbidden. In truth, what is restricted is only the study of *Sitrei* Torah, because it is too powerful for the novice.

The other aspect of Kabbalah, which we will be discussing, requires no prerequisites of any kind; somewhat like skin diving or snorkeling, it is called the study of *Ta'amei* Torah. *Ta'amei* Torah is not only permissible, but has been encouraged by the spiritual leaders of Judaism until only fairly recently, when, mostly for political reasons, they began to discourage and even forbid its study. The secrets of *Ta'amei* Torah are available to all of us.

Ta'amei Torah not only answers why we are supposed to fulfill certain precepts, it explains the very reason we are here in the first place: why the universe was created, why we are here, where we are going, and where we fit in the grand scheme of things, that is, what our function is in living as physical beings on earth.

It is for this reason that the study of Kabbalah always begins in the beginning—in fact even before "In the beginning . . ." so that we know why there was a "beginning" in the first place. All this will be discussed in chapter 1.

THE MEANS TO CONTROL OUR DESTINY: FREE WILL

More important to us today than why things are the way they are is how we can change the way things are so that instead of negativity controlling us, we can control the negativity and be masters of our destiny.

According to Kabbalah, humankind was subject to the power of nature until Abraham came along. Abraham (eighteenth century B.C.E., per *Yudaica Lexicon*), who was the first Jew (a term that needs to be defined, as we shall do in chapter 6), is, among other firsts, considered the first astrologer and to whom is attributed the writing of the first book on astrology, the *Sefer Yetzirah*, The Book of Formation.

In Genesis, chapter 15, Abraham seems to shoot the breeze with God and expresses how at the age of one hundred he still wants a son to continue his spiritual endeavors. God then tells Abraham to go out and count the stars. Kabbalists explain that what God was telling Abraham was not to go merrily stargaze, but instead was teaching him cosmology, the power of the stars, or astrology. Abraham, as an adept astrologer, had seen by the stars that, per his destiny, he was not going to have any children. What God was then showing him was how to transcend the power of the stars, his destiny, and effect a different life. And, in fact, transcending the natural laws of the physical body, Abraham, then one hundred years old, and Sarah, who was then in her nineties, conceived and gave birth to Isaac.

The power revealed to Abraham was free will, which is what enables the individual to transcend the powers and dictates of the cosmos. Even when all seems chaotic and uncertain around us, we can learn to take control of our lives. It would be as if we could walk with a bulletproof bubble around us that protects us from all the chaos and devastation that reins around us. (From this we can get a glimpse into the internal message of the book of Noah and what it means to float above death and destruction, even of the entire world!) This is also where we come to understand the saying from the Torah that "as above, so below." This is a reciprocal force: Through our endowment of free will, we humans have the ability to engender changes in the upper worlds (the spiritual—

metaphysical worlds) from our lower world (the physical realm). This is also the meaning of man's "dominion" (Genesis 1:28) over the world: Man's free will can transcend the forces of nature and even control nature, as we will discuss.

This knowledge is what Judaism gave to the world when it came into existence almost four thousand years ago. This is the power that Abraham revealed for the world. And it is from this seed that Christianity, Islam, and the doctrines of the Far East evolved. (We will discuss various spiritual doctrines in chapter 6. We will also discuss more on the means to control our destiny in chapter 4, when we discuss *Tikkun* and reincarnation.)

THE SEED OF ALL SPIRITUAL DOCTRINES

While Christianity and Islam are known to branch from Judaism, one may wonder how we can say that the doctrines of the Far East evolved from Judaism as well. And how can we be sure that God wasn't really telling Abraham to go stargazing? After all, God did tell Abraham to count the stars, and that passage makes sense on its literal level. Why should we have to interpret it further?

What Kabbalah proffers is not an interpretation, but rather a deciphering of the encoded Bible.[11] In fact, a passage from the book of Genesis, chapter 25:5–6, answers the above questions.

5. And Abraham gave all that he had unto Isaac.
6. And to the sons of the concubines that Abraham had, Abraham gave gifts; and he sent them away from Isaac his son, while he was yet living, eastward, unto the east country.

---

11. Although Dr. Gerald Schroeder supports the term "interpretation" from a scientific perspective:

On the basis of a literal 'reading' of the physical world, we might discard the claims of scientists to a deeper understanding of our universe. But such literal interpretations of the heavens or of biology are never used by scientists. Interpretation is an integral, indeed essential, part of scientific inquiry . . . [Likewise,] A literal reading of the Bible reveals only a part of the wealth of information held within the text (*Genesis and the Big Bang,* p. 20).

If one looks at this passage carefully, analytically, one sees a physical impossibility. Abraham gives all away, and then he gives some away again. To explain, let's first lay out the metaphysical principle that will decipher this passage: In the spiritual, metaphysical world, there is no loss of energy and no loss of original form.

In physics there is the principle of the conservation of mass and energy, which means that no physical property (or its energy equivalent) is ever created out of nothing, nor can it disappear; it can merely change form. For example, if one has a cup of water and freezes it, the water then turns into ice—that is, it changes form. But once it becomes ice, it is no longer liquid. One cannot obtain both a cup of water *and* a cup of ice from the original one cup of water.

Now if that cup of water were metaphysical energy, and we were to freeze it, in the metaphysical we would then have a cup of ice (as there is no loss of energy), but we would also—still—have a cup of water (as there is no loss of original form). This is true of all energy that is of spiritual or metaphysical nature. To illustrate this from our daily lives, knowledge is a metaphysical or spiritual energy. If I possess, say, 100 units of knowledge of Kabbalah and teach someone (i.e., transfer) 75 units, I am not left with 25 units. Instead, in the second stage, that other person would have 75 units—but I would still have 100 units, simultaneously.

This is a key principle that will help us understand various concepts regarding Creation (discussed in chapters 1 and 2) and reincarnation (discussed in chapter 4). But for now, we can apply this principle to understand the above passage.

Let's say that Abraham's total estate is 100 units. Per verse 5, he gives "all" to Isaac, which in the physical would translate to the entire 100 units. However, in verse 6, Abraham gives "gifts" to the sons of his concubines. Now if in verse 5 he gives all (and we take into consideration that in the eighteenth century B.C.E. when he lived, there were no cash advances or extended credit programs), then by verse 6 he should have nothing left to give anyone, even as gifts.

If what Abraham were transferring was of physical substance, the laws of physics would apply. But as we learn from the passage, his bestowal could not have been of physical nature. What this short passage shows us is that Abraham conveyed purely spiritual energy, being the entire body of knowledge that he had acquired, to Isaac: "all that he had unto Isaac." What Abraham gave to the sons of his concubines were parts or pieces—"gifts"—of this body of knowledge before sending them "eastward," which means to the Far East.[12]

Rabbi Matityahu Glazerson, in his book *From Hinduism to Judaism*, writes about Jews that he spoke with who returned to "the Jewish faith after encounters with such Eastern schools of spiritual practice as Yoga, Transcendental Meditation and even levitation" (p. 1). He quotes the "words of Rabbi Menashe Ben Israel on the influence of Judaism on the Wisdom of the East (per the Soul of Life section 4, chapter 21.)":

And similarly, when [Abraham] went down to Egypt and lived there, he taught this philosophy, after which he sent the sons of his concubines away from Isaac while he was yet alive towards the East to their holy land, India. They also disseminated this faith. Behold, you may see there the Abrahamites, who are today called Brahamans; they are the sons of Abraham our patriarch and they were the first in India to spread this faith. . . .

Then, in his fifth chapter, Rabbi Glazerson shows how Hinduism is actually a derivative of Judaism. His title alone reveals the root from its branch, as the chapter is entitled: "Brahan and Abraham, Veda and Knowledge [from the Hebrew word for knowledge, *Yeda*], Prana and Glory [from the Hebrew root of glory, *P-A-R*]" (p. 16).

Isaac was his father's successor in the lineage of Judaism. It is for this reason that Abraham conveyed to Isaac the knowledge of the complete structure of the universe before he died. And it is also for this reason that Kabbalah—the body of knowledge of "Abraham, Isaac, and Jacob"—and only Kabbalah can provide the view from above of all spiritual doctrines.

---

12. Rabbi Berg, in discussing this passage notes, "The Zohar [the central text of Kabbalah] questions the meaning of the word gifts, and replies as follows: "The word 'gifts' refers to the stages of spirituality which do not include the 'emendations' and subsequently these people (sons of the concubines) moved eastward to what is known as the Far East" (xv). From: *The Kabbalah: A Study of the Ten Luminous Emanations,* from Rabbi Isaac Luria, vol. I.

In chapter 6, we will define the energy of Kabbalah, why the Oriental doctrines are *fragments* of the system at large, as we will also see where the system of the ancient Egyptians fits in, as did that of what is considered "the generation of the Tower of Babel," which would also include Atlantis.

Parenthetically, with regard to the above hypothetical argument about the textual reading of the Bible, in the chapter in which we discuss reincarnation, additional textual examples will be provided from the Bible, which require deciphering, as they make no sense on a literal and physical level.

KABBALAH AS A SCIENCE

According to Kabbalah, Judaism is a spiritual doctrine whose precepts are based on cosmic law. Like most other disciplines and studies, metaphysics requires its own language to understand and discuss, and which we will discuss shortly. Also, like physics, metaphysics, or cosmic law, is a systematic body of law; it is a methodical information system. Its principles are observable, although for the kabbalist, physical manifestations never serve to "prove" cosmic law, they only illustrate. In Kabbalah, there is no place for superstition, old wives' tales, or even flat statements like ". . . because God hath commandeth it such." Neither is Kabbalah a playground of mathematical acrobatics, although in chapter 5 we will touch on the function of *Gematria* (numerology), as a kabbalistic tool.

There is a concrete reason for each precept in Judaism, defined by the energy exchange it involves. For example, in chapter 4 we will discuss the energy exchange resulting from an act of murder to understand why it is given as a negative precept. Kabbalists believe that if people knew what happens to them metaphysically—what energy exchange resulted from such acts as murder or stealing—if they *really* understood, they would not do it. They wouldn't want to!

ETHICS AND MORALS

As we can see in society today, rules of ethics and morals do little to detract crime and bring people to behave in a humane way toward their fellow human beings. Common sense does not really appear to be very common. Thus, the *why*'s of murder, stealing, or bestiality and why they are forbidden by the Bible need to be spelled out—not from a moral perspective, but a metaphysical one. According to Kabbalah, ethics and morals are end results—that is, the *effects* of studying and internalizing Kabbalah—and are some of the fringe benefits reaped from its practice.

Kabbalah transcends those disciplines that concern themselves only with the physical realm, which is just a speck compared to the vastness of the real, spiritual world. Kabbalah looks beyond into the root cause of all that exists, of what we can see and what we cannot. Thus Kabbalah transcends politics, racism, fads, and fashions. It explores why a phenomenon of any nature in any field or discipline arises in the first place and does not merely describe how it looks once it has materialized. For example, we can succinctly state:

> Stress, neuroses, *burn-out*, these terms from the modern vernacular describe conditions in which the flow of energy is uneven. . . . An even flow of energy is essential to a person's physical, emotional, and spiritual well being (Berg's *Kabbalah for the Layman,* vol. II, pp. 50–51).

Vis-à-vis medicine, Kabbalah offers reasons for phenomena that are only documented as observation, testimony of the five senses. Medicine may tell us there are red and white cells in the blood, but it does not tell us why. Why not pink and purple, or why not just one type? The answer to this will be touched on in chapter 3. Similarly, in chapter 7 we will explain the reason why a woman's menstrual cycle is *not*, in contrast to biology's assertion, an expression of inefficiency in nature. Everything exists for a reason and serves a purpose. We just need to discover it.

Vis-à-vis science, physics, and astrophysics, Kabbalah offers much information and insight into the creation of our universe and the reasons for it. In discussing why, which we will do in chapters 1 and 2, we witness Kabbalah's ability to define the source of evolution and pinpoint the age of the universe. Many questions that modern science renders inexplicable or simply unanswered have actually already been answered and explained by Kabbalah. In his conclusion to chapter 1 of his posthumous book on immortality, resurrection, and the age of the universe, Rabbi Aryeh Kaplan maintains:

> Classical Torah sources not only maintain that the universe is billions of years old, but present the exact figure proposed by modern science. There are two accounts of creation in the Torah, the first speaking of the spiritual infrastructure of the universe, which was completed in seven days. This took place some 15 billion years ago, before the Big Bang. The second account speaks of the creation of Adam, which took place less than six thousand years ago.
>
> What is most important is that there is no real conflict between Torah and science on this most crucial issue. If anything, Torah teachings are vindicated by modern scientific discoveries (p. 12).

We will also explain such details as the metaphysical reason physical bodies, when they fall to earth, bounce before settling at their point of impact. We will also understand why the universe is composed of ten dimensions. Yes, ten. (Interestingly, Dr. Stephen Hawking notes that the astrophysics "String theories . . . seem to be consistent only if space–time has either ten or twenty-six dimensions" [*A Brief History of Time,* p. 173]. Parenthetically, we will understand the relationship between ten [the ten *Sefirot*] and twenty-six [the Tetragrammaton] in chapter 5.) Just as this is not a sales pitch, it is neither a theory nor science fiction. Kabbalah is an information system that teaches us how to access the energies of the universe (and knowledge is energy), so that we can use them and benefit from them individually and globally.

With all the similarities between Kabbalah and modern science, it is important to understand where science fits into the grand scheme of things. There is a reason why science has not been able to formulate a single, unified theory that explains all of existence. In fact, by chapter 5—under our discussion of the structure of the atom—we will understand how the theories of relativity and quantum mechanics are really part of the same structure—how they are actually one and the same. Moreover, Dr. Stephen Hawking, who may be considered the representative of all of science, proffers a different angle of physics' limitation when he writes: "General relativity is only an incomplete theory: it cannot tell us how the universe started off, because it predicts that all physical theories, including itself, break down at the beginning of the universe" (*A Brief History of Time,* p. 55).

In his article "Physics vs. Metaphysics,"[13] Jeffrey Marsh points out, "Disillusionment with science—or at least with its inability to deal with the spiritual side of man's nature—has led to a growing backlash" (p. 50). Marsh presents three recent books[14] in the field of physics that offer "a response to the perception that the journey of physics as we have known it since Newton is coming to an end" (p. 50).

The reason science has reached its limit is because (1) it evades the root cause of existence, and (2) because science constitutes only the testimony of our five senses. As Kabbalah teaches, when one does not understand the root, the branches appear to differ. (Since the concept of root vis-à-vis its branches is a central idea in Kabbalah, this will be discussed shortly.) Dr. Hawking touches on the limitation of science and hence where it needs to pursue, when he notes that science has "as yet, had little success in predicting human behavior from mathematical equations!" (*A Brief History of Time,* p. 179). However, Dr. Hawking just misses the mark when he asserts (as quoted in Michael Lemonick's article), "'You don't need to appeal to God to set the initial conditions for the universe.'"[15] As we will understand from our discussion on creation, God (or the "Light") is very much a part of the picture. In fact, without Him, there is no creation or any comprehension of it!

With regard to science's focus and approach to the universe, as Dr. Hawking explains: "A scientific theory is just a mathematical model we make to describe our observations" (*A Brief History of Time,* p. 147). Science occupies itself with only one percent of

---

13. *Commentary,* vol. 96, no. 5, 1993. 48–51.
14. The three books Marsh refers to are:

    1. Steven Weinberg, *Dreams of a Final Theory*, Pantheon.
    2. David Lindley, *The End of Physics: The Myth of a Unified Theory*, Basic Books.
    3. Bryan Appleyard, *Understanding the Present: Science and the Soul of Modern Man*, Doubleday.

15. Michael D. Lemonick, "Hawking Gets Personal," *Time,* Sept. 27, 1993: p. 80.

reality. Thus it actually can *prove* nothing. ("Any physical theory is always provisional, in the sense that it is only a hypothesis: you can never prove it" (ibid., p. 11).

Conversely, to the kabbalist, the physical world, and hence any of the disciplines dealing solely with the physical realm, are never looked at to *prove* anything. The physical can simply *illustrate* metaphysical principles. The physical realm is merely an expression of its metaphysical root and actually comprises only a small amount of "reality." Put differently, since it is not of the causal level, the branch can never prove—it can only illustrate.

BRANCH AND ROOT

As we have already said, the concept of "branch versus root" touches on a central principle in Kabbalah—that of cause and effect. Kabbalah looks to the root of all existence and is why it is the system that unifies all of the theories of physics: It shows how they all stem from the same root and shows just where everything fits in the grand scheme of things. Thus, for one thing, as we will explain in chapters 4 and 5, time, space, and motion are illusions. Instead of such finite, linear concepts, in the metaphysical realm what exists is cause and effect. Memories, flashes, and even daydreams are phenomena that offer a small indication of why time, space, and motion are illusions. Therefore, to the kabbalist, it is not surprising that, as Dr. Hawking notes, the "laws of science do not distinguish between the past and the future" (ibid., p. 152). Moreover, physics has even defined that there are three "arrows" of time! (ibid., p. 153).

The concept of the videocassette, as Rabbi Berg helps us understand, best demonstrates how things really exist: all at once! The beginning, middle, and end—as we perceive it—of all stories on video actually exist simultaneously in their little plastic boxes. The fact that we need to sit down and watch each frame unfold in a linear fashion only indicates the limitations in our physical bodies. In fact, our five senses filter out much of the information and stimuli that we are confronted with daily. And even science has discovered that our brain only uses about five to nine percent of its capacity.

CREATION

Everything there is to know about the universe begins with an understanding of creation, which we will summarize in chapter 1. Science's inability to explain the universe prior to the big bang is precisely why it can go no further than it has gone to date and why its various theories do not conflate.

Interestingly, the arts, academia, and science all began connected to theology in one way or another, be it in the name or service of Dionysus, the church, etcetera. Their evolvement or detachment from God is what—as Dennis Prager expresses in his essay "The Case for Ethical Monotheism"—has rendered such disciplines as false gods in our modern society. In his essay, Prager, a radio talk-show host in California and founder of the Micah Center for Ethical Monotheism, demonstrates how values and disciplines of all and any kind, when divorced from their "God-based" soil (p. 29) become an end in themselves and thus become "a god, a false and dangerous god" (ibid., p. 11). With all else, such disciplines and values—and science included—must swing full circle, back to their root, which is with "God" the "Light" or the "Source."

Vis-à-vis the social sciences, Kabbalah solves the academic riddle or "feud" between Sigmund Freud, Friedrich Nietzsche, and Viktor Frankl regarding the ultimate ingredient that motivates Man—the ultimate question of "What makes man tick?" The answer to this will be understood better by chapters 3 and 4. Moreover, with regard to the field of psychology and psychiatry, Kabbalah also offers insights into the existence of phobias and "irrational" behavior in otherwise so-called normal people, as discussed in chapter 4 on reincarnation. The metaphysical root cause of depression, kleptomania, and even compulsive shopping, is discussed in chapters 3, 4, and 8.

In addition, other controversial issues of the day, such as homosexuality, are discussed (chapter 7 on sex, marriage, and soul mates) as they are understood from their root level. According to Kabbalah, there is a distinct definition of homosexuality that once understood—and from the metaphysical root level—will cease to exist as a moral or ethical problem. Most problems exist as problems and fester into bigger problems simply because they are not defined from a root level. And, in turn, these issues need to be acted upon on an equally metaphysical–spiritual level.

In Kabbalah, nothing is taken for granted. The root (metaphysical reason) is explored for everything we do and don't do. In modern, Western society, for example, we no longer question why human sacrifice or cannibalism are no longer practiced. In chapter 3, though, we define precisely why human sacrifice is prohibited by Judaism or Judeo–Christian doctrine, as we discuss the reason for the prohibition against cannibalism in chapter 4.

Basically, Kabbalah teaches the flow of energy in the universe. And by learning how to flow with it and act accordingly, we enhance our lives. Working *with* the current as opposed to against it not only enables us to better our individual lives but also to contribute to a global state of consciousness whereby peace on earth and goodwill toward our fellow human beings results. The kabbalistic word for such a state is *Moshiakh*, the Messiah, which we will explore further in chapter 8.

Nomenclature: All terms—"destiny," "free will," and "Messiah"—need to be defined. And what does it mean to be a "Light for all nations"? Kabbalah is a science. It utilizes a certain body of nomenclature that also enables it to provide concrete definitions to its subject, as do all discrete disciplines like (man-made) law, medicine, computers, etcetera.

THE LANGUAGE OF THE BRANCHES

We humans have a difficult time dealing with abstractions. In math, we assign letters or symbols to the unknown, which are understood in the mathematical context, but may mean something else in a different context—especially in their various, original, alphabetic (English, Greek, etcetera) context. The same holds true for metaphysics, or in particular, Kabbalah. In the language of Kabbalah, everyday words, like *light*, *vessel*, or *branch* are used, which represent a distinct, intangible, metaphysical energy. Thus, *light* does not refer to the physical emanation from a lightbulb, although physical light would be the closest thing, in parallel form, to the metaphysical "Light."

In the physical, as in the metaphysical, we cannot observe the seed or roots of a tree, only its branches, leaves, and fruit. That is to say, we cannot see the cause, but we can see the effect. What we perceive in our world through our five senses are the effects, or "branches," of the root cause. What we can say is that by looking at the fruit (the effect), we can understand what exists at the seed level (cause). If, for example, we observe a pear tree, we know the seed of that tree contains the DNA of pear. We can also know that if we discern pears on a tree, the seed of that tree could not be, say, a lemon seed (containing the DNA of lemon). Moreover, what is contained in the root necessarily manifests in the branch. A lemon tree cannot come from a pear seed or vice versa. This is a law of nature as it applies to physics (the branch), as it does to metaphysics (the root).

Kabbalah establishes that there are basically two worlds: the spiritual world and the physical world. Almost like an upside-down tree, all causes—or the seed—exist in the spiritual realm, whereas the branches and leaves manifest themselves in the physical. The physical realm is never a cause for any phenomenon or process. It is for this reason that, for example, Dostoyevsky, in his novel *Crime and Punishment*, can map out the mental and physical process preceding and following an act of murder. But such a depiction does not explain the source of those processes. Dostoyevsky's story begins only *after* a desire has already been aroused in Raskolnikov to commit murder. The book does not explain where that desire came from in the first place. That is because desire (as we will discuss in chapter 3) stems from the metaphysical realm, not the physical.

Yet these two worlds, the metaphysical and physical, are fused and work together. Thus, we can engender change in the spiritual from the physical level. We can also discern the metaphysical cause or spiritual root of phenomena—being its branches—on our realm.

Moreover, since we have no access to the seed of all existence and have limited access to the spiritual realm in general, the language used to discern such phenomena and processes (which are rooted in the spiritual and affected in the physical) relates only to the "branches." That is, the language reflects the branches of existence.

The Language of the Branches is also the language of the Bible, as we will demonstrate throughout this volume. It is through the use of this language that Creation and all that evolved from it can be explained. With this in mind, we can understand why Kabbalah defines reality as the totality of all that we can perceive through our five senses and all that we cannot: *Reality* encompasses the physical and the metaphysical worlds.

THE TWO METAPHYSICAL SYSTEMS

Kabbalah defines two metaphysical systems by which one can draw energy from the cosmos: (1) the System of the Vessel, and (2) the System of the Channel. Again, terms like *vessel* and *channel* need to be defined. For now, suffice it to say that the difference between the two lies in the object of each one's focus.

One of the first principles we learn in Kabbalah is that of cause and effect, or *root* and *branches*. This is significant because if we want to effect a change, we can only do so from the root or seed level. An illustration of this would be if we wanted to effect a change in the color of, say, a watermelon. We could create the impression or illusion of change by taking the fruit itself (the final product, the branch), and painting the rind and injecting dye into the fruit. But the color of the watermelon, by definition of the information contained in its DNA, will not have been altered. That is, (in Kabbalistic/metaphysical terms), the watermelon has not been changed on the seed level.

To effect real change in the watermelon's color, we would have to work not with the watermelon itself, which is the end effect (branch), but with the seed (root) that is in line to produce that watermelon. Once we work with the seed and fiddle with the DNA contained in it, we can rest assured that what grows later from that seed will conform to the definitions we have set for it. Thus, it is easier and more effective to work from the seed level—also called potential energy—than to struggle with the fruit, which by definition is no longer potential. That is not to say that the fruit does not contain in it seeds that constitute potential for yet a new and separate series of effects; it does, but we are looking at one particular frame or sequence at a time.

Under the System of the Vessel, what one connects to spiritually is the effect, the branch; whereas what one connects to under the System of the Channel is the cause or the root (the seed). Once we understand what free will is (as we will in chapter 3) and what its function is in the universe and vis-à-vis our individual lives, we can understand why Judeo–Christian doctrine forbids the preoccupation with anything of the System of the Vessel. The focus should be on the cause, not the effect.

Examples of the employment of the System of the Vessel can be found in any religion or spiritual doctrine that draws on the

forces of nature. Certain religious practices that, from their externalities, appear similar are actually polar opposites when catego-
rized as being from the System of the Vessel or the Channel. For
example, in Judaism as in the Wiccan (the modern term for witchcraft) religion, there exists a ritual that draws on the power of the
moon. In Judaism, it is called *Birkat HaLivana* (the blessing of the
moon) or *Kiddush HaLivana* (the sanctification of the moon) and
in Wiccan it is called "drawing down the moon." The difference
between the two practices lies in the object of the prayer—however "prayer" is defined by either religion. The Wiccans work to
"draw down" the energy of the full moon. The spiritual work the
Jews engage in is to connect to the positive aspect of the new moon.
This requires a bit more explanation.

All energy has the potential of both positive and negative,
almost like an absolute number—say $|2|$—that remains poten-
tially positive or negative until we define it as being either a $(+2)$
or a (-2). The point here, however, focuses on the fact that the
doctrines of the System of the Vessel, like the Wiccans, connect
with the effects (the branches) of nature, here being the full moon.
By the System of the Channel, on the other hand, the connection
is with the energy of the seed level that contains the potential of
positive and negative energy.

KABBALISTIC ASTROLOGY

With the above in mind, we can begin to understand what distin-
guishes the various principles and tools in Kabbalah from other spiritual doctrines, between conventional astrology and kabbalistic astrology, for example. Conventional astrology tells you what has been
defined by the stars as the nature of the individual. It, therefore, also
offers divinations of the future, since the stars can expose what destiny the forces of the stars have mapped out for the individual.

In kabbalistic astrology, on the other hand, the character traits
and revelations offered by the stars, per the positioning of the stars
at the moment of one's birth, are only a stepping-stone. From it
the individual can define what his or her "tools" and obstacles are;
but it is from that point that the individual is directed in changing
his or her destiny to transcend the control of the stars. It is from
this perspective that Rabbi Berg asserts:

The restrictions placed upon us in our present lifetime are direct results of mistakes and errors of the past. . . . However, once the individual has escaped the original state of reincarnation and has entered a higher level of spirituality the natal restrictions no longer apply (Berg's *Reincarnation*, p. 156).

Therefore, in kabbalistic astrology, the future, as defined by the stars, is never divined. That would only limit the individual in realizing from the infinite possibilities of the potential, what he chooses to do with his free will. It is for this reason that Judeo–Christian doctrine forbids divination of the future in any form.[16]

It is also for this reason that the teachings of the System of the Channel, Kabbalah, are not only permissible (as they do anything but interfere with the interplay of one's free will), they have been encouraged. By understanding the language, structure, and workings of the system, we acquire better use of our free will. After all, you can possess a telephone, but if you do not know what it is used for, what kind of communication it permits, or how to operate the device, it cannot provide you with the maximum service it was designed for, if it proves helpful at all.

In the final analysis, Kabbalah deals with what really matters in life.

---

16. As Christianity is a derivative of Judaism, it has assumed many principles and practices indirectly from Kabbalah, or Judaism in general. This will become more discernible as we discuss Kabbalah and compare its concepts to Christian practices.

I

Creation

1

Creation

The study of Kabbalah always begins with "In the beginning . . ."—not for historic reasons, but because we learn about Creation to raise our consciousness to ultimately improve our well-being. The beginning, Creation, constitutes the seed of our universe. If we recall the discussion in the Introduction on the difference between connecting to the seed of something and connecting to its branches, we can understand how connecting to the seed of all existence gains us control of what is produced from that seed. As Rabbi Berg discusses in his recorded lectures on Genesis,[1] we all want to establish various aspects in our lives that are considered the seed or root level of things: a new business contract, a new house, a new personal relationship, and so on.

The word *knowledge* is defined in the Language of the Branches as *connection*. Therefore, when we learn (knowledge) about Creation, we connect to that level, being the seed level of existence. The connection we make to the seed, in turn, effects the nature of the things we "plant," as it puts us in control of their outcome.

Parenthetically, it is for this reason that in the Jewish liturgy we are told to "remember" the act of Creation, *Ma'aseh Beresheet.* "Remembering" means to connect. Thus, for instance, over the

---

1. Rabbi Philip S. Berg, "*Zohar:Bereshit,*" nos. 1–6.

Friday night *Kiddush* (blessing over the wine) the term *Ma'aseh Beresheet* is actually recited. As we will learn in the chapter on *Sefirot*, when we say something, when we bring that energy to the physical level of "*Malkhut*," we implement it, by the mere act of saying it.

The subject of Creation alone is dealt with in many books and comprises many volumes. This is partly because, as it is the seed of the universe, Genesis, and especially its first chapters, is most concealed: it is the most encoded part of Torah. In fact, every single word of its first verses, if not chapters, are code words. For this reason, this chapter will merely provide a rough sketch of the totality of Creation—the structure of the picture at large. This, in turn, will enable us to see where all pieces fit in.

The study of Creation begins with an axiom—the only axiom in the science of Kabbalah:

> There is one source or cause. This one source is the cause of all causes. And this source is completely positive energy.

This is considered an axiom, because as physical beings, we can never know anything about the source (the root). All we can perceive and experience are the emanations of this source, which are its branches. There is, however, one term that requires definition before we go any further, and that is "positive."

In Kabbalah, when the words "positive" or "negative" are used, they do not refer to subjective terms like good and bad or right and wrong. They refer to metaphysical energies, like the physical energies we would find in a battery or an electrical circuit. The positive and negative poles represent two distinct kinds of energy; and in the battery we can see them separated with the positive side clearly marked with a plus (+) sign.

Positive energy, like the positive pole, gives off energy, whereas negative energy, like the negative pole, draws energy to it. In the Language of the Branches, positive energy is called the *Desire to Give or to Impart* while negative energy is called the *Desire to Receive*.

Other spiritual doctrines use similar terms in describing the two fundamental energies of the universe. For example, the Oriental doctrines usually refer to them as yin and yang. In the Language of the Branches, however, because the terms use words that are familiar to us, they enable us to define and thus get a clear understanding of the various phrases encoded in the Bible.

One example of this would be the Angel of Death. Disregarding all personifications and caricatures associated with this term, Kabbalah offers an unequivocal, non-Halloween-like, definition. An angel is simply a channel for a specific unit of metaphysical energy. Like an absolute number, energy requires definition of being either positive (like a positive ion) or negative (like a negative ion). The Angel of Death is a channel of a unit of negative energy—Desire to Receive—so strong that it can take away (receive) physical life. An equally positive energy—Desire to Give—would enable or give life.

The Language of the Branches employs many synonyms for positive and negative energy. The Desire to Give or Impart is also called the Right Column or Right-Column energy; whereas the Desire to Receive is also called the Left Column or Left-Column energy.

This original positive source, in the Language of the Branches, is called the *Ohr*, Light, as it is the emanation of the source and is all that we can talk about with regard to the source. Therefore, for us mortal beings, the Light *is* the source. In the military, this would be somewhat like a general from a private's perspective. For the private, the general is basically synonymous with the chief of staff because of their difference in rank.

That the Light is totally positive energy, a pure Desire to Share, means that it is whole, perfect, and lacking nothing: It has no Desire to Receive in it. That it is the cause of all causes means that all energy ever emanated into the universe all comes from the Light, the single source. Experienced on our level today, Light translates into anything that gives us pleasure and fulfillment—a sense of wholeness, physically, mentally, emotionally, and spiritually. This is all energy that stems from the Light.

In fact, as kabbalists always explain to us, everything we want in this world, our physical world, is all of a spiritual nature. While health and happiness are understandably spiritual forces, even the money that we may aspire for, for example, is not the physical property of money, the paper bills, but rather the buying power that money represents that we desire. That power translates as fulfillment, or one form of fulfillment. The totality of fulfillment, as the human race collectively perceives it, all derives from the positivity of the Light.

The Light is also infinite, as it existed even before time did. Therefore, the Light is also termed the *Ohr Einsof*, the Endless Light.

Now, if the Endless Light is whole, perfect, and lacking nothing, then what it lacks is lack! And "lack" translates as a Desire to Receive.

The Endless Light then created an infinite energy of lack— a Desire to Receive, called the Endless *Kli*, or Vessel. Just as the word itself indicates, the Vessel (or Endless Vessel) was created to receive and contain all the endless positive energy of the Light. That is, the Vessel contained all of the Light: positive, fulfilling energy. Moreover, since we are still talking about the Endless world, the Vessel, like the Light, is not a physical entity. In our minds, we may imagine a vessel, say a bowl; but, in the Endless, the Vessel existed without the physical limitations of time, space, and movement.

Since the Light is completely positive energy—or Desire to Share—and contains no negative energy (Desire to Receive), we say that the Endless Vessel was created out of nothing, *Yesh MeAyin* (Something From Nothing). This creation of something from nothing, being the Vessel, constitutes the totality of creation. The Vessel was the only entity *created*. Per the law of the conservation of energy, all else merely evolved from this single creation.

Since at this point none of this seems to have any bearing on our immediate life, it may be worth pointing out that the Endless Vessel constitutes the infinite aggregate of all souls today: All the souls that have ever roamed this planet, ever will, and are now are all pieces of this Endless Vessel. Since the Vessel denotes an energy of lack, this is also the definition and composition of the soul, our soul—the Desire to Receive. Our desires are what drive us or make us tick, just as the nature of our desires defines the individual that possesses those desires. The differentness of individuals' desires is also what makes people different.

The study of *Ta'amei* Torah really begins here, with the creation of the Vessel, since knowledge of the Light is beyond the means of this physical realm, while we are in physical bodies. It is also for this reason that Kabbalah is called as it is. The word "Kabbalah"[2] is the Hebrew noun of the verb "to receive." It defines everything there is to know about receiving: how to receive, what is the Desire to Receive, why to receive, and so on. And since our very being is comprised of a Desire to Receive, Kabbalah relates to every aspect of our lives.

The creation of the Vessel is said to require four specific phases or Aspects to be initiated.[3]

THE FIRST ASPECT

The First Aspect, or phase, is the picture we arrived at above. It is the state in which the Endless Light and the Endless Vessel were in perfect harmony. Here there was a balanced flow of positive and negative energy. Moreover, the moment the Vessel was created it became immediately filled with Light. The Vessel was endless and so could contain endless bounty: every want and need the Vessel could ever desire was already fulfilled in this phase, filled by the Light. So that even though the Vessel is an energy of lack and, per se, has no Light of its own, in this phase it had never felt "hungry" or lack; it had received all passively since its inception.

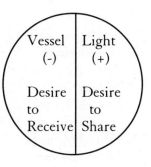

The Endless World

THE SECOND ASPECT

What then happened was that the Vessel, being so stuffed and never having known what hunger or lack means, never having really desired anything, decided it wanted to be like the Creator,

2. The Hebrew terms are more significant than their denotative function. We will discuss the power of the Hebrew letters in chapter 5.

3. *Ten Luminous Emanations*, vol. I, xviii.

the Light. The Vessel wanted to share. But the Vessel, by definition as a container for the Light and an energy of lack, had no Light of its own. And in addition to its innate inability to give, it had nothing or no one to give to!

Here the Vessel no longer wanted to be passive. It wanted to play an active role in its receiving Light. In the Language of the Branches, we say that what aroused in the Vessel was a feeling of *Lekhem Bizayon*, Bread of Shame. Bread of Shame is a feeling of getting something for nothing or receiving energy without having earned it and for which one cannot pay back.

THE THIRD ASPECT

To stop its receipt of Light, the Vessel constricted itself, somewhat like shutting its eyes. This had no bearing on the Light, as the Light is an eternal constant. But this created a situation in which the Vessel depleted itself of Light. In the Language of the Branches, the Vessel's self-induced constriction is called *Tzimtzum*, or *Restriction*.

In essence, the *Tzimtzum* created a vacuum in the Vessel. A vacuum is not an entity in itself, but rather is merely a lack of Light. And from this vacuum evolved a whole chain of effects, which will be discussed in the following chapters. However, for the purpose of this initial synopsis, what warrants being noted is that the interval immediately following the *Tzimtzum*, the Restriction, has been termed by modern science as the Big Bang. As Rabbi Berg explains, the result of the Second and Third Aspects "was the rejection or restriction of the Light which created a vacuum; this vacuum, in turn, permitted the emanation and creation of all the worlds through the process of progressive revelation" (*Kabbalah For the Layman*, I, p. 89).

THE FOURTH ASPECT

This stage completes the Thought, or purpose, of Creation. By this stage the Vessel has corrected[4] its Bread of Shame and now returns

---

4. The issue of "correction," or *Tikkun*, will be discussed in chapter 4 under *Tikkun* and Reincarnation. The Fourth Aspect constitutes the state of "Final Correction," or *Gmar Tikkun*.

to the Endless to rejoin the Light. This is a return to the state of the First Aspect, of perfect balance and harmony between the energy flow of Light to Vessel. By the Fourth Aspect, however, the Vessel, having experienced a real lack and desire from the Restriction, truly desires, appreciates, and craves the Light that completely fills and fulfills it.

With this, it is important to note that the Thought of Creation was for the Vessel to come to truly want and receive the Light. A real desire, or craving was necessary so that the Vessel's enjoyment and fulfillment from receiving would be real. The only way for the Vessel to appreciate the Light was by losing It and feeling existence without It. Therefore, Bread of Shame and the Third Aspect were necessary and, in fact, part of the Thought of Creation—not mistakes or flaws.

Actually, we should say that the Third Aspect *is* necessary, as this is the stage that we, the Vessel, are at now: We are working to return to the Endless. The work that needs to be done to return to the Endless is called *Tikkun,* or Correction (to be discussed in chapter 4). What we are correcting is the Bread of Shame of the Second Aspect of Creation. And the means by which we fulfill *Tikkun*, which is our goal, is by exerting Restriction (to be discussed in chapter 3). The Vessel's ability to achieve *Tikkun* via Restriction is the experience it needs, per its choice, to reach the Fourth Aspect of Creation.

It should also be noted that while, as physical beings, we cannot fully comprehend concepts that are not linear and finite, it is still important to remind ourselves, and especially at this stage, that the Endless contains no physical-illusory concepts such as time, space, or motion.[5] The Endless is not a place in the physical sense; it is a state of metaphysical energy. Therefore, each aspect of creation exists simultaneously (remember the example of water versus knowledge?).

From our linear existence, for example, we can draw upon the energy of each of these aspects and bring them into our individual reality to help us. The energy, for example, of the Fourth Aspect—what we are all aspiring for—is called in the Language of the Branches the *Shekhina*, meaning the corrected physical

---

5. We will discuss how this came into existence and why this is in chapter 4.

world.[6] It is also a good idea to bear in mind that all concepts discussed until now—Light, Vessel, Restriction, *Shekhina*, etcetera—are all energies: intangible, insensible, timeless, and spaceless.

This point will be further discussed in the next chapter. However, what we can note now is that from the Big Bang came the evolution of the worlds and *Sefirot*, the last of which is our physical plane. What also resulted was the shattering of the Vessel into fragmented pieces or *sparks*, which, in the physical world, became covered with an illusory covering or body.

This illusion of the body is important, since it now gives us the impression that when we give something to another, we are giving to something foreign to us. But per the *Quantum effect* (as we will discuss in chapter 5), the other is actually part of us, part of the complete Vessel. All our souls are still connected to their unified, completed seed, which is the Endless Vessel.

Suffice it to say at this point that the evolution of the physical world resulted so as to provide the Vessel (all souls collectively) with the opportunity to remove Bread of Shame and to earn the Light. This, in a nutshell, constitutes the purpose of our existence.

To offer the above basic sketch of Creation and the picture at large, the main thrust of Kabbalah has been glossed over. The bulk of Kabbalah deals with the Third Aspect—the phase that we ourselves are now at as it deals with its various ramifications. The knowledge of all of this together can aid us, us being the pieces of the composite Vessel, to return to the Endless—that is, to achieve the Fourth Aspect.

A SYNOPSIS OF SOME DIRECT RAMIFICATIONS OF CREATION

The Endless is the seed of all existence. What evolved from the Endless was *branches* and *leaves* whose existence is defined and determined by their metaphysical DNA in the Endless. Thus, what is voluntary on the upper level becomes mandatory on the lower level. The Endless Vessel *chose* to restrict its receipt of Light; there-

---

6. The corrected physical world, as we will learn under the subject of *Sefirot*, is called *Malkhut* or Kingdom. Therefore, the *Shekhina* is actually defined as the "corrected *Malkhut*."

fore, we, as the evolution and pieces of the Vessel, are now subject
to that choice. As a result of the *Tzimtzum*, a number of principles
govern our mortal lives:

1. Spirituality (a term we will define in chapter 3) and one's
    receipt of Light are unenforced and unenforceable. The
    Endless Vessel chose not to be coerced into receiving Light;
    thus, there is no such thing on our level as coercion in spiri-
    tuality. Put differently, (A) if there is no desire on the part
    of the recipient, then there is no real receiving or fulfillment;
    and (B) one cannot force another to become spiritual.
2. The Endless Vessel did not want to be passive in receiv-
    ing, as it wanted to be able to share what it received, being
    the Light. Therefore, to receive Light today, we must
    share or give. To give and be active about our giving, we
    need to be conscious of the fact that we are giving when
    we do so. And to be conscious of our giving, we need free
    will, a term we will define with its related term, Restric-
    tion—the central principle of Kabbalah—in chapter 3.
3. Everything that ever existed, exists, or will exist has al-
    ready existed, or was "contained," in the Endless in the
    First Aspect. Today, we merely long for what we once
    had. For example, when we hear a new song that we like,
    our connection to that song is merely a recognition of
    something we have already known from the Endless, and
    we feel a sense of fulfillment from the lack our soul felt
    from having lost it. Therefore, there is really no such thing
    as human creation, as the only creation was *something
    from nothing*—the Endless Vessel. All we can do is reveal
    energy in its various forms (what we dub as an invention)
    or release energy from being concealed (what we dub as a
    discovery). As Ecclesiastes 1:9 reminds us, "There is noth-
    ing new under the sun."[7]

The next chapter will delve us deeper into the issue of Creation, after which, in chapter 3 we will discuss the central prin-

---

7. And, parenthetically, *sun* refers to the *Sefirah* of *Zeir Anpin*, which is
directly above our level, *Malkhut*. Thus, to rephrase, there is nothing new on
our physical level of being.

ciple of Kabbalah, and thus of Judaism, being Restriction or its synonym, Resistance. Restriction and *Tikkun*, the latter which will be discussed in chapter 4, together are what enable us to activate Light in our lives. Proceeding these chapters we will discuss how to establish the necessary "wiring" to the Light. For this we will discuss the *Sefirot* and the Hebrew alphabet.

A working understanding of the concepts of these discussions equips us with the necessary tools to help us with every aspect of our lives. And as we shall see, we can also apply these tools to understand specific topics that pertain to and are indicative of our modern, physical existence (as we will do so in section IV).

2

Creation, Expounded Upon

Among kabbalists, there are basically two points that, in addition to the act of Creation per se, as discussed in chapter 1, have been discussed over the centuries with regard to Creation: one regards the age of the universe and the other regards evolution. The topic of Creation and its many ramifications are discussed and revealed to us in different forms. They also reveal a wealth of information and understanding far beyond the simple story line that the biblical story of Creation purports to be.

THE AGE OF THE UNIVERSE

A number of works bridge the apparent gap between the story of Creation related in the Book of Genesis and science's assertion that the universe is billions of years old. The following offers a brief examination of some of them to show how all reconcile what has been deemed to be an irreconcilable conflict.

Dr. Gerald Schroeder, veteran scientist in nuclear physics and oceanography, is one such author. In his book *Genesis and the Big Bang*,[1] Schroeder derives his thesis—that the "biblical

---

1. *Genesis and the Big Bang: The Discovery of Harmony Between Modern Science and the Bible* (New York: Bantam, 1990).

narrative and the scientific account of our genesis are two mu-
tually compatible descriptions of the same, single, and identical reality" (p. 12)—on essentially two main points. His first
point is that there is "overwhelmingly strong evidence, both
statistical and paleontological, that life could *not* have been
started on Earth by a series of random chemical reactions"
(p. 25). Biologist, biochemist, and Nobel Prize winner George
Wald

> was 100 percent correct in his thesis. Given *enough* time ran-
> dom chemical reactions would lead to life. Wald assumed that
> the needed time would be found. But it was not. Life appeared
> almost immediately on the newly formed Earth. Those
> people who assume that the fossil record provides proof for
> the theory of evolution through natural selection have fallen
> into the same trap as did Wald. . . . The fossil record of the
> mid-1800s, the time of Darwin's *On the Origin of Species*, in-
> deed contained organisms ranging from the primitive to the
> complex. But there was no continuity within this record. With
> its gaps in fossil evidence, it did *not* demonstrate an evolu-
> tionary flow from the primitive to the complex. Darwin re-
> alized this and acknowledged the deficiency. . . . [And]
> today's fossil record is as discontinuous as that of Darwin's
> (and Wallace's) time. . . . A gradual, or slow, evolution of a
> new species from one that predates it, is *never* seen in the fossil
> record (pp. 133–135).

Thus, through the discoveries of modern science, the theory
of evolution through natural selection is dissolved!
    With this, one might also consider that a running theme in
Schroeder's book, regarding science and the laws of nature, is:

> At the key junctures the specialists do *not* have the an-
> swers. The fact is that the laws of nature as we experience
> them *fail* to account for the forces that in effect formed the
> universe. These same laws, which form the basis of our lives,
> also *fail* to account for the most central phenomenon of our
> lives, the appearance of life itself (161, sic).

15 Billion Years = Six Days

Schroeder's second main point states:

> The Bible gives God six days to form mankind from the
> material produced at the creation. Current cosomology [sic]
> claims, it even proves, that nature took some 15 billion years
> to accomplish the same thing. . . . Both are [correct]. Liter-
> ally. With no allegorical modifications of these two simulta-
> neous, yet different, time periods (p. 29).

This is explained as follows:

> The biblical calendar for the time *after* Adam presents no
> problem to archeology. . . . [And we can] integrate the [pre-
> Adam] biblical data with that presented by cosmology and
> paleontology for the period extending from "the beginning"
> to Adam . . . but only if we practice . . . "stretching time." This
> is the very heart of the matter (p. 33).

To understand this, we need to incorporate the law of relativity, which states that "there is no absolute passage of time. It is
as flexible as the possible differences in the force of gravity and the
speed of motion across a boundary separating the observer from
the observed" (p. 157). That is to say, "The difference in perceived
time is called relativistic time dilation, the dilation that makes the
first six days of Genesis reassuringly compatible with the 15 billion years of cosmology" (p. 44).

Thus, as Einstein demonstrated, "when a single event is
viewed from two frames of reference, a thousand or even a billion
years in one can indeed pass for days in the other" (p. 34).

Sanford Aranoff[2] presents a similar argument in his essay,
"The Age of the World," when he shows how "the truth in the
Torah framework does not mean the same thing as truth in a sci-

---

2. Aryeh in Carmell and Cyril Domb, editors, *Challenge: Torah Views on
Science and its Problems*, second revised edition (New York: Feldheim, 1978),
pp. 150–163: "The Age of the World."

entific framework" (p. 152). Aranoff begins his explanation by stating:

> Anything which is impossible to measure or to observe is considered meaningless in science. Note carefully that this does not imply that prophecy [for example] is false; it is asserted only that prophecy cannot enter into science" (p. 153).

The same holds for the example given of the revelation per quantum mechanics, namely, "It is impossible to measure *both* position and momentum with complete accuracy" (p. 153, emphasis added). Thus, if one knows either the position or momentum (speed), the other factor is rendered "a meaningless concept . . . and that consequently we are not allowed to speak about it scientifically." Similarly, "[t]ime can thus be meaningless scientifically" (p. 153).

Moreover, "According to the Torah, God created everything, including the scientific laws. *It is meaningless to speak of the creation of the scientific laws in terms of scientific laws.* This shows that Creation is a scientifically meaningless concept (pp. 156–157, italics in original).

Dr. Schroeder presents the flip side of this point in noting:

> The biblical commentators on whom we rely said explicitly that the first six days of Genesis were six 24-hour days. This means that whoever was in charge recorded the passage of 24 hours per day. But who was there to measure the passage of time? Until Adam appeared on day six, God alone was watching the clock. *And that is the key* (p. 49, sic).

With this in mind, as Aranoff notes, "Many concepts in the Torah are meaningless in science" (p. 154). For example:

> There were six days of creation. During this period, there were arbitrary violations of scientific laws. We know this because the world was created with ten "sayings". . . . During these days scientific laws must have existed, except for the violations (p. 154).

Universe's Age = 5735 + Six Creation Days

Rabbi Simon Schwab[3], from a slightly different approach, poses the question, "[W]hat could possibly be the simple *meaning* of *yom* [day], when there was nothing visible in the sky which could indicate a lapse of time?" (p. 165). That is, "How can one tell time as long as the earth consists of naught but a dark undefined mass? When did the first day start and when did it end?" (p. 166). To this Rabbi Schwab takes into consideration:

> The time-span of each of our days here and now on earth can be defined by two methods:
>   a) the rotation of the earth; and
>   b) the appearance of the creation Light.

> These two time systems are synchronized *since the seventh Day*, the first Sabbath (p. 168, italics in original).

Thus:

> *Before* the Sabbath . . . [d]uring the period of creation . . . the earth could have turned around its axis much more rapidly. This would mean, that while the creation Light would register only one day, the earth could have experienced any number of days (p. 169).

In short, Rabbi Schwab writes: "Our question is: How old is the Universe? Answer: the Universe is 5735[4] years old, *plus six Creation Days*" (p. 168).

1,000 = 1

In 1993, Rabbi Aryeh Moshe Eliyahu ben Shmuel Kaplan's ("Aryeh Kaplan") manuscript, which discusses, among other topics, the age of the universe, was published by the Association of

---

3. Rabbi Simon Schwab, "How old is the Universe?" pp. 164–174. Carmell and Cyril's *Challenge*.

4. Specifically, 5735 in 1975, when Rabbi Schwab's essay was evidently written.

Orthodox Jewish Scientists.[5] In his posthumous book, Rabbi
Kaplan reveals a particular writing of "Rabbi Isaac of Akko
(1250–1350) [who] was a student and colleague of the Ramban
[Nahmanides], and one of the foremost Kabbalists of his time"
(p. 9).

In explaining Rabbi Isaac's writings, Rabbi Kaplan begins by
saying:

> The *Sefer ha-Temunah* [written around 1270[6] and which, per
> Kaplan, "establishes the age of the world, at least according
> to some classical interpretations, at forty-two thousand years"
> (p. 9) speaks about Sabbatical cycles (*shemitot*). This is based
> on the Talmudic teaching that "the world will exist for six
> thousand years, and in the seven-thousandth year, it will be
> destroyed" [per Sanhedrin 97a]. The *Sefer ha-Temunah* states
> that this seven-thousand-year cycle is merely one Sabbatical
> cycle. However, since there are seven Sabbatical cycles in a
> Jubilee, the world is destined to exist for forty-nine thousand
> years.

Rabbi Isaac of Akko writes:

> One of God's days is one thousand years, as it is written, "For
> a thousand days in Your sight are as a day" (Psalms 90:4).
> Since one of our years is 365¼ days, a year on high is 365,250
> of our years. Two years on high is 730,000 of our years. From
> this, continue multiplying to 49,000 years [7 years of 7 sab-
> batical cycles; each year being 1,000 years], each year consist-
> ing of 365¼ days, and each supernal day being one thousand
> of our years, as it is written, "God alone will prevail on that
> day" (Isaiah 2:11) (p. 13).

Rabbi Kaplan basically spells that out for us:

> Rabbi Isaac of Akko writes that since the Sabbatical cycles
> existed before Adam, their chronology must be measured, not

---

5. Rabbi Aryeh (Moshe Eliyahu ben Shmuel) Kaplan, *Immortality, Resurrection, and the Age of the Universe.*

6. Per the *Yudaica Lexicon.*

in human years, but in divine years. Thus, the *Sefer ha-Temunah* is speaking of divine years when it states that the world is forty-two thousand years old. This has some startling consequences, for according to many Midrashic sources, a divine day is 1,000 earthly years long, and a divine year, consisting of 365¼ days, is equal to 365,250 earthly years.

Thus, according to Rabbi Isaac of Akko, the universe would be 42,000 x 365,250 years old. This comes out to be 15,340,500,000 years, a highly significant figure. From calculations based on the expanding universe and other cosmological observations, modern science has concluded that the Big Bang occurred approximately 15 billion years ago. But here we see that same figure presented in a Torah source written over seven hundred years ago! (p. 9).

In Dr. Hawking's book *A Brief History of Time*, the age that he gives the universe is only vaguely "about ten or twenty thousand million years (1 or 2 with ten zeros after it)" (p. 114). When one considers the vagueness offered by modern science compared to a thirteenth-century rabbi, the magnitude of such a statement is phenomenal!

Showing the complexity of such studies, Rabbi Kaplan also unfurls:

There is a question as to which cycle we are in today. Some authorities maintain that we are currently in the second Sabbatical cycle. Others maintain that we are currently in the seventh cycle. According to the second opinion, the universe would have been forty-two thousand years old when Adam was created (p. 6). . . . According to *Sefer ha-Temunah*, then, there were other worlds before Adam was created. These were the worlds of previous Sabbatical cycles (p. 7).

Rabbi Kaplan then refers to a number of allusions to this concept of sabbatical cycles in the Midrash:

1. God created universes and destroyed them[7] (p. 7).
2. According to the Talmud, and some Midrashim as well,

---

7. Per *Sefer ha-Temunah* 314.

there were 974 generations before Adam.[8] The number is
derived from the verse, "Remember forever His covenant, a
word He commanded for a thousand generations" (Psalms
105:8). This would indicate that the Torah was destined to
be given after one thousand generations. Since Moses was the
twenty-sixth generation after Adam, there must have been
974 generations before Adam (p. 7).

3. The concept of pre-Adamic cycles was well known
among the *Rishonim* (early authorities), and is cited in such
sources as *Bahya, Recanati, Ziyyoni,* and *Sefer ha-Hinnukh*.[9]
It is also alluded to in the *Kuzari*, and in the commentaries of
the *Ramban* and *Ibn Ezra*[10] (p. 7).

4. In the same vein, the Midrash states that before this creation "God created worlds and destroyed them."[11] As these
teachings are interpreted by a number of sources, especially
among the Kabbalists, they refer to earlier cycles of creation.
Adam was merely the first human being created in the latest
cycle (p. 21).

A solution to the questions these theories raise may be found
from the second point studied, regarding Creation, and that is:

EVOLUTION

It is important to understand the place of "creation" and evolution
in the grand scheme of things, as outlined in the last chapter. The
only creation that actually occurred, was *Yesh MeAyin*, something
from nothing, which was the Desire to Receive, or the Endless
Vessel. The "creation" that the Bible begins with in chapter I is the
Big Bang—that is, the Bible explains what went on from the particular point that science has termed the Big Bang. As explained
in the last chapter, the Big Bang occurred immediately following

---

8. Per Hagigah 13b–14a; *Kohelet Rabbah* 1:15, 4:3; *Tanhuma Lekh Lekha*
11, *Yitro* 9; *Midrash Tehillim* 105:3; *Yalkut Shimoni* 2:863.

9. Per Bahya, Ziyyoni, and Recanati on Leviticus 25:8.

10. See *Kuzari* 1:67, Ramban on Genesis 2:3, Ibn Ezra on Genesis 8:22.

11. Per *Bereshit Rabbah* 3:7, 9:2; *Kohelet Rabbah* 3:11; *Bereshit Rabbah* 10:2.

the *Tzimtzum*, the Restriction, in the third aspect of the creation of the Endless Vessel.

As the Endless Vessel was the one and only creation, all else is an effect of that primal creation. There are many "replicas" or microcosms of the ultimate macrocosm, being the Endless Light and Vessel, and they are all parallel and derived from their parent macrocosm.[12]

Outside of kabbalistic study, the Biblical commentary most widely read and referred to is that of Rabbi Shlomo Yitzkhaki, who is better known by the acronym of his name, Rashi (1040–1105 C.E.[13]). Rabbi Adin Steinsaltz,[14] who is a 20th-century, world-renowned Jewish religious and spiritual leader, summarizes the magnitude of the stature of Rashi. In Rabbi Steinsaltz's book, introducing the Talmud to a general audience,[15] he simply states that "the greatest commentator was undoubtedly . . . Rashi" (p. 67).

Interestingly, though, Rashi was also a kabbalist. In fact, Rashi even quotes Rabbi Shimon Bar Yohai (second century C.E.), who revealed the *Zohar*, the central text of Kabbalah,[16] all through his commentary. It is also Rabbi Shimon who is the authority quoted the most in the Talmud. But this point is only parenthetical to the discussion at hand.

---

12. Two examples, as we will see in chapter 5, are the human body, which is a miniature parallel of the Ten *Sefirot* and the atom, the latter being a miniature parallel of the "lower seven" *Sefirot*.

13. per *Yudaica Lexicon*.

14. Rabbi Adin Steinsaltz is the first in history to translate the *Talmud* to English and heads the Israel Institute for Talmudic Publications in Jerusalem, Israel.

15. Adin Steinsaltz, *The Essential Talmud*.

16. Kabbalists say that the *Zohar* is "attributed" to Rabbi Shimon, since, like other authorities of his time who employed scribes, his student Rabbi Abba was the one who actually transcribed the words of his teacher. Moreover, the fact that Rashi quotes Rabbi Shimon and the *Zohar* is significant, because it refutes some academics' claim that the *Zohar* was not written by Rabbi Shimon, but rather by thirteenth-century kabbalist Moses de Leon or by others of the latter's contemporaries. In "proving" their point, however, such academics will claim that when Rashi refers to the *Zohar*, it is not the kabbalistic work he is referring to but to something else.

Needless to say, practicing kabbalists, who appreciate the spiritual stature of Rabbi Shimon, all agree that no one but Rabbi Shimon could have and

Basically, Rashi[17] discerned the Lamarckian or Darwinian idea of evolution through the first verses of Genesis, chapter 1: "And God called the light Day, and the darkness He called Night. And there was evening, and there was morning, one day" (Genesis 1:5). Unfortunately, many translations of the Bible have erroneously translated *Yom Ekhad* as "first day." Ekhad means "one"; "first" would be *rishon*, but the word in Genesis is unequivocally *ekhad*, thus "one." Rashi picks up on this key word that will later explain the source of evolution, and that word is *one*:

According to the order expressed in this portion [of Scripture] it should have been "the first day," as it is written of the other days, "the second [day]," "the third [day]," "the fourth [day]" (ibid., p. 4).

Further on, Rashi comments on Genesis 1:14: "And God said. Let there be lights in the firmament of the heaven to divide be-

---

thus did "write" (dictate) the words of the *Zohar*. Kabbalists even maintain that, per Rabbi Luria's (the Ari's) *Gate of Reincarnation,* Rabbi Shimon was the reincarnation of Moses. Just as Moses channeled the Wisdom of Kabbalah in its oral form, Rabbi Shimon channeled this wisdom in its written form (see Rabbi Berg's chapter on "The Origins of Kabbalah" in *Layman* I).

In this context, one might note Rabbi Kaplan's words:

Until the rise of the Jewish Enlightenment, mysticism and intellectualism had equal status within Judaism. The ostensible goal of the Enlightenment, however, was to raise the intellectual level of Judaism, and positive as this may have been, it was often done at the expense of other Jewish values. The first values to fall by the wayside were Jewish mysticism in general and meditation in particular. Anything that touched upon the mystical was denigrated as superstition and occultism and was deemed unworthy of serious study. Even *Kabbalah*, which contains mysticism par excellence, *was reduced to simply an intellectual exercise; its deeper meanings were totally lost* (*Jewish Meditation*, pp. 40–41, emphasis added).

Moreover, as Rabbi Berg points out, the writings of Rabbi Asher Ben David (c. 1229) and Rabbi Isaac Ben Jacob HaKohen (c. 1260) indicate that kabbalists already knew of Rabbi Shimon's *Zohar* well before Rabbi Moses de Leon made it public at the end of the thirteenth century (Rabbi Berg's *Reincarnation,* pp. 182, 187).

17. *The Pentateuch and Rashi's Commentary,* by Rabbi Abraham Ben Isaiah and Rabbi Benjamin Sharfman in collaboration with Dr. Harry M. Orlinsky and Rabbi Dr. Morris Charner.

tween the day and between the night; and let them be for signs, and for seasons, and for days, and years. . . ." (ibid., pp. 8–9). On this he explains:

> On the first day they were created, but on the fourth day He [God] commanded them to be suspended in the firmament. So also all the creations of heaven and earth were created on the first day, and each one was put in its proper place on the day that was decreed for it (ibid., p. 8).

Yet even further on he notes for Genesis 1:24, "And God said: Let the earth bring forth (the) living creature after its kind, cattle and creeping thing and beast of (the) earth after its kind. And it was so" (ibid., pp. 12–13). Rashi refers to his point made for Genesis 1:1, when he expounds: "That is what I explained [under verse 14] that everything was created on the first day and it was necessary only to bring them forth" (p. 12).

In short, what Rashi explains is that, per the literal reading of the first chapter of the Bible, all was created in one day, called "one day" and not "first day." And then each entity was brought forth (that is, actualized) in its respective or appropriate time. This basically amounts to the theory of evolution.

> In the beginning, God created the heaven and the earth. . . . And God called the light Day, and the darkness He called Night. And the evening and the morning were one day. . . . And God called the firmament Heaven, And the evening and the morning were the second day. . . . And God said, Let be there lights in the firmament of the heaven to divide the day from the night. . . . (Genesis 1:1–8).

Rabbi Berg demonstrates and expands on the evolution process when he discusses the following:

> The first question we have to ask is why there appears to be so much repetition in this description; we are told, for instance, that Heaven was created on the second day, yet it is also referred to in the first verse, where we are told that it was created on the first day. In the same way we learn that day and night were established on the first day, yet the process

seems to be repeated on the fourth day, when the lights came into being to distinguish day from night. Another strange feature of this passage is that the first day is called *"yom ehad,"* meaning "day one," as opposed to all the subsequent days, which are called the second, third, fourth, etc.

These problems begin to unravel themselves only when we recall that the essence of Creation is the progressive transformation of energy levels, which are known as the *Sefirots*. Now we know that this process of transformation does not alter the root of the energy at all; it merely reveals a different aspect of the energy, just as when water is poured into a number of different coloured glasses, we see a different colour in each glass, but know that the water has not been altered. The *sefirot* or vessels, operate in the same way, diversifying the original energy of the *En Sof* (Berg's *Layman* I, 94–95).

While the topic of *Sefirot* will be discussed in chapter 5, even at this stage its mention proves helpful in explaining the evolution of the world. Very briefly, there are six particular *Sefirot* that act together as a channel or link between the spiritual and physical worlds. The first three correspond to energy that is only potential, while the lower three correspond to energy that is actualized or materialized in our corporeal world.

With this in mind, we can understand what Rabbi Berg means when, in his recorded lectures on Genesis,[18] he explains that the first word, *Beresheet*, misleadingly translated to "In the beginning," means *bara sheet*. *Bara* means "He created," while *sheet* is Aramaic[19] for the number six. Therefore, the very opening word of the Bible means "He created six."

---

18. Rabbi Philip S. Berg, *"Zohar: Bereshit,"* nos. 1–6.

19. Aramaic and Hebrew share the same alphabet, many words, and are in many ways the same. Both languages are used in Biblical study, but are used for different spiritual purposes, as each connects to a different level of metaphysical energy. The *Zohar* and the Ari's writings, for example, are written in Aramaic.

Moreover, as a parenthetical observation, it is interesting that most swear or curse words are of a religious tone, possibly including the above-referenced Aramaic word for *six*. While *Genesis* in Hebrew is usually transliterated *Bereshit*, this author purposely transliterated it so as not to evoke any modern, colloquial connotations!

The words "Heaven" and "earth" in this same opening verse, are translated by the Language of the Branches as the first being positive energy and the second, the energy of the negative pole. The opposition of these conflicting energies produced a spark, which emanated as "one day." And "day" is the code word for *Sefirah* (the singular of *Sefirot*).

Rabbi E. Dessler[20] presents a similar explanation when he quotes Ramban (Nahmanides, 1194–1270 C.E.) in the later's commentary on Bereshit 1:3, which is as follows:

> "[T]he days mentioned in *Maaseh Bereshit* [the act of creation] were . . . actual days, composed of hours and minutes; and they were six, like the six weekdays, according to the plain meaning of the text. But in [relation to] the inner meaning of the matter, "days" refers to the *sefirot* emanating from on high . . ."—referring to the six *sefirot* from *hesed* to *yesod*, Rabbi Dessler's note (p. 139, italics in original).

Rabbi Dessler points out, by quoting Rabbi Nehunia ben HaKaneh, that the Bible reads: "'Because six days did God make heaven and earth' . . . Surely it should rather have said '*in* six days' . . . The answer is that what God made was the *days*, which we understand mean *sefirot*—the days themselves were what were created" (p. 139).

That is, what is described in the book of Genesis is the formation of the six Sefirot from the created Endless Vessel plus the concept of "rest." (Rabbi Berg discusses this concept of rest in his recorded lectures on *Beresheet*; however, in short, "rest" refers to a metaphysical state whereby the opposing forces of the positive and negative poles cease to conflict.)

One Day

As we have discussed before, the DNA intelligence, contained in a seed on a physical as on a metaphysical level, represents the entire evolution of whatever stems from that seed. Everything that

---

20. Rabbi E. Dessler, "The Inner Meaning of the Creation," pp. 138–140, in Carmell and Domb's *Challenge*.

there is to ever be known about an entity is concentrated within its seed.

The same holds true for this group of six *Sefirot*. It is for this reason that what we think of as the first day of Creation, as Rashi has already pointed out, is actually one day; although all subsequent days of Creation are called "second . . . third . . . fourth . . . fifth," and so on. This is because day one constitutes the seed for all that stems from it. It is "one day" because it is a whole and unified conception of energy. This, again, encapsulates the theory of what is called evolution.[21]

Since "day" refers to a particular concept of energy and because the first three *Sefirot* in this group of six correspond to the spiritual world and to potential energy only, the physical concept of time does not exist. In his recorded lecture on the Torah portion of *Shoftim*, Rabbi Berg even points out that the enumeration of years, as per the Hebrew calendar (whereby this year, 1994, would be 5754), began with the fourth day of creation: The fourth day, as one of the lower three of the group of six, corresponds to the first of actualized energy. The fourth day is the "day" in which the means to measure time came into existence, which was the implementation of the sun and the moon.[22]

Spiritual energy is infinite. Genesis I discusses pure spiritual or metaphysical intelligences and, therefore, discusses only the spiritual-metaphysical energies of the creation/formation of the world (the ninety-nine percent). In fact, nothing in Genesis chapter one is of a physical, corporeal nature. Everything that is created/formed is what Rabbi Berg calls "bottled-up energies," referring to the *Sefirot*.[23] Genesis II, on the other hand, discusses the physical aspect of Creation (the one percent).

---

21. Rabbi Berg discusses the terms of these first verses in depth. Those interested in obtaining a deeper understanding of this particular focus of Kabbalah can consult Rabbi Berg's recorded lectures on Genesis and *"Talmud Esser Sefirot."* For the purposes of this brief discussion, however, what is important to note is the nature of these "days."

22. Rabbi Schwab concretizes this point by noting that it was not "until the fourth day did the sun become visible in the sky thus becoming a regulator of time. During the first three days of creation the sun and the stars were not recognizable from the earth" (p. 166).

23. See chapter 5 on the *Sefirot* to understand Adam's level before and after the Fall and hence what the Fall means.

Therefore, Rabbi Berg not only defines the process of evolution from its absolute beginning, but, from his explanation of the first verses of Genesis per the *Zohar*, he inadvertently provides a kind of umbrella solution to the question regarding the age of the universe. It goes something like: Since the first part of evolution took place in the infinite, potential state, even before time came into being, the absolute age of the universe is infinite or non-finite.

THE WRITINGS OF THE ARI AND RABBI ASHLAG

Second to Rabbi Shimon Bar Yohai—who "had no karmic reason to walk this earth 2,000 years ago" but to reveal "the wisdom of the *Zohar*"—was Rabbi Isaac Luria who "appeared solely to interpret the *Zohar* and spread its wisdom" (Berg's *Reincarnation*, p. 59). Rabbi Luria (1534–1572 C.E.), who is usually referred to by the acronym of his name, the "Ari,"[24] is the founder of the school of Kabbalah known as the "Lurianic System." This essentially is the school of Kabbalah that has survived until today. One of the reasons this school and not others continued is primarily because "[a] prime objective of the Ari's commentary was that truth should be presented in a logical, consecutive manner" (Berg's *Layman* I, p. 37). Hence, his method and the modern, scientific method of written dialogue are compatible.

---

24. The Ari is also considered by Kabbalists to be the reincarnation of Rabbi Shimon, as Rabbi Berg, a practicing Kabbalist himself, expresses: "Anyone familiar with the writings of the Ari will realize that his clarity and depth of thought and understanding could only come from one blessed with the spirit of Rabbi Shimon: only Rabbi Shimon's soul would have been capable of the feats of transcendence that are clearly indicated in the Ari's writings" (Berg's *Layman* I, p. 35).

Moreover, though parenthetically, the Ari demonstrates that the prerequisites for the study of *Sitrei* Torah (which are adamantly claimed by some, though erroneously so, to pertain to the study of *Ta'amei* Torah as well) are not such hard and fast rules. "The Ari was a Talmudic authority before he had reached the age of twenty" (ibid., p. 34), after which he went on to become a master of Kabbalah. He "completed his task on earth and ascended to the place waiting for him" (ibid., p. 36) before he even reached the minimum age of forty for studying *Sitrei* Torah, as he passed on at the age of thirty-eight.

Among the legacies the Ari left was his book *Etz HaHaim* (*The Tree of Life*), which defines the process of Creation and its resulting evolution. The Ari's writings, however, as logical and methodical as they are, are also on what a Kabbalist would say is a "seed" level. Each word is encoded in the Language of the Branches and is why each sentence seems so cryptic. The following is all of chapter one, as quoted from the Research Centre of Kabbalah's translated edition:

1. [Know] that before the emanations were emanated and the creatures were created, the upper simple Light had filled entire existence, and there was no empty space whatsoever namely as empty atmosphere, hollow, or pit for everything was filled with that simple, boundless Light, and there was no such part as head, and no such part as tail; that is there was neither beginning nor end, for everything was simple or smoothly balanced evenly and equally in one likeness or affinity, and that is called the Endless Light.

2. And when in His simple and smooth will the desire to create the world and to manifest the emanations, to bring to Light the perfection of His deeds and His names and His appellations, which was the cause of creation of the world.

3. Behold He then restricted himself, in the middle point which is in Him, precisely in the middle, He restricted the Light, and the Light has withdrawn to the sides around the middle point.

4. And there have remained an empty space, atmosphere [and air and empty space], and a vacuum surrounding the exact middle point. And behold, this restriction was equally balanced around that middle empty point in such a manner that the vacuum was circular and in complete balance and sameness all around. It was not in the shape of a cube, which has straight angles, the boundless also withdrew His Light in a circular form equally on all sides.

5. [The reason was] because the Endless Light itself is equal: that is, since the Endless Light is in complete omniparity, it follows that it must contract itself in omniparity on all sides. It is a well known fact that in mathematics, or geometry, a sphere or circle is the most balanced and uniform figure. This is not true of the cube with its angles, or of the

triangle, or any other form that might be considered. (It was therefore necessary for the middle point to be restricted in the form of a circle) and behold after the restriction mentioned above it drew from the Endless Light one line, direct from His circular Light from above downwards, and it gradually descended by evolution into that hollow or vacuum. The upper head of the line was extended from the Endless, Himself, and it contacted Him. Verily, the end of that line below did not contact the Endless Light. The line was drawn and extended below, and in that vacuum He emanated, created, formed and made all the collective worlds. [*The Tree of Life*, Chapter 1,1 as quoted in Rabbi Berg's *Ten Luminous Emanations* 55–87].

It would be almost four hundred years before someone could decipher and thus unlock the wealth of knowledge contained in the Ari's writings. This person was Rabbi Yehuda Ashlag (1886–1955).[25] As Rabbi Berg sums up in his introduction to the above translation, "Rabbi Ashlag left three legacies" (p. 26). The first was his translation of Rabbi Shimon's *Zohar* into Hebrew (the *Sulam*) from its original Aramaic. This alone was a tremendous doing, not only because the *Zohar* had never before this been translated from the original Aramaic, but in his translation Rabbi Ashlag deciphered much of the crypticness of the *Zohar* "into clear, flowing Hebrew" (ibid.). The *Sulam* edition of the *Zohar* comprises twenty-four volumes.

His second legacy was the founding of the Research Centre of Kabbalah in Jerusalem in 1922. Rabbi Ashlag, head of the Centre, was then succeeded by his chief disciple, Rabbi Yehuda Brandwein (1904–1969), a family descendant of the Maggid of Mezhirich. The Maggid of Mezhirich was the successor to the Ba'al Shem Tov (the *Besht*), who was the founder of the Hassidic movement. In 1969, Rabbi Brandwein handed over the directorship of the Kabbalah Centre to his chief disciple, Rabbi Dr. Philip Berg.

Rabbi Ashlag's third legacy was the compilation of "his sixteen-volume textbook, the *Study of the Ten Luminous Emanations (Talmud Eser haSfirot)*" (Berg's *Layman* I, p. 44). In these vol-

---

25. Whom kabbalists consider to be a spark (reincarnation) of the Ari's soul.

umes Rabbi Ashlag deciphers the writings of the Ari, and it is from this work that texts, like the above, are explained and taught today. The study of *Talmud Esser haSfirot* is an advanced course, which spans years of study if not an entire lifetime. The above-quoted chapter is studied over a period of a number of sessions, if not months.[26]

The above is given not only to whet the reader's appetite, but in the context of this discussion, the Ari's and Rabbi Ashlag's writings provide the direction one needs to find the answers to all of our questions about Creation and the beginnings of our planet and cosmos.

In his monumental astrophysics book for the masses, Dr. Stephen Hawking, who to many today represents the entirety of modern science, poses a number of questions, which for science remain unanswered. One such question (without getting into the details of its answer) can be understood or at least be perceived to exist in the Ari's above-quoted chapter. The question is Dr. Hawking's question number two, which begins as follows: "Why is the universe so uniform on a large scale? Why does it look the same at all points of space and in all directions?" (p. 127). It is interesting that Dr. Hawking, in asking today, and the Ari, in answering four hundred years earlier, even use the same terminology.

In fact, Kabbalists will go on to say that science can learn much more and find the answers to the questions raised by its empirical studies in all fields from Kabbalah—and all based on the Bible. We will continue to explore various points regarding Creation in this volume as we go along and acquire more tools.

EVOLUTION AND MAN

Evolution denotes an emanation from the Source (God or His emanation, the Light) in parallel form. The rings that emanate around a stone thrown into a body of water illustrate this concept. Evolution is *not*, however, a change of one form to another. Thus

---

26. A couple hundred of these sessions are recorded and available through the Research Centre of Kabbalah, whose main branch is in New York and can be reached at (718) 805–9122; they also have two small volumes on the Ten Luminous Emanations for the novice.

the rings that emanate from the stone's impact point will all be circles; neither triangles nor squares will just pop up amid the circles.

Kabbalah expounds that the Vessel, as expressed on earth, contains four levels or forms. These levels are expressed as "higher" and "lower" forms according to their level of Desire to Receive. The lowest form is the inanimate, lowest because it expresses the least amount of Desire to Receive and in fact is almost independent of this world for its existence. The next level is the "growing" or plant life. The next level is called "living," meaning the animal kingdom, and the highest form is the "speaking," meaning humans. Evolution occurs as an emanation within each of these four forms but never crosses forms. Thus, what is of the inanimate level remains inanimate, what is "growing" will always be "growing," and so on.

There may be different kinds or levels within each form, but they nevertheless remain within their form. Coral, for example, is defined by *Webster's II New Riverside University Dictionary* as a "marine coelenterate . . . rocklike structure," where a "coelenterate" is defined as an "invertebrate animal" (pages 311 and 278 respectively). Thus, coral is an animal that acts like a plant ("growing") or even as inanimate; but it is of the "living" (animal) form all the same. The Venus's-flytrap, on the other hand, is "an insectivorous plant" (ibid, p. 1281), meaning it is a plant that acts like an animal. Regardless of its behavior, it remains a plant all the same.

The same holds true for the various types of monkey that many purport to have "evolved" into man. According to Kabbalah, this is an impossibility, and such a cross of forms never occurred, since what is animal remains within the animal level and what is human remains within the human level. These types of monkeys, like the Venus's-flytrap, evidently demonstrated abilities or behavior like the form above them, being "speaking" (human); but they are nevertheless only higher forms of monkey (animal), not human ("speaking").

In continuation of his argument regarding the age of the universe, Sanford Aranoff[27] relates to such theories of "man's evolution":

---

27. "The Age of the World," pp.150–163, in Carmell and Domb's *Challenge.*

The entire question [the problem of the evolution of man] loses much of its force if we realize that there were arbitrary violations of scientific laws before the first Sabbath. If such violations were involved in the making of man, we cannot say that man "naturally" evolved (pp. 158–159).

After the Restriction, that aspect of "speaking" in the Endless Vessel evolved into Adam. While, in Genesis I, Adam acquired "physical" form, he did not have a physical body as we do today. In Genesis 1:27, Adam is created androgenous, "male and female." These male and female aspects are separated in Genesis II and thus Eve appears.[28]

Midrash tells us that Adam was so tall that his head reached the heavens while his feet walked on the earth. We are also told that Adam and Eve, at that stage, were made entirely of nail—the material of our finger- and toenails. That is to say, Adam and Eve were completely transparent; nothing about them was opaque that could obscure the Light and thus cause them limitation of any kind. In fact, as Rabbi Glazerson notes: "Our sages tell us the radiance from only Adam's heel made the light of the sun seem weak in comparison" (*From Hinduism To Judaism,* p. 41).

In chapter five we will define the spiritual level at which Adam and Eve existed before and after the Fall and how exactly the Fall is defined. However, in terms of our discussion on evolution, we said that Adam was a giant whose head was in the heavens. In fact, all of existence before the Fall was large, from the inanimate to the "living" levels. Kabbalists even express that as large as the living kingdom was then, including the dinosaurs, they were merely small pets for Adam and Eve!

------

28. We will discuss this point more in chapter 7, when we discuss male and female and soul mates. In chapter 5 we will also be better equipped to define what the Bible means by saying that "God created man in His image, in the image of God created He him" (Genesis 1:27). However, the reason Adam and Eve were separated as discrete beings is because, as androgenous, the positive and negative or masculine and feminine energies, were "back-to-back," meaning there was no communication between them. Since androgenous Adam could not utilize his energies as such to create a circuitry of energy, Eve, the feminine aspect of androgenous Adam, was removed so that the two poles, represented by Adam and Eve, could then communicate "face-to-face."

After the Fall the entire universe shrank. Everything from the inanimate and growing to the living and Adam and Eve. All shrank spiritually and physically. All shrank spiritually, as the Light in everything became concealed. All of the Light that Adam and Eve had revealed to them became concealed, and it became their duty to reveal the Light Force from all existence after the Fall. The state that the Vessel (manifested in Adam and Eve) exists, whereby the Light is not concealed, is called "Paradise". Once the Light became concealed, the universe was rendered, to use John Milton's terminology, "Paradise Lost."

The universe also shrank physically. All was reduced to miniaturized form. Thus, today we still find living replicas of the dinosaur but in miniaturized form: these would be the lizards and other forms of reptile. They never completely disappeared; they were just reduced in size.

Physically, Adam's body also shrank to the proportions we have today. After the Fall, he acquired a physical content of flesh and blood, which is what we have today. The only remnants of Adam and Eve in our physical body are our finger- and toenails, as they are the substance from which Adam and Eve were made.

Incidentally, on Saturday evening, in Judaism there is a ritual (in the *Havdalah* service) in which one looks at the reflection of light off his fingernails. This is to connect us to our state of perfection before the Fall. What we essentially connect to is not Adam's physical state as much as to Adam's spiritual state. Leaving the Garden of Eden meant leaving an elevated state of consciousness. The reduction of the physical aspect was merely an effect of the spiritual reduction that took place.

We will discuss these different levels of consciousness and spirituality throughout this book. By the time we get to chapter 8, we will also be able to define what the snake was that got Adam and Eve into this mess in the first place, as by then we can define how paradise can be regained. As our Sages remind us, the remedy is always in the problem itself.

II

Activating the Light

3

Restriction

The Vessel's act of *Tzimtzum*, or Restriction, in the Endless created a paradox in our world: there is no revelation of Light without a vessel, that is, without something to cover and to contain the energy. Actually, there are many paradoxes in this universe, and kabbalists explain that wherever there is a paradox, that is where you will find truth. From a different angle, Rabbi Kaplan points out:

> [I]f we look at God as the creator of all things, then God must also be the creator of logic. This has important ramifications: if one discovers paradoxes in relation to God, it is not a problem. Paradoxes are merely ideas that transcend logic, and since God is the creator of logic, He can use it as He desires, but He is not bound by it (Rabbi Kaplan's *Jewish Meditation*, p. 89).

In short: "Logic is a tool of God's, but He is never bound by it" (ibid., p. 126).

The paradox that energy needs to be concealed to be revealed can be illustrated using simple geometrical figures. An infinite number of circles may exist on a blackboard. But it is only when we put chalk to board and outline a particular circle that that circle becomes revealed. It is only when we confine the abstract circle to physical form that we can not only perceive the circle with our five senses, but, more importantly, we can make use of it.

MASCULINE (POSITIVE) AND FEMININE (NEGATIVE) ENERGIES

In this context we can understand why the terms positive and negative are also referred to as masculine and feminine energies. Masculine energy, being positive energy, is potential energy. Feminine energy, which is negative energy, is the energy that implements masculine—potential—energy. The sun's rays of light, for example, are masculine (potential) energy. Although the sun's light is essential for all life on earth, there is no life on the rays of light themselves. The earth, on the other hand, is feminine (negative) energy, which is also why she is called Mother Earth. It is only on earth that the potential energy of the sun is implemented.

There are countless examples of the workings of this duo—masculine and feminine energies—in nature, the most obvious being the reproductive system. The male, a physical expression of masculine energy, supplies the potential energy to the female, a physical expression of feminine energy. Conception takes place in the woman, and it is only the woman who can implement the potential energy. It is also for this reason that the *Shekhinah* is referred to as a feminine energy. Aside from the grammatical fact that the name *Shekhinah* is feminine in Hebrew, the *Shekhinah* represents the implementation of the whole Thought of Creation. While she is a metaphysical energy, she is the energy of implementation, of the final product.

There are a number of pagan religions that worship the *Shekhinah*, although maybe not by her Hebrew name, but rather as a god or "the Goddess." According to Kabbalah, and hence Judaism, the *Shekhinah* is *not* a god: She is the energy of the completed Vessel. There is only one God, and He is referred to as the Light.

The *Shabbat* is also considered a feminine energy. She is even referred to as the Sabbath Queen (*Shabbat HaMalka*), because she crowns the entire week, or as the Sabbath Bride (*Shabbat HaKalah*). The *Shabbat* is the implementation of all the spiritual energy that we have worked to achieve that week. She bears the fruit of our toil.

With this in mind, we can also understand what a memory is. The word "memory" in Hebrew is *Zikaron* from the root *Zakhar*, and *Zakhar* is Hebrew for "masculine." Therefore, a memory, by definition, is an influx of positive (Desire to Give) energy that *gives* us the energy of a particular event or place or whatever is contained in that memory. As there is no time, space, or movement in the "real" world, we may be in one place at a specific time, but through the power of memory or thought, we can draw on the energy of a place on the other side of the globe from many years ago. The minute the energy is drawn, the memory is recalled, and we are there.

This is what is meant in the Friday night *Kiddush* that we mentioned in chapter 1. In the liturgy, we say, "*Zikaron LeMa'aseh Beresheet*," which literally translates as "memory of the Act of Creation." But now that we have the necessary tools, we can understand that the real translation would be an "influx of the energy of Creation," while Creation is the energy of the seed level of the universe.

In the same prayer, we invoke another influx of energy, that which brought freedom to the enslaved Israelites who were in bondage over three thousand years ago in ancient Egypt. We say, "*Zekher LiTzi'at Mitzrayim*," which literally translates as "memory of the exodus from Egypt." As Rabbi Berg constantly reminds his students: If all we are being asked to do in Judaism is, literally, to *remember* the Act of Creation or the Exodus from Egypt, then we could simply mark it on our calendars! Such "memories" as just memories would offer no direct benefit to our lives today. It is, instead, the energy that effects freedom that we draw on Passover to help release us from whatever type of bondage we may be enslaved to in the modern world today.

RELATIVITY OF LIGHT AND VESSEL IN OUR WORLD

In addition, it is also important to note that the terms Light and Vessel, from our perspective, are relative. The Endless Light and Endless Vessel are absolute Light and Vessel, respectively. However, the farther we go from the Light, the more everything in between has the potential to be a Light from one stance, yet a vessel from another.

Our soul, for example, is a spark or sparks of the Endless Vessel. And yet, vis-à-vis our body, our soul is Light, while the body is a vessel for the soul. The Endless Vessel is the vessel for the Endless Light, yet the Endless Vessel for us now, is Light, since in the First Aspect it was completely filled with Light. A soul, vis-à-vis the Light, is a vessel. Yet every soul (as we will discuss in chapter 7) has two parts—a masculine and a feminine aspect. Thus, in relation to each other, the masculine aspect is Light for the feminine aspect, which is the vessel for her masculine counterpart. The physical sun may be the physical expression of the Light, and thus a vessel of the Light, but as regards the earth, the sun is Light, physically and metaphysically.

Moreover, there are vessels that are contained in vessels. As we said in chapter 2, there are many forms or microcosms in the universe that parallel the Endless Light and Vessel, but which are merely evolved forms of their parent macrocosm. The body, for instance, is the vessel of the soul. But clothes are another form of vessel for the body. One's home is yet another form of vessel, for the soul, or people living within its walls.

Light cannot be revealed in this world without a vessel to contain it. But that is only a prerequisite. The means of actually revealing the Light, per the Tzimtzum, is through Restriction. This is why Restriction is the central and key concept of Kabbalah and hence of Judaism. As Rabbi Berg emphatically states, "Restriction is the essential feature of the whole study of Kabbalah. And if you ever learned Kabbalah and you never came across the word Restriction, you learned nothing!"[1]

One can learn all kinds of fancy terms and intricate charts; but if one does not learn, and more important *integrate and internalize*, the concept of Restriction or Resistance (as these two terms are used interchangeably), one is missing the whole essence of Kabbalah.

Many occult practices have taken on various aspects of Kabbalah. For example, Robin Skelton notes that witchcraft employs "tarot, cheiromancy [sic], herbalism, astrology, numerology or kabbalistic methods" (p. 14); and many witches:

---

1. From Rabbi Berg's recorded lecture *466: Talmud Esser Sefirot* (lesson no. 466).

use the symbolic and mystical system of the kabbalah (Quabalah) which derives from a Jewish book, the Zohar . . . and Gemetria [sic] as well as the system of numerology which also derives from Hebraic mysticism. Although the authoritative monotheism of Judaism and its codes of behaviour are unacceptable to followers of the Old Religion, some parts of the kabbalah—though not all—fit perfectly with traditional Wiccan belief and practice (*The Practice of Witchcraft Today*, p. 31).

The Gematria that witchcraft has borrowed, though, is only a *tool* employed in Kabbalah. Gematria is far from being the essence of Kabbalah (as we will discuss in chapter 5). And, with such, witchcraft has adopted a means to draw metaphysical energy, but is operating such tools without also employing the "safety measures" of Restriction, which is what gives Kabbalah its spiritual distinction.

The basis of the Nazi doctrine—Ariosophy, Theosophy and Darwinism—was formed essentially from the writings of "two Austrian occultists, Jorg Lanz von Liebenfels and Guido von List" (Sklar's *Gods and Beasts*, p. 5). List had studied "the origins of Jewish Mysticism" (ibid., p. 13)—that is, he had *supposedly* studied Kabbalah. Moreover, "the race struggle was [Lanz's] major concern, but the order also dabbled in astrology [and] the Cabalah" (ibid., p. 20).

Aleister Crowley (1875–1947), a self-proclaimed satanist, who would become "the most infamous black magician of all times . . . was active in the Hermetic Order of the Golden Dawn . . . [which among other practices, engaged in the study of] Cabala" (Larson's *Satanism: The Seduction of America's Youth*, p. 151). As Carr notes in *The Twisted Cross*, "Crowleyite neo-paganists busied themselves with the practice of witchcraft and magic with astrology, Tarot cards . . . (Cabalism) and other such works" (p. 105).

But the abuse of metaphysical knowledge has not just been confined to pagan, Nazi, or satanic use. As we will discuss in the next chapter, the self- and world-destruction wrought by the building of the Tower of Babel was undertaken by people who had Jewish souls. And then there were the 24,000 students of Rabbi Akiva (15–135 C.E.), the teacher of Rabbi Shimon Bar-Yokhai, who revealed the *Zohar*. Rabbi Akiva's students were "giants" in their knowledge and facility of the wisdom of Kabbalah. However, it is said that eventually the students began to compete with one another about who knew the most, and they no longer showed respect for one another. This demonstrated the opposite of the key principle of Judaism—Love Thy Neighbor as Thyself—the negation of which creates a deadly imbalance of energy. It was for this reason, that all 24,000 students were killed by the Romans.

There are misuses of energy even today. As Rabbi Kaplan exposes:

> Unfortunately, a number of groups also involved in "Jewish meditation" were practicing something far from Judaism. Some of them attempted to adapt Eastern practices to Jewish audiences, or to Judaize Eastern teachings. Although these groups attracted a following of sorts, they were not teaching Jewish meditation (*Jewish Meditation*, viii).

One might even argue that some of the European Jewish communities from the Middle Ages up through the twentieth century engaged in various practices that intentionally challenged and thus abused natural law through their use of magic, amulets, and wonderworkings.[2] Per the Lurianic teachings, the use of amulets and magic causes the recipient of such energies Bread of Shame as the drawer of such energies is rendered a (negative) channel for that Bread of Shame. And Bread of Shame is antithetical to the Thought of Creation. Nevertheless, as Nigal points out in his book, Jewish magic has been used with the intention to heal and help people—to restore positivity as opposed to revealing negativity.

The difference between the use and abuse of the power of the cosmos, through the wisdom of Kabbalah, lies in the use of Resistance. And that is why Resistance/Restriction is the key.

Because Restriction is the key principle in Kabbalah, its many facets must be discussed. Therefore, the rest of this chapter will discuss why Restriction is so important, when Restriction should be exerted and when it should not, what the connection is between free will, the Golden Rule, and being "spiritual." We will also analyze where Restriction is discerned in nature, where it is not, and how we are to interact with these aspects of nature that do and

---

2. See Gedalyah Nigal's *Magic, Mysticism, and Hasidism.*

do not. We will then discuss specific ways that each of us can exercise Resistance in our daily lives.

RESISTANCE ENGENDERED
BY OR AGAINST OUR WILL

Nature is balanced and strives to maintain balance. When we do not exert Resistance by our own free will, nature—physically and metaphysically—steps in to gain her due balance. Because the Thought of Creation was only to provide fulfillment to the Vessel, the moment it, or *we*, want to receive, Light enters immediately and automatically: because a Desire to Receive constitutes a vessel for the Light. However, per the concepts of Bread of Shame and the *Tzimtzum*, when we receive immediately, a veil of negativity, called *Klipot* (Husks) or a *Masakh* (Curtain) is effected and covers the Light. That is, we can always draw energy; but when we draw unbalanced energy, we inevitably blow a (cosmic) fuse, which immediately shuts down the flow of energy/Light.

Basically what this means is that whenever we act to gratify our desires immediately, we draw what is called Direct *Direct Light* and cause a "short circuit" in the spiritual flow of energy from the Light to the Vessel, which is ourselves. Drawing Direct Light is very much like going out in the sun without sunscreen. One can get the most rays without sunscreen, but one

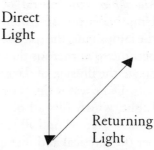

Direct Light

Returning Light

will also burn. Aside from the pain of a sunburn, the skin then peels, and the initial goal of suntanning is forfeited. Instead, we strive to create Returning Light, which is Direct Light on which we have exerted Resistance—by pushing some of the Light away, like sunscreen: resisting (our drawing of) some of the physical sunlight. It is only Returning Light that can be retained and thus enjoyed indefinitely. And it is only by resisting the Light that we convert Direct Light into Returning Light.

People who create a short circuit in themselves, by drawing Direct Light, often speak of feeling "burned out." After the 80s big sexual revolution, for example, a good number of people began expressing a feeling of being burned out from one-night stands. Sex is a very powerful means of drawing energy, and for this reason we will discuss sex in more detail in chapter 7.

But suffice to say for now that where there is not a balance of giving and receiving, of positive and negative energy, which is the essence of Returning Light, a short circuit inevitably results. A one-night stand basically translates as an immediate gratification of a desire, or Direct Light. The same would hold true for the Direct Light of overnight successes, or receiving a windfall of money or fame. Of course, there are many examples of this from our everyday lives and surroundings. But the point is, if the energy, the money—and money is a powerful form of potential energy—or the status is not converted into Returning Light, whereby it is shared, it will burn the recipient.

With every short circuit, another *Klipa* (Husk) or *Masakh* (Curtain) is automatically erected, which in turn dims the Light from shining through. Direct Light causes a burnout; and what is burned out is the Light from that drawing Vessel.

It is important here to remind ourselves that the Light is a constant: It never changes nor ever ceases to shine. The *Klipot* or *Masakhim* (the plural of Husk and Curtain) would be like lampshades put up around a lightbulb. With each layer added to the lampshade, the (physical) light appears to dim. The layers may become so numerous that they in essence block out the light and create the illusion of darkness.[3]

Darkness is thus always referred to as an illusion, since the Light, which fills all of existence, has and never does cease to shine—even behind all of those lampshades, or Husks.[4] In fact, as per the physical and metaphysical law of conservation of energy, darkness cannot be an entity. As Rabbi Berg emphasizes, if darkness were an entity, it could not just disappear from a dark room when we turn on the lights.[5] What the erection of each Husk does is stunt the Vessel (us) from actualizing our desires, since the fulfillment of all desire is in the Light; it is the energy of the Light.

---

3. This allusion to lampshades basically equates with Rabbi Berg's allusion to colored glasses, as noted in chapter 2.

4. We will discuss the power of the illusion of darkness as Satan in chapter 8.

5. Rabbi Berg's recorded lecture, "How to Bring Moshiach Into Our Lives."

No part of the Vessel, whether it be of the mineral, vegetable, animal, or human kingdoms, can control the desires that arise in him or her. But unlike the first three kingdoms, man[6] has the ability to control his desires. Or rather, the control that man has exists between the surfacing of his desire and its realization: Man can say no to his desire and resist the Light that fulfills it. This is an experience and phenomenon that did not exist in the Endless and which the Endless Vessel wanted. And it is the very reason we are here. In short, we have no control over our desires; the only control we do have is what we do between the surfacing of a desire and its realization.

There is even a proverb in the book of Ecclesiastes whose translation reads: "the preeminence of man above the beast is naught" (3:19). The word *naught* (in Hebrew *Ayin*) simply means no. That is to say, the difference between man and beast is man's ability to say no, and thus control his desires. And saying no, resisting our impulsive desires, constitutes Resistance or Restriction. Restriction means resisting our desires and thus controlling them. This principle is so simple, and yet it is so difficult to internalize— to the point that it takes most of us years, if not several lifetimes, to master it, if at all.

Moreover, restriction constitutes the effort we need to exert on the spiritual level to remove Bread of Shame when we want something.

If the effort that we exert is only on a physical level, we will only get the physical property of what we wanted to receive. As Karen Berg, Rabbi Berg's wife, explains in her introductory tape to Kabbalah, the things that we want in this world are all spiritual. This applies even to money, because what we want is the buying power of money and not the physical property of the bills. What we want is the pleasure felt from things, situations, and people, not their physical property. That pleasure is always the Light in everything. Therefore, what we want is Light.

As an aside, this would explain such phenomena as compulsive shopping or anything done in a compulsive manner. First we need to remember that the cause of all things in the universe is rooted in the metaphysical or spiritual world and never in the

---

6. "Man" and its equivalents here connote "humankind"—that is, both men and women.

physical. In this particular example, psychological factors may offer some indications of the problem, but the indications merely relate to the physical expression (branch) of the root, which is of spiritual nature.

Compulsive shopping would then indicate that that person's soul is looking for Light in things. As vessels, we exist and flourish by the Light in all the things and activities around us. So we look to draw Light our entire lives. But here, what usually occurs, is that initially the newly bought item possesses that pleasant feeling (Light) of newness. However, that feeling wears off because the spiritual part of the item was never firmly rooted in a vessel. This is the nature of Direct Light: It gives an immediate high but then leaves the drawer of the energy burned and empty (i.e., without Light). Lack of Light, or darkness, expresses itself as depression, disease, unfulfillment, and so on, so this leaves the drawer looking in desperation for more Light. In short, the Light in everything is what gives us pleasure. Therefore, what we want and look for is Light.

HOW TO EXERT RESISTANCE

What Kabbalah basically advocates is that if one wants something, he or she should not deny that the want exists, but should rather resist that desire by saying, "I don't want it *now*." Put differently, Restriction means negating our desire: for example, when a drive says "yes," we resist by saying "no"; or if we do not want something to tell ourselves that we actually do. By resisting the immediate influx of energy that is affected (Direct Light), we create, by definition, Returning Light.

Evil: According to Kabbalah, all evil derives from a person's desire to receive for himself alone, that is, receiving without restriction or sharing. Put differently, "the nature of evil is the unfulfilled desire to receive" (Berg's *Layman*, I, p. 80). In fact, the Hebrew word for "evil" is Rah: the letters R(esh) and A(yin). Kabbalah explains that *Rah* is an acronym for *Ratzon [Le]Atzmo*, meaning desire [for the] self. What we strive for is what is called Desire to Receive (–) in order to Give (+). What then happens is that, as in a battery, there is a balanced flow of energy created as both poles work in sync.

Receiving in order to give is also likened to, say, a water pipe. The pipe can receive an infinite amount of water, but only if it dispenses with that infinite amount of water. If at any point that pipe decides to hog some of the water/energy for itself, it creates an imbalanced increase of the negative pole. Then its receipt automatically diminishes as it creates a clog in itself.

Channel: A clean, "clog-free" pipe, in the language of the branches, is called a *Tzinor*, or channel. We strive to be channels of the Light, which means desiring to receive, but only in order to give, which in turn creates within us the capacity to receive more. Remember, as per the principle of the Thought of Creation, when a vessel is created and a desire exists to receive, the Light fills it automatically. But, as per the dictates of the *Tzimtzum*, only Returning Light, or Light that has been resisted, can be retained and enjoyed.

Holy: Moreover, when a channel is a pure one for the Light, we say that it is *holy*. *Pure*, from the Hebrew *Zakh* actually means transparent, clear, lacking any opaque quality. A place can be holy, as we say Israel is the Holy Land. An object can be holy, as we call the Torah holy or the ancient Holy Temples of Jerusalem. A person can even be holy, as a saint only receives in order to give; he or she has no element of a Desire to Receive for the Self Alone, which would clog his or her ability to channel Light in a pure manner.

The term *holy*, therefore, connotes an infinite flow of energy. Electricity is a good example of holy's parallel on the physical level. The positive and negative poles, when working together, on an equal level, produce an endless flow of (physical) energy. Holy, thus, means circuitry. With this in mind, one can understand that a phrase like *holy war* is an oxymoron, a contradiction in terms. War is a form of negativity where human life is taken away (left column, the Desire to Receive or to take); whereas holy denotes an endless flow of energy. Thus, by definition of the terms, there can be no such thing as "holy war."

The word for holy in Hebrew is *Kadosh* (of the root *K-D-Sh*). With this, we acquire an automatic understanding of, for example, the Friday night *Kiddish* or *Kiddush* that we mentioned in chapter 1, which comes from the same root, *K-D-Sh*. We can also get an immediate understanding of the gist of what the Bible means when it says that "God blessed the seventh day, and made it holy" (Genesis 2:3). God created the *Shabbat*, the seventh day, in which during it there would be an automatic, balanced, circuitry of Light.[7]

"REGAH" AND CENTRAL COLUMN

Kabbalists always talk of the need to insert a *Regah*, literally a moment, into our impulses to fulfill our desires. This is because the word *Regah* encapsulates the whole gist of Restriction or Resistance. Just as the concept of the Desire to Receive is called the Left Column, and the Desire to Give the Right Column, the concept of Resistance is termed the Central Column, as it embodies the very notion of balance.

Left Column	Central Column	Right Column
(−)	(−) + (+)	(+)
Desire to Receive	Desire to Receive in order to Share	Desire to Give/ Share

The number three in Kabbalah, and hence in Judaism, always indicates the Central Column; and there are many examples, such as the three *Matzot* on the Passover plate or the three divisions of duties in the Temple—Cohen, Levite, and Israelite. There is even

---

7. That is obviously an oversimplification of the meaning of *Shabbat*, the sabbath. It is the day we do not have to work to balance the two poles, or Columns, by Resistance. It is the only day we can receive Light automatically, without Bread of Shame. The energy of the Central Column, which we will discuss shortly, prevails and all we need to do is not disturb or disrupt its balanced flow in the cosmos. For more on *Shabbat*, the reader is referred to Rabbi Berg's recorded lectures on the Torah portion of *Pinkhas* (re: the meaning of *rest*) and *Beresheet* (re: the meaning of *rest* and the energy of the seventh day) and to cassette no. 20 of the Kabbalah Beginners Course, on *Shabbat*, given by Moshe Rosenberg.

a ritual whereby in the morning, upon rising or after one has handled "profane" material, one performs what is called *Netilat Yadayim*, which is translated as the washing of the hands. But the washing is not of the physical impurities (in fact there is a different word in Hebrew for washing, as in bathing or washing dishes). What is washed is metaphysical impurities, which the *Netila* does by our splashing tap water three times on each hand. Spiritual balance is achieved as one makes the mental focus that the first splash on each hand is the Right Column, the second round the Left, and the third the third, the Central Column.[8]

NUMERICAL VALUES

Alef	–	א	–	1
Bet	–	ב	–	2
Gimel	–	ג	–	3
Dalet	–	ד	–	4
Heh	–	ה	–	5
Vav	–	ו	–	6
Zayin	–	ז	–	7
Chet	–	ח	–	8
Tet	–	ט	–	9
Yod	–	י	–	10
Kaf	–	כ	–	20
Lamed	–	ל	–	30
Mem	–	מ	–	40
Nun	–	נ	–	50
Samekh	–	ס	–	60
Ayin	–	ע	–	70
Peh	–	פ	–	80
Tzadi	–	צ	–	90
Kof	–	ק	–	100
Resh	–	ר	–	200
Shin	–	ש	–	300
Tav	–	ת	–	400

---

8. This is not to be confused with the *Netilat Yadayim* performed before the blessing over the bread. For this purpose, water is splashed first twice on the right hand and then twice on the left, as 2 x 2 makes a connection to the Tetragrammaton. The Tetragrammaton will be discussed in chapter 5.

But getting back to the word *Regah*, using the guide to the Hebrew alphabet on the previous page, one can see that the Hebrew letters are also used as numbers, as each letter has a specific numerical value ascribed to it. The letter *Gimel* has the numerical value of three. Now, at a closer look at the word *Regah*—R(esh), G(imel), A(yin)—we can see that *Regah*, literally meaning "moment," inserts a three (Gimel)—the third, Central Column—in the middle of *Rah*, which literally means "evil." When we take a *Regah* (a moment/Resistance), we reveal Light that can be retained and enjoyed, because through the Resistance (moment) we have converted It from being expressed as Direct Light to being Returning Light.

FREE CHOICE

The concept of *Regah* also helps define the concept of free will, or *Khofesh Bekhirah*, which then translates back as free choice.[9] As we said before, we have no control over our desires: desires are predetermined. This is, for example, what inclines people toward a particular occupation, vocation, or avocation. It is also what invokes an urge for things like alcohol, drugs, or crime.

Free choice is endowed exclusively in human beings. It is the power we possess to act on each desire in one of two ways: with either (1) *Rah*, denoting evil (Desire for the Self Alone) or selfishness; or with (2) *Regah*, a moment, connoting an exertion of Resistance. Put differently, the second choice connects us to and achieves for us the Endless, while choice number one achieves end—finality. That is our choice. The first option creates a short circuit, while the second prepares a vessel, into which the Light automatically flows in a balanced manner. The second choice is also the very thing we, the Vessel, lacked in the Endless; it constitutes the very heart of the Thought of Creation.

The existence of free choice in man means that while animals, plants, and inanimate objects are predestined with either positive or negative energy, people have the potential for both positive and nega-

---

9. Remember, it is the Hebrew word for an object or idea that reveals that thing's internal essence. This will be explained in chapter 5 in discussing the Hebrew alphabet.

tive. By virtue of having a human vessel (body), we have the innate potential to be either channels of positivity or of negativity. It is for this reason that Judaism forbids human sacrifice. Even without completely understanding the issue of the sacrifice of minerals, plants, and animals, we can see that those things that were brought to the Holy Temple for sacrifice had no innate free choice.[10] Humans, on the other hand, do. Therefore, when a human being is murdered in the name of religious practice, the victim is being denied his innate right and obligation to exercise free choice, which is the very purpose of our existence.

Technically speaking, once Resistance has honestly been exerted, it does not really matter what one then decides to do, since the main goal is to exert Resistance as a means and an end. This is not to say that one is not responsible for his proceeding action: We are all responsible for everything we do. This is why it is important to understand the energy exchange involved in our desires, regardless of which choices we opt for: Our decisions may create a situation whereby a short circuit will become inevitable, as the action taken creates a new imbalance of energy. Everything we do

---

10. The word sacrifice in Hebrew is *Korban*, from the root *karev*, meaning to bring near, connoting bringing the object sacrificed closer to the Endless. Since only humans have free choice, humans are obligated to do *Tikkun* for those kingdoms—inanimate, growing, and living—that do not. The meaning of *Tikkun* will be discussed in the next chapter. There are a number of ways that *Tikkun* is fulfilled for the other kingdoms; sacrifice was one, but it is no longer performed since the vessel needed to perform it, the Holy Temple, no longer exists. In the next chapter we will expand on how humans can fulfill *Tikkun* for the lower kingdoms and why, for instance, cannibalism is forbidden—why it creates a short circuit.

It is also important to note the erroneous translation of the event in Genesis, chapter 22, that has been translated as "the sacrifice of Isaac." The term in its original Hebrew is *Akedat Yitzkhak*, the *binding* of Isaac. The concept of binding is that of the Right Column binding the Left to create balance or the Central Column. For a more in-depth understanding and analysis of this biblical passage, the reader is referred to the Kabbalah Centre's "Kabbalah Beginners Course" also available on audiocassette—in particular, cassette no. 9, in which it is discussed how the energy of the binding is continued today through the use of *Tiffilin* (phylacteries). In short, however, neither the event nor the term referring to the biblical passage were ever deemed to be "sacrifice," and it is this point that is crucial for our present discussion.

is the result (effect) of the choices we have made (*Rah* or *Regah*) and leads to a new string of cause and effect.

We may choose the path of evil or selfishness, Desire for the Self Alone. However, in addition to creating an immediate short circuit, the choice of selfishness also causes more Curtains to be erected, which, by definition, block out the Light. This puts the individual on a cycle of negativity. Moreover, it keeps the individual on the same destiny line as before—or even on a more difficult one. By choosing to restrict, one gains three advantages: (1) it reveals Light; (2) it aids in fulfilling the purpose of Creation, that being to remove Bread of Shame; and (3) it puts the individual in a different, and necessarily better, personal track.

Each choice we make, while being an effect of one process, also constitutes the cause of a new series of events that then defines our future. Each choice lines us up on a new predestined path. It is almost like being on a westbound highway but wanting to go north. Each choice we are confronted with enables us to change highways. An act of Desire to Receive for the Self Alone either keeps that individual on the same westbound path or even puts him on one that heads farther south. An act of Restriction, on the other hand, would put one on a highway that is going, say, northwest or west-northwest and closer to his goal.[11]

A person's destiny[12] line may be, for example, to commit a heinous crime or to be the victim of such a crime. The destiny of ruthless criminals puts them on a wayward "highway"; the destiny line of the victim would be toward pain and suffering or death. Crime, pain, suffering, and death are all phenomena that do not exist in the Endless; they are indicative of the opposite of the Endless—finality. A person who connects to the Endless automatically detaches from such phenomena of end.

People often ask how they will know if and when they have connected to the Endless—when they are *there*. Connecting oneself to the Endless means connecting to endless circuitry in accordance with the flow and forces of the cosmos. When we connect to the Endless, our level of consciousness is raised and we begin to

---

11. For a brilliant, metaphoric illustration of this idea, read Richard Bach's *One*.

12. And we will discuss how destiny is determined in the next chapter, under Tikkun and Reincarnation.

see how the cosmos assists us in maintaining circuitry. We may, for instance, miss our exit off the highway only to find out later that had we turned on time and as planned, we would have been caught in a major traffic jam for hours. Or we may "just happen" to find an item we were looking for—and on sale.

Things *appear* to happen by chance. But such things serve as road signs on our journey back to the Endless. Nothing happens by chance. When things are really tough and nothing is working out, the cosmic system is actually helping us and is in essence warning us that that is the wrong way or a dead end. When we head in the right direction, the system assists in the flow of "traffic" and we find "things just working out." It will assist us in retaining our connection to the Endless and avoiding those phenomena indicative of end.[13]

Free choice can, therefore, also be defined as the choice that we have to connect either to our destiny, per the dictates of the zodiac, or to what enables us to transcend the power of the stars and thus of our destiny. The free choice is between pulling our own reins or being pulled by them.

We *do* have the power to control our destiny. We can always better our lives, if we only steer our lives in the right way. Moreover, whether we are conscious of it or not, we are all aiming for the same goal: to return to the Endless. The question is merely how we chose to get there.

WHY NOT DIVINE THE FUTURE

Because of this ability that we all have, the Bible tells us (in Leviticus 19:31 and Deuteronomy 18:10–11) not to divine the future. The future, as defined by the zodiac, tells us what the outcome is of the particular destiny line or highway we are on at a particular time. This is harmful for two reasons: (1) When we become conscious of a particular destiny line, we become bound to it, as the connec-

---

13. In the next chapter, when we discuss *Iburim* and *Dibbukim*, we will see that actually the cosmic system "assists" us in whichever choice we make—evil or circuitry. If we chose to harm ourselves, the system will even assist in that. The cosmic system, therefore, also serves as a mirror for us to see our choices more clearly.

tion has been made on a soul level. Overcoming and changing that line will be that much harder, because we are already set on one particular outcome; (2) The future divined is good only if nothing else happens to change our direction and thus destiny. Since we are constantly confronting choices (either *Regah* or *Rah*), our destinies keep changing. Therefore, if we hear a divination of the future, that future may be obsolete and inapplicable just a few hours later or after doing only a small deed.[14]

Divining the future is prohibited by the Bible because it opposes the very purpose of our existence. It diminishes the mental activity necessary for exerting free will, if it does not also totally eliminate our use of free will completely. And this negates the very Thought of Creation. If one hears a "good" future, one may cease to exert free will and resistance in an effort to realize the prediction. Relinquishing free will relegates us to robotic consciousness, which, as we will discuss in chapter 8, constitutes the realm of "Satanic Consciousness."

Related to the issue of fortune-telling is that of mediumship, seances, and regression. In the first book of Samuel chapter 28, King Saul goes to a witch to call on the spirit of Samuel. Samuel appears and is angry (1 Samuel 28:15). Kabbalah explains that such mediumship practices are harmful primarily for two reasons. The first is that any time there is a third party between the individual and the spiritual realm, the individual's free will is taken away. In essence, the patient or individual is eliminated.

In his book *Gate of Reincarnation*, the Ari establishes that there are five levels of the soul: *Nefesh, Ruakh, Neshama, Khaya,* and *Yekhida;* although within these levels there are gradations as well. A medium can only draw the lowest grade/level of the lowest level of the soul (*Nefesh*). It is for this—the second—reason that Samuel, although a kind and saintly priest during his life, appears angry after his death to Saul and the witch at En-dor. With this

---

14. We learn, for example, that giving charity saves one from death. During the time that people could still read foreheads, kabbalists explained that an individual was born with the letter *Aleph* (the first letter of the Hebrew alphabet) on his forehead. A month before death, the letter *Tuf* (the last letter of the Hebrew alphabet) would appear on that individual's forehead. Giving *Tzdaka* (charity) causes the letter *Tzadi* (the first letter of *Tzdaka*) to appear and replace the *Tuf*, thus saving the giver from the then-fated death.

we can express that the witch at En-dor did *not* channel Samuel: because she only drew on the lowest level of Samuel's *Nefesh*, she did not connect with his true essence.

Seances are not a game either, especially when one considers that one relinquishes free will during such a practice and draws only the lowest of negative energies. In the next chapter we will explain what a *Dibbuk* is. But suffice to say for now that when one exposes himself by engaging in mediumship/seances, he opens himself up to negativity. And negative (i.e., desiring for *themselves* and harming the individual), noncorporeal "guests" do not necessarily go away when the corporeal players decide the fun is over and it's time to go home.[15]

LEANING TO THE RIGHT AND CONNECTING TO CENTER

This is not political propaganda. Since Kabbalah does not play politics, the Right referred to is the Right Column—the Desire to Give. Because we are from the Endless Vessel, we naturally have in us Left Column energy, the Desire to Receive. This is what is meant when we say that man is innately evil. Evil is a term of art, and the art here is the Language of the Branches.

The aspect of the Right Column, however, is not in us innately. We need to exert ourselves, by making a conscious effort, to connect with the Right Column—the Desire to Give. The effort itself is Resistance, and once we make contact with the Right Column, it converts, almost automatically to Central-Column energy.[16]

With this in mind, we can understand some seemingly insignificant *Halakhot* (Jewish procedure). We are told, for instance, to be conscious of first putting on the right shoe in the morning. The Torah scroll is always placed on its bearer's right shoulder when it is removed from the ark during prayer and carried around. The wine glass and bread are always held in the right hand during the blessing. On Passover, we lean to the left. By doing this, the right

---

15. For a more in-depth understanding of this point, refer to the Kabbalah Centre's advance course on "Reincarnation."

16. "Almost," because, as we will discuss, even on giving one needs to exert Resistance.

side is raised over the left, thus creating a dominance of the right (column) over the left. This is especially significant during Passover, as the goal is to connect us to the energy that promotes our freedom, our acquisition of control over our destiny, so that we are not slaves to our destiny.[17]

It is for this reason that kabbalists make a conscious effort never to cross their left arm or leg over their right. Similarly, they make a conscious effort to always give with their right hand. Giving with one's left hand denotes giving with a Desire to Receive of what is being offered. Therefore, giving with the left hand is not pure giving. We can assume that it is on this basis that the Catholic Church once declared left-handed people to be emissaries of the devil. Satan, as we will discuss in chapter 8, is a form of negativity, a Desire to Receive for the Self Alone energy, whereas writing is a form of giving.[18]

A good deal of handshaking takes place during Jewish communal prayer, especially among kabbalists. When a man is called up to the Torah, he receives a large amount of energy. A person who has received a large amount of energy will then go around and shake everybody's hand.[19] That person distributes the energy he received through his right hand, while the recipient receives through his right hand—in effect, resisting some of the energy being given. Of course, by now we know that the only way to receive energy that we can enjoy and retain is by resisting it. Moreover, the fact that handshaking has become a social gesture is incidental. As we have already said, the question that kabbalists ask is why something is done in the first place and what is the energy exchange involved.

---

17. The importance of this point—of right over left—may become more apparent in chapter 8 when we see, for example, that Adolf Hitler intentionally reversed the direction of the sinistrogyrate swastika to that of the dextrogyrate swastika to create the Nazi symbol.

18. Kabbalah would merely define that left handedness is a sign that the left-handed individual has a *Tikkun* with the left column. *Tikkun* will be discussed in the next chapter.

19. That is, the men among the men. The reasons men do not exchange energy with women during communal prayer will be discussed shortly in this chapter. Moreover, as we will discuss in chapters 5 and 7, only men go up to the Torah, because men correspond to the *Sefirah of Ze'ir Anpin,* while women correspond to *Malkhut.*

The idea is that everything we do on the physical plane can be done either just for its physical significance (out of rote, by destiny), or it can be converted into a spiritual act that, in turn, elevates the doer.

THE GOLDEN RULE

In Leviticus 19:18, the Bible proclaims a phrase of three words (in Hebrew) which has been labeled the central precept of Judaism: *VaAhavta LeRe'ekha Kamokha*, "Love thy neighbor as thyself." The translation is a bit misleading, since the Hebrew for *neighbor* which is *Re'ekha* actually better translates back to what is dubbed in psychology as the *Other*. *Other* is more correct than *neighbor* and more logical, since the latter seems to imply that someone living on the next block isn't entitled to my consideration, simply by virtue of his address.

The Golden Rule, as defined above, is said to be the central precept of Judaism, a precept that Christianity later adopted as its central principle, too. There is a famous account of a convert to Judaism who approached Rabbi Hillel (first century B.C.E.–first century C.E.):[20]

> When a convert came to [Rabbi] Hillel, he said, "Teach me the whole Torah while I am standing on one leg." Hillel replied, "That which is hateful to thee, do not do to your fellow man," (This is the translation of Love Thy Friend) "The rest is commentary, go out and learn."
> We have before us a clear *Halakha* (Jewish law). None of the 612 *mitzvot* or other principles of the Torah is more important than "Love Thy Friend As Thyself." They only come to explain and permit us to keep the commandment of loving another as it should be kept (Rabbi Ashlag's *Gift of the Bible*, pp. 30–31, italics in original).

Love: The reason "Love thy Friend as Thyself," as Rabbi Ashlag puts it, is the ultimate principle is because it embodies the

---

20. Rabbi Hillel was the "*nassi*" (president) of the "supreme spiritual authority," being "the Great Assembly . . . or the *Sanhedrin*," per Adin Steinsaltz's *The Essential Talmud*, pp. 17, 25.

cosmic principle of the Central Column, Restriction. In analyzing this coded principle for its energy composition, the first word we need to decipher is "love."

When two people are "close," we say that they are close even though physically or geographically they may not be in each other's immediate proximity. A beloved on the other side of the ocean is considered close to us, while a stranger sitting right next to us on a bus is considered far or distant. The reason for this seeming paradox is that the concept being conveyed is of a spiritual nature, not physical. In Kabbalah, when two people or entities are on the same wave length, think alike, or are close, it is said that they have *Shivu'i Tzurah*, Similarity of Form.

Two people who are just not on the same wave length and are very distant to one another, despite any physical, biological, or any other physical sign of seeming closeness—if two people are spiritually far away—in the Language of the Branches, it is said that they have *Shinu'i Tzurah*, Difference of Form. In short, Similarity of Form is the spiritual parallel of the physical term closeness, whereas Difference of Form is the spiritual parallel of physical distance.

The Hebrew word for hate is *sin'ah*, which comes from the root *shaneh* (*Sh-N-H*), meaning different.[21] Hate and evil are caused by entities being different in form—a state opposite of that state in the Endless[22] where the Endless Light and Vessel were fused as one. Anything that is of or causes fragmentation is from this root of Difference of Form.

In the spiritual, when there is a Similarity of Form between two entities, we call that *love* (or in Hebrew *Ahava*). Note that in the physical what we call love is a rather selfish emotion; but in the Torah *love* means being on the same spiritual wave length. Remember those "strange" verses in the book of Genesis when Isaac is said to *love* Esau (Genesis 25:28) or when Jacob is said to *love* Joseph (Genesis 37:3)? When we understand that Isaac and Esau embodied different aspects of the Left Column and Jacob and Joseph of the Central Column, we can rest better knowing that

---

21. The Hebrew vowels are not considered when evaluating the root of a word because, as we will discuss in chapter 5, the energy that forms or defines the particular word, concept, or object is contained only in the actual letters.

22. In the first aspect of Creation—see chapter 1.

what was conveyed in these verses is not a demonstration of parental preference of one child over another.

Incidentally, this also explains why we are told to love God. If we love God, which for us is the Light, that means that we are to create a Similarity of Form with the Light. The Light is positive energy, the energy of sharing. When we share—"love our neighbor as ourselves"—we create that Similarity of Form with the Light and thus "love" Him.

The second component to examine in the Golden Rule is "as thyself." This means that a desire (–) must first exist for myself. Let's say a seat becomes available on a crowded and stuffy bus. I must first feel a desire to sit down in that seat myself. I must then feel a Similarity of Form with someone else in that what he wants is what I want—but I want it for the other. Only then can I exert Resistance on my desire and offer it (the seat) to that other person (+). If I offer something I dislike or for something I do not feel a desire, then no Restriction would have been applied. The activation of the Central Column through both positive and negative poles is what creates a balanced flow of energy.

Thus the central principle of Love thy Neighbor as Thyself is just another means of saying exercise Resistance. And this, in turn, is comprised of the same two energies—positive and negative —by which the entire universe came into existence. As Rabbi Berg notes:

> As miraculous as it may seem, the computer operates on a binary system, which means that each of its circuits has but one operation to perform: on or off. Each of the tiny circuits within the computer is conducting electricity or not conducting it, depending on the given commands. On or off, positive or negative, restricting or not restricting, fulfilled or unfulfilled, such was the world view expressed by sixteenth century kabbalist Isaac Luria, the creator of Lurianic Kabbalah (Rabbi Berg's *Kabbalah For the Layman* II, p. 20).

Indeed, the entire universe operates on the binary system of positive and negative poles, the two forces that prevail in nature. The Central Column is something that we need to reveal for ourselves.

The entire content of the Torah, its laws and commandments, are nothing more than instruments for the improvement and development of self-control. Therefore Hillel chose the one precept of "love your neighbour" as the one specific idea that can guide men to this final goal. The precept reveals the inner spirituality of the individual (Rabbi Berg's *Kabbalah For the Layman*, I, p. 123).

OTHER GOLDEN RULES COMPARED

It is in this context that we can compare the "holy" flow of energy prescribed by Judeo–Christian teachings, with, for example, the Wiccan as well as various satanic golden rules. Again, we are only examining them for their energy composition.

One might say that the least nocuous of the pagan golden rules is that of witchcraft. Robin Skelton defines "the Witch's Law," as "Do what thou wilt, and harm no one" (*The Practice of Witchcraft Today*, p. 37). The second part, "harm no one," means not effecting a chain of short circuits. The first part, "Do what thou wilt," denotes the Desire to Receive (–). But this Desire to Receive is unaccompanied by a resisting factor; thus, it formulates Direct Light, which equates with a short circuit to the doer.

In *Gods and Beasts: The Nazis and the Occult*, Dusty Sklar exposes the Nazi golden rule to be "love thy racially similar neighbor as thyself" (p. 55). In chapter 8, we will define why racism of any kind is endemic of satanism. As Sklar and Joseph Carr reveal, the Nazis actually *were* practicing satanists, who performed various satanic rites, including human sacrifice (of their own Aryan race). Moreover, "[t]o get the right kind of offspring, [Heinrich] Himmler even ordered the kidnapping of racially pure children from occupied countries" (Sklar, p. 115). Ritual murder, kidnapping, and rape—while the Nazis may have called these acts of love, they are actually the epitome of short circuitness. These acts generate negativity not only on the doer, but effect a chain of short circuits that pervades the entire cosmos.

Self-proclaimed satanists, on the other hand, do not even feign love. Aleister Crowley (1875–1947), who was "a neo-pagan fancier of Egyptian gods and a practicer of magic (which he routinely spelled 'magick')" (Carr's *The Twisted Cross*, p. 104) proclaimed the satanic golden rule as "'Do what thou wilt shall be whole of the Law'" (Larson's *Satanism: The Seduction of America's Youth*, p. 152). Doing only "what thou wilt" means acting on desires as they arise. This translates as Direct Light drawn by a Desire to Receive for the Self Alone. And this inevitably effects a short circuit, if not also a chain of short circuits generated throughout the cosmos.

In his book *The Satanic Bible*, Anton LaVey, "the king of Satanists in America today" (Sklar, p. 63), states the satanic golden rule as "'Do unto others as they do unto you'" (*Man, Myth and Magic*, p. 2477). This devised rule relates to the dichotomy of proactiveness versus reactiveness.[23] Being reactive means relegating oneself to the realm of the Tree of Knowledge of Good and Evil, where one is played like a ping-pong ball by the forces of nature and destiny. This is robotic consciousness.

When a person purposely relinquishes free will, the means by which one controls his destiny, he negates the very Thought of Creation. When one relinquishes free will, as we will discuss in chapter 8, that person is relegated to what is called "satanic consciousness." At such a level of consciousness, one inevitably becomes burned out metaphysically as it causes a whole string of short circuits. Moreover, the only time someone already inclined to act out his natural impulses (Desire to Receive) when another "does unto them" is when a negative act has been committed. Reacting in the same, if not worse, negative manner creates more negativity, causes a short circuit, and inevitably burns out the doer.

Thus, the only way to create a balanced flow of energy is to—as God's given Bible to us tells us—"Love thy neighbor as thyself." With this, we can now also understand exactly what "spiritual" really means.

BEING SPIRITUAL

Spirituality is not restricted to only an elect few, nor does it equate with cults, social misfits, street preachers, or simple weirdos with strange hairdos and hip first names. Being in tune with nature or the world or meditating do not in themselves render one spiritual.

---

23. Rabbi Berg touches on this in his recorded lesson no. 466, July 1993.

These practices may help in one's work to become spiritual, but they are not, per se, spiritual acts. Conversely, though, spiritual people will necessarily be in tune with all around them and they will usually meditate in one form or other.

The focus of spirituality is not on the self or the individual, but rather on the other: everything outside of the self. It is for this reason, for example, that the "me" attitude is, despite what it purports to be, is actually antispiritual. An egocentric person who engages in meditation to gain benefit just for himself is only delving deeper into the self and away from spirituality. Being spiritual means thinking of the other at my expense. Larson indicates one of the dangers of self-absorption, when he writes:

> Involvement in occultism encourages an introspective individualization process. The emotionally dysfunctional will become more self-absorbed and less likely to deal realistically with life's problems. This is especially problematic with youth (*Satanism: The Seduction of America's Youth*, p. 59).

There are meditations and other practices that are of the System of the Vessel and there are meditations and other practices of the System of the Channel. And as we discussed in the Introduction, these two systems are not the same. The first, also called the *Impure System*, draws energy in a one-way direction—to the self, for the self. The System of the Channel, also called the *Pure System* or the *Holy System* strives to turn its practitioners into channels: to draw energy for the whole world.

Thus, spiritual people concern themselves not only with the implementation of urges and desires but also with the entire process of a desire: from its source and function to the many possible outcomes or forms of its implementation. This would take into consideration all around them. For while in the physical realm actions and words are all that count, in the spiritual, everything is taken into consideration. It is on this level that we can understand the commandment prohibiting coveting. Purity of action stems from purity of soul and of thought.

Self-induced thought control that forces out negative thoughts, which themselves constitute negative energies projected into the cosmos, is an extremely difficult level of discipline to acquire. As we have already said, man by nature is "evil," that is, he has a Desire for the Self Alone. Kabbalah, thus, offers a support system by which the individual can progress spiritually. Positive thinking and a positive demeanor are merely fringe benefits of applying oneself to the System of the Channel. It is also for this reason that Rabbi Ashlag bemoans, "Everyone thinks that a single excursion to delve into and consider these lofty issues during a free hour is sufficient" (Rabbi Ashlag's *Gift of the Bible*, p. 19).

Spirituality, and hence Kabbalah, is a total way of thinking, a total attitude toward life, a total way of living.

Thus, also, being spiritual and being psychic are two different things altogether. Bending spoons or reading another's mind do not in themselves make this world a better place. Being spiritual means living according to "Love thy Neighbor as Thyself." A person who can bend spoons by telekinesis or read another's mind by telepathy is not necessarily spiritual, just as a spiritual person may not be able to demonstrate telekenesis or telepathy.

Along the same line: a word about drugs. Being spiritual means being aware and conscious of all around oneself. Being intoxicated falls out of the realm of being spiritual. When one is intoxicated, he lacks proper perspective of the world, as he is totally involved only with himself. Moreover, he is a menace to society, on the roads and in the home. One may attain an altered state of consciousness through intoxicants, but the energy of drugs and alcohol cannot be shared nor prove beneficial to others while one uses them.

Rabbi Berg touches on the root cause of the rise and prevalence of drug abuse when he inquires:

> And why is the drug scene prevalent now? The Kabbalah states that in the time of the Messiah (also known as the "age of Aquarius") there will occur a tremendous spiritual awakening, the cause of which is the violent revolt of the soul against the governing limitations of the body. . . . Man wants to *get away* from the insatiable "desire to receive" for oneself, and from the clutches of our limiting factors. For drugs do simulate this experience; one *does* become oblivious to his physical surroundings. However, one thing is wrong. On the return to his present surroundings the individual is back to where he started from (*A Study of the Ten Luminous Emanations*, xxvi, italics in original).

In short, all forms of intoxication—substance abuse, alcohol, food, etcetera—are an attempt by the soul to free itself from the body. Therefore, spirituality and substance abuse, by definition, do not equate. Period.[24]

Incidentally, the soul's revolt against the body unfortunately finds expression in many negative forms. Rabbi Glazerson exposes another of these forms that is next in line if not equal in its destructiveness to drugs. He refers to cults.

The longing for communion with supernatural forces arises from the depths of a soul which yearns to unite with its divine source . . . [thus many] impetuously join any sect which promises this result (*From Hinduism to Judaism*, p. 52).

Test of Spirituality: Kabbalah says that it is important to live among people, not only to contribute to community social and spiritual efforts but also because it is primarily through the interaction with people that one has the opportunity to exercise Resistance. Meditating atop an open mountain, one has very little opportunity to develop Resistance skills. Opportunity usually exists when one is the least comfortable, or the situation will put one in an uncomfortable situation.

Thus the test of spirituality is in everyday, mundane living. Not that there is someone to judge; each can only judge himself. It's the little things we do in our everyday living that we tend to overlook. But it is the little things in our everyday lives that are that much more significant, because they are so difficult to improve. And it is difficult just to recognize the opportunities for Restriction.

The test really refers to an opportunity that is presented to reveal Light where there is at that moment a lack of Light. It is when we aren't ready for it, when we haven't had preparation to get psyched up for it, that the test is most genuine. Take, for instance, a traffic jam: You want to get home; it's late, but you're stuck in rush-hour traffic. You're honking, cursing, zig-zagging in and out of lanes. A typical thought is, "I will be late getting home and I am uncomfortable." That's egocentricity. What about the

---

24. In chapter 8, we will also discuss why drugs are typically used with satanic practice.

people you've just cut into or the headache you're causing others by honking?

There is a phrase in Hebrew that says *"Kol HaAkava LeTova,"* "Every delay is for the best." If you've done everything that you can to get somewhere on time and something happens to make you late, like an unanticipated traffic jam, the delay is for the best. When someone has put his best foot forward and made every effort to do something, that is all that matters; the result, whether or not it will work out, is left to the cosmic system: What is meant to be?[25]

The unspiritual person in the jam is getting more and more worked up. The spiritual person is working to exert Restriction, which in this case translates to restraint. Who knows? By inconveniencing you, maybe the system is making sure you are staying out of harm's way, when, per your destiny, you were supposed to be the next victim. Our limitation in seeing only the here and now prevents us from seeing the full range of cause and effect. Maybe the delay will cause you to meet someone you need to meet. Or maybe you were never supposed to get to where you planned to go that evening anyway. There are an infinite number of such possibilities. The spiritual person recognizes that such an opportunity is a sign, is thankful for the sign, and remains restrained, because he knows he is working with balance in the cosmic flow of things.

And what if the traffic jam is because of an accident? Sitting in your car, are you only thinking of how inconvenienced you are, or are you also considering everyone around you, from the car in the next lane to the poor souls involved in the wreck? Or their families? Maybe it's a holiday, and the medical staff rushing out to the scene got called off on the emergency. Are you also thinking about them, or is your mind solely on yourself? And, per the quantum effect, how will this effect the entire world? And what are you contributing to the world in this situation?

All of these "test" questions merely demonstrate the nature of the opportunities that confront us. We will discuss this more when we discuss various ways that we can discern Restriction in our life and what we are to do when trouble has already befallen.

---

25. For more on this principle, the reader is directed to Rabbi Berg's recorded lesson, *Talmud—Baba Metzia,* which applies this principle to a discussion on "what is meant to be" with regard to one's physical possessions.

But, in short, the spiritual person is one who lives by "Love Thy Neighbor as Thyself." The spiritual person is one who takes the whole world into account in everything he does. Now that we know the formula for spirituality, we can call a spade a spade and recognize what is not.

WHERE RESTRICTION EXISTS IN NATURE

While the universe is composed of only the two poles of energy, the positive and negative, nature also exerts Restriction in various ways to reveal Light. Resistance in nature may be considered like the filament in the lightbulb. In the electrical current, the two opposite poles work and yet do not create a short circuit solely thanks to a filament that is even called a *resistor*. The resistor does exactly what its name suggests: it resists the current, enabling the opposite forces to work in sync.

In the body, the ear exerts Resistance on the sound waves it receives, by means of the eardrum; and with such we can translate the waves to sounds—that is, the Resistance reveals a certain facet of Light, being sound. The eye does the same thing: it reverses the picture received in the lens and then reverses it again. The whole maze that the light waves go through for us to see a picture right-side-up is for the purpose of exerting Resistance, which in turn enables us to see. And to inhale more air (receive) we first need to exhale (give: resisting our desire for more) the air we already have.

The earth is feminine energy—being a Desire to Receive—which is evident by her natural pull toward herself: her gravitational force. On the other hand, nature as a whole, and thus earth, too, is balanced. And balance is always from the Central Column. This is why, for instance, although the earth pulls towards herself (Left Column), once a body falls and makes impact with the earth, the object bounces slightly up off the earth before falling again. This is indicative of Resistance. Moreover, although gravity pulls downward toward earth, Mother Earth also resists her natural tendency by enabling plants and trees to grow upward.

In fact, the entire solar system demonstrates Resistance. Rabbi Berg, in his recorded lectures on Genesis, explains that all of the planets in our solar system revolve around the sun, because the sun possesses the internal intelligence of balance. A millennium ago,

Rabbi Shabbtai Donolo (913–982) explained that the sun is the energy provider for the entire universe.[26] This is why all the planets (as the electron[s] around the nucleus of the atom) rotate around the sun. The planets contain the energy intelligence of a Desire to Receive; they revolve around the sun, which contains the energy intelligence of balance, to receive their nourishment.

The planets, however, do not collide, because they exert sufficient Resistance. Therefore, the solar system, as one frame of reference or unit within the universe, is balanced. In chapter 5 we will understand the structure by which all of the universe is manifested on its physical and metaphysical level. This is the system of the *Sefirot*. The solar system, is thus one reflection (of the many, as we will see) of this structure in the universe.

But probably the best example of balance, the Central Column at work in nature, is in the very building block of all physical matter: the atom. The atom has a proton (+), electron(s) (–) and a neutron (Central Column). In fact, the atom represents the structure of balance to such a degree that if that Central Column agent were removed—a process known as the splitting of the atom—despite its size, we have the formula for an atom bomb. And why is it only the neutron that causes this effect and not the proton or the electrons? The answer is that the energy intelligence of the neutron, the metaphysical energy that it expresses in physical form, is balance itself. And it is the fragmentation of that balancing agent, on the physical and metaphysical levels, that destroys our world.

Aside from the destructive nature of fragmentation, Nature can teach us something else about Resistance. The physical level is, as we have said, the level where Light is revealed, but only after it has been concealed. The place of impact (where Light is received) is concealed, whereas the space around that place of impact is where the Light is revealed. Take a stone that is thrown into a body of water. At the place of impact (parallel to Direct Light), no influence can be seen; it is the concealment. However, pushing away (Restriction) from the place of impact, we can see waves emitting in circular form from the impact point (which is parallel to Returning Light).

---

26. Reference to Rabbi Shabbtai Donolo made by Rabbi Berg in Rabbi Berg's recorded lesson on the Torah portion of *Shoftim*—"Shoftim: Four Kinds of Judgement; Witnessing in Court."

This can teach us a valuable lesson. When something happens, we need to restrict and step back to see the big picture. When we zoom in and continue focusing on the point of impact (on that which happens to us) with all kinds of questions, we lose the forest for the trees. This is like a black hole: very intense but black, because that is the point of impact where the Light is concealed. If we step back, away from the point of impact, we step into the realm where the Light is revealed, like the rings in the water around the stone. And stepping back, which is where we can see the picture at large, is also an exercise of Resistance. Therefore, the paradox that Kabbalah recommends is that when you really want to understand something, say to yourself you don't want to understand and push it away.

WHERE THE FILAMENT
IS LACKING IN NATURE

Where a natural filament is lacking in nature, with regard to things that we use, Judaism flatly states that the elements of the positive and negative poles need to be separated. This is the hard fast rule of the cosmos to prevent a short circuit. One example of such will be discussed in the next chapter under *Tikkun*, and that is the law of *Kashrut* (the state of being *kosher*) regarding animals. But under the laws of *kashrut* there is also the law of *Shatnes*. Torah basically says that one is not to mix wool and flax (or linen) together in the same garment or worn together as different layers of clothing. That is the *Halakhah*. Kabbalah then explains the why.

The law on *Shatnes* derives from the passage in Genesis 4:2–5 where Adam and Eve's son Abel, who was a shepherd, makes an offering to God of the "firstlings of his flock, and the fattest thereof." Abel's brother, Cain, who was a "tiller of the ground," offers God "the fruit of the ground." Then the scriptures tell us that "the Lord had respected" Abel's offering, but not Cain's. As per the Aggadah, what Cain brought as an offering was flax,[27] whereas what Abel brought was wool.

---

27. See Rashi, *The Pentateuch and Rashi's Commentary*, by Rabbi Abraham Ben Isaiah and Rabbi Benjamin Sharfman, p. 38.

First of all, Kabbalah explains that every story in the Bible serves as a physical medium to convey a spiritual message to us. What is described in this passage about Cain and Abel concerns an offering of two entities that are of opposite energy intelligences. Flax, or linen, has the internal energy intelligence of the Desire to Receive—negative energy—whereas wool has the internal energy intelligence of the Desire to Share—positive energy. It is also for this reason that we wear wool in the winter, because wool *gives* (Desire to Give or Share, positive energy) us warmth, whereas we wear linen in the summer, because linen (flax) has the internal quality that *takes* (Desire to Receive, negative energy) the heat (Light) from us. And since there is no filament in nature that synthesizes these entities, as the resistor does in the bulb, we do not wear wool and linen together. That is, we prevent assuming on, in, or around us anything in a constant state of struggle between the two energy poles due to its lack of a natural filament.

Another example of where separation is required of the two opposite poles because a natural filament is lacking is during communal prayer. The positive pole is established by the presence of a minimum of ten men[28] who together act as the positive pole. In such a circumstance, where such a tremendous amount of energy is drawn, the positive pole (men) is separated from the negative pole (women). All that is required for such separation of the poles is a nominal, symbolic yet physical demonstration of separation. *Halakhah* tells us that the separation, or *Mekhitzah*, is to be about five and one half feet high.[29] But, the separation can be effected by even a sheet or lace (see-through) material. The idea is that we establish a distinction of the two energy poles on the physical level—that's all. Unfortunately, this requisite has been exaggerated over the centuries to such an extent that today in some synagogues the separation between men and women has unnecessarily become a wall, or the women are even seated in a back room.

The same separation is required for dance, as dance is a means of drawing spiritual energy. It is also for this reason that dance within a circle, as most dances in Jewish tradition are, turn counterclockwise. The counterclockwise rotation demonstrates right over left.

---

28. Men constitute the parallel, human, physical expression of the Right Column, and ten per each of the ten *Sefirot*.

29. Baruch Litvin, ed., *The Sanctity of the Synagogue*, p. 123.

Color

One last example of our need to prevent assuming what exists in nature in a constant state of struggle between the two poles of energy relates to food. In chapter 5, after we understand the metaphysical structure of the body, we will be able to understand why we eat and, specifically, why we eat (animal) meat. For now, however, we will touch on one aspect of the spiritual dietary laws that demonstrate an example of opposite energies in nature without a filament.

The Bible tells us in Exodus 34:26 and 23:19 "not to boil a goat in its mother's milk." Our sages have deciphered this cryptic message that (per *Halakhah*) milk and meat must be separated, in cooking and in ingestion. Kabbalah then explains why.

In explaining this aspect of *Kashrut* (being kosher), it may be helpful to incorporate the kabbalistic understanding of colors. First of all, color is an energy; it is an expression of energy translated and perceived by the eye as color. All color is contained in white light. The element of white light that reflects (Resistance) from an object is the color we see. Thus, for example, when white light shines on a ripe tomato, the red aspect of the light is reflected or resisted by the tomato; thus the tomato appears red. This is an additional example of the cosmic rule that where there is Resistance, there is revelation of Light.

Colors, therefore, expose the internal essence of the object from which the color is being reflected. While color is itself energy, it merely serves as an indication or reflection of the object's energy; but the color is not the object's energy per se. The *Zohar* explains that white is the color indicative of Right Column energy. An object that is white reflects *all* the rays of white light. White, therefore, indicates a pure form of giving.

Red is the color indicative of Left Column energy, and green is indicative of Central Column energy. Green is a further indication of the balance in nature, as most flora is green. While flora takes (–) from nature what it needs to exist, it also gives (+) animal and human life oxygen, by which we exist. Thus, in general, plants are in a perpetual state of circulating a flow of energy or of balance (Central Column).

In addition to these three basic colors, which represent the three fundamental energies (positive, negative, and Central Column), there are two colors indicative of the Vessel itself: black and blue. Black indicates that there is no circuitry of energy, as black absorbs (or takes (–)) all of the rays of white light. Black indicates that there is a connection to either the Right Column or the Left Column, but not to both columns. Blue, on the other hand, indicates a state of Restriction, and thus a communication or flow of both Right- and Left Column energies.

As an aside, despite the earlier disclaimer to politics and mundane preoccupations, this fact of physics and metaphysics is not to be construed as racial. With this, it might be pointed out that "black" means black and not olive-toned or brown. Interestingly, those whose skin pigmentation really is black are actually "blue-black," to use Nettie's terminology from Alice Walker's *The Color Purple*. *All* human beings, by virtue of their possessing free will, possess the potential to reveal either positive or negative energy. "Blueblack" merely serves as a manifested, physical expression of the metaphysical or spiritual potential that all humans have.

This duality of potential positivity (Desire to Share) and negativity (Desire to Receive) is also expressed in our blood, which contains both red (–) and white (+) cells. Blood is the filament between our body and our soul. Concurrent with the color analysis above, blood, as it remains concealed from our sight and exists in a "potential" state, is red and white. However, when blood becomes manifest on the skin, it appears as "black-and-blue" marks.

With this, we have a better indication of the *Halakhah* requiring a separation of milk and meat: the colors of milk and meat, respectively, help us perceive their internal energy intelligence. Milk is white, and thus of positive (Desire to Share) energy intelligence. Milk is life *giving*, being what mammals *share* with their offspring. Milk also demonstrates the continuity of positive energy as milk cannot be wasted: from milk we get soured milk, from which we make cheese, yogurt, butter, and other dairy products.

Meat, on the other hand, is red, indicating that its internal energy intelligence is of the Desire to Receive, negative energy. Meat demonstrates the polar opposite nature of milk's continuity. To obtain meat, the life of an animal is taken away (–), taking away any life continuity. Moreover, meat lacks continuity: once it spoils, it becomes (poisonous) waste.

Since we are on the topic of Restriction, it is also appropriate and now comprehensible to mention the physical attributes of the animals that the Bible, in Leviticus chapter 11, specifies are "clean" or "pure"[30]—those animals from which kosher meat is obtained. The Bible offers a list of signs that we can use to detect an animal's internal energy. Animals of the "clean" category have split hooves and chew their cud. The split hoof indicates the existence of the (+) and (–) energy poles in the animal but that the poles are separated (as in a battery). Chewing cud is an expression of Restriction or Central Column energy, as giving back what it takes (eats), means receiving in order to share (Central Column).

For a fish to be kosher it must have fins and scales. The two fins indicate separated Right and Left Column energies. Fins are also what give fish balance (Central Column) in their aquatic locomotion. Scales reflect light (and thus Light), indicating an existence of Central Column energy, or Returning Light.

The point, for the purpose of this chapter's discussion, is that milk and meat are physical expressions of the two opposite poles, respectively, and do not possess a natural filament to synthesize. It is for this reason that milk and meat must remain separated, to prevent a metaphysical short circuit. As Rabbi Berg explains:

> There is a clear and grave warning here that death and life must be respected in this world for what they represent—two separate and irreconcilable elements [per *Zohar III*, p. 79a] (*Layman*, I, p. 129).

An additional example of such opposites and whose internal energies are identifiable by their colors, are (menstrual) blood, which is red, and semen, which is white. No natural filament exists that synthesizes these entities of opposing energy either and is why *Halakhah* requires their separation as well. This last example will be discussed more in detail in chapter 7, when we discuss "Personal Relations" and sex in particular.

WAYS TO EXERT RESISTANCE IN OUR LIFE

Now that we know a little more about Resistance or Restriction, especially its crucial requisite in all we do, we can look at a few

---

30. In the next chapter, we will discuss *Tikkun*. "Clean" and "unclean" refer to being "clean" or "unclean" in a karmic, spiritual sense, and have nothing to do with physical hygiene.

specific means of applying it in our lives. In short, Resistance means resisting our immediate impulses and desires as they surface. The first moment we want something, we need to say to ourselves that we really do not want it and push the object away in our mind. What is important is the (sincere) mental process. Resisting means resisting our natural tendencies—not denying or annihilating them, but rather simply resisting them.

First of all, Restriction is an individual issue because each of us has a different Desire to Receive. There are an infinite number of forms that human desire takes. Thus, each of us needs to determine his own form and amount of Restriction. And this is what each of us needs to calculate and determine for ourselves, using our own free will. Even in the same individual, the same desire, under different circumstances, may require different amounts of Restriction. Resistance is, therefore, something we need to determine with everything we do as it comes up. And it is also for this reason that there are no set formulas for exerting Resistance. That is also why Resistance is so difficult.

The key to Resistance is the understanding that every exchange of energy must be balanced. For this reason, Restriction is necessary both in receiving and in giving. It is important to share; but there needs to be an equal Desire to Receive on the part of the recipient. Giving to someone who does not want to receive is not sharing.

Similarly, not all sharing is good. If, say, A gives to B, who has a Desire to Receive for Himself Alone, then A has become a channel for B's Bread of Shame. Thus A's giving to B is bad for A, too! In exerting Resistance, one is essentially practicing being considerate of the other. One way we exert Resistance is by applying the *Regah*—the "moment"—by stopping to evaluate the circumstances. Such evaluation also gives us the opportunity to check how we are interacting with others: tolerantly? considerately? as we would want them to act towards us?

Resistance requires of us a constant awareness of our surroundings and of what is inside of us. It demands that we constantly evaluate and reevaluate what we do. The minute we give in to robotic consciousness, we relinquish our free will and thus oppose the very Thought of Creation, being the reason for our existence. And we all have things we need to work on to improve, by the very virtue and proof of our having a corporeal body! So no one is excluded from this necessity.

Resistance also translates into giving the other a second chance. No one is perfect; we all make mistakes. And this is what the Endless Vessel (we!) wanted from the Light in the Endless: The Vessel asked for time to be able to rid itself of Bread of Shame to earn the Light. If the Light could give us a second chance, then we can certainly afford a second chance to our fellow human beings.

Resistance is mostly between man and man.[31] When someone is insulted, for instance, it requires a great deal of Restriction, because the person who is insulting may actually be offering the person being insulted a crucial message (consciously or not). The question is whether the person being insulted is listening. In short, Resistance asks that we do not judge others so fast or react right away. When someone reacts right away, the response is usually not balanced and many times is the ego speaking as opposed to the soul.[32]

Resistance connotes discipline: one needs to check whether what one is doing is only for himself or is benefiting others—even indirectly. Whenever something is done or consumed *too* much—eating, drinking, and so on—it becomes relegated to the realm of Desire For the Self Alone. Such discipline also requires that when all looks like it is going smoothly and easily in our life, it denotes the greatest danger. If we no longer see lack in our life, we are completely engulfed by the illusion of this world, and that spells danger! Therefore, when we think we have mastered all forms of Restriction in our lives, we need to look for new forms of Restriction to exert. Thus, Restriction should always require a conscious effort and should not be easy nor come naturally.

HOW TO EXERT RESISTANCE WHEN THINGS ARE ALREADY GOING BAD

Kabbalah asserts that Restriction is the solution for all problems, in all areas of life. While pain medication can only provide *temporary* relief, Restriction engenders a total removal of the problem. Pain, of any kind, is an indication that something is wrong; it is a sign. As paradoxical as it may sound, instead of acting on the ob-

---

31. Again, the use of the male gender refers to both male and female.
32. The danger of the ego will be discussed in chapter 8, regarding Satan.

vious and most convenient impulse (i.e., resist that desire), ask for more pain!

For example, when we get sick, symptoms are signs that something is wrong, and they show us where the wrong is. It is in human nature to take for granted the things that are going right while they are, like teeth that do not ache, or a toe, back, finances, family, and so forth that do not ache or cause grief. We tend to direct our attention or consciousness to such aspects of our lives only when they hurt. Pain, disease, or anxiety are all expressions of metaphysical darkness, which is merely a lack of Light. The root of all physical phenomena and processes is in the metaphysical. Therefore, the *cause* of any pain is not in the physical expression, but rather in the energy that corresponds to that pain in the metaphysical.

For this reason, when something happens to us—"good" or "bad"—it is important to deal with the matter on its physical level. But more importantly, we need to deal with it on its root, metaphysical, level. A trying time is trying because it is offering us an opportunity to overcome a "husk." And the way to remove husks is by Restriction. Yet, to be sure, when one passes such tests, one elevates to a higher level.

Similarly, when we get involved with a troublesome situation that affects us directly, confront it instead of shying away from it. The convenient and easy thing to do is not to get our feet wet. Restriction advocates that we do get our feet wet, in an attempt to remedy or at least better the situation. By restricting, one only takes the positive part of the situation and eliminates the negativity. Put differently, proactivity corresponds to positivity, because it acts on an opportunity for spiritual elevation, while reactivity corresponds to negativity, because it relegates us to robotic consciousness.

4

Tikkun *and Reincarnation*[1]

Tikkun means *correction*. To fulfill *Tikkun* is essentially the purpose of our existence: to correct the Bread of Shame that we (the collective Vessel) felt in the Second Aspect of Creation. When we do not fulfill this goal, the soul comes back to try it again, as it were.[2] This is the basis of Reincarnation: The soul returns to this plane in a continuing effort to fulfill *Tikkun*.

Tikkun works within the natural laws that instill balance in everything. What this means is that every situation is the result of human actions that precede it. In this universe there are no accidents, as there are no technicalities (legal or mechanical) on which exchanges of energy can go off unbalanced. The *Tikkun* process or system works within the cosmic system very much like a meticulously monitored bank account: Energy that is taken is eventually demanded back—and with interest. Therefore, *Tikkun* connotes the cosmic law of fair play. "All misfortunes or 'accidents' encountered in the present are but the logical outgrowth of some action in a past life or in the present one (Berg's *Reincarnation*, p. 99).

---

1. The Kabbalah Centre offers an entire advanced course on Reincarnation, also available on audiocassette.

2. Different ways that the soul can come back will be discussed in this chapter. Women's return or reincarnation will be qualified in chapter 7.

REINCARNATION IN THE BIBLE

Since the Bible is our cosmic guidebook, the first question kabbalists ask in discussing an issue is "Where is it written in the Bible?" And, in fact, in discussing reincarnation, a number of passages show us the workings of reincarnation in this world. Rabbi Berg, in his book on reincarnation, offers insight into the following biblical passages:

1. Ecclesiastes 1:4: One generation passeth away and another generation cometh and the earth abideth forever.

    The *Zohar* [which reveals for us the soul, or internal essence of the Bible] tells us [Per *Zohar Hadash*, p. 33a] that what this verse really means is that the generation that has passed away is the same generation that comes to replace it (p. 23).

2. Exodus 20:5: The sins of the fathers are remembered even unto the third and fourth generations.

    This does not imply, as some erroneously have contended, that God is so full of wrath that He is not content to punish merely the sinner, but that he will inflict punishment for sin upon the sinner's innocent grandchildren and great grandchildren as well. Who could rationally love and worship so fierce and vengeful a deity? The *Zohar* reveals that the truth of that verse is that the third and fourth generations are, in fact, the first—one soul returning in the form of its own descendants so that it may correct the sins cited as 'sins of the fathers' (p. 23).

Rabbi Kaplan, in his posthumous book, *Immortality, Resurrection and the Age of the Universe*, includes a translation of a sermon given by Rabbi Israel Lipschitz in 1842, in which the latter offers "proof" of reincarnation, per the following Torah passages:[3]

---

3. From "*Derush Or ha-Hayyim*: A Theological Reflection on Death, Resurrection, and the Age of the Universe," a sermon preached by Rabbi Israel Lipschitz in the German–Polish city of Danzig (Gdansk) in 5602 (1842) (p. 65), translated and annotated by Yaakov Elman and contained in Rabbi Aryeh Kaplan's book, *Immortality, Resurrection and the Age of the Universe*.

3. After Cain murders Abel, God calls to Cain in Genesis 4:10: The sound of your brother's blood cries out to Me from the earth.

   But if Abel's soul was cut off entirely upon leaving his body, where is there sound or utterance? (pp. 94–95).

4. Genesis 9:6: One who sheds human blood—his blood will be shed.

   [T]hat is to say, I will demand this from one who kills himself. But if after death the soul dissipates like a cloud, and becomes as nothing, when will He demand [punishment] for this terrible sin [of suicide]? (p. 95).

5. Genesis 17:14: And any uncircumcised male, who circumciseth not the flesh of his foreskin, that soul shall be cut off from his people.

   If the soul ceases to exist when it issues from the body, what warning is this for one who violates the covenant [of circumcision]? (pp. 95).[4]

As kabbalists will point out, the Bible is replete with such examples and the above is only a small sample. Parenthetically, one might even note the prayer said before going to bed (the *kriyat shma al hamita*) in which one offers forgiveness to anyone who has wronged him *bain begilgul ze bain begilgul akher*—"whether in this lifetime or in another lifetime." But the point is not so much to prove the existence of reincarnation in the Bible as it is to provide a stepping stone for an understanding of where reincarnation fits into the grand scheme of things.

In this context, we might clarify a few terms of art that will further aid us in understanding the cosmic design.

THE "NEXT WORLD": HEAVEN AND HELL

This term originates in the Hebrew, *HaOlam HaBa,* but has evolved into terribly misleading translations: "next" becoming "after" and

---

4. We will discuss circumcision in chapter 5.

"world" becoming "life." The term is *next world*. It is not a place in the physical sense of the word, nor is it necessarily reached (or not) after one's physical life is over.

Instead the "next world" is a state of consciousness that the individual, even while in this physical world and in the living state, can choose or not choose to be in. Since consciousness never ceases for the soul, what is called *heaven* and *hell* can exist for the soul, whether incarnated in a body or not. While in a physical body, if one connects only to the physical world and believes that events here occur by chance, he is in what is known as *Gehenom*, hell.[5] But if he raises his consciousness to the spiritual world, the "next world," the world that is above the physical where the picture at large can be seen, then he elevates to what is called heaven.

Both heaven and hell are states of consciousness whereby the husks or curtains are removed and the soul sees its state (of *Tikkun*) vis-à-vis the picture at large. A soul that has succeeded in eliminating Bread of Shame and in connecting to the Endless will rejoice in the state of heaven. Despite the various notions of hell, it, too, is a state of consciousness that a soul must merit. Hell is like an express *Tikkun*. It is a state whereby the soul comes face to face with its own negative (Desire to Receive) actions while in a body. Since the soul knows that its purpose on earth is to share (Desire to Share (+)) and to eliminate Bread of Shame, the soul *suffers* in such a state from the harsh truth of real self-reflection.

This is Heaven and Hell according to Judaism. Either one exists for the individual according to what he or she chooses to connect to.

TREE OF LIFE VERSUS TREE OF KNOWLEDGE OF GOOD AND EVIL

Heaven, which is also called the Tree of Life or Tree of Life consciousness, is the connection to the spiritual realm, where there is only good. All is positive, because everything brings us closer to our final goal: the removal of Bread of Shame and the return to the

---

5. We will note exactly where the consciousness level of hell is located on the cosmic map in chapter 6 when we discuss UFOs.

Endless. Hell is the connection to the illusory, physical world, also known as the Tree of Knowledge of Good and Evil (or Tree of Knowledge of Good and Evil consciousness), because from this stance, all appears to happen by chance. At this level, there is, therefore, the illusion that there is both good and evil.

What is important to note here is that both of these "trees" are terms in the Language of the Branches for specific realms or states of consciousness. Thus, they are neither a physical place nor an actual, physical tree. One can then understand why the great kabbalists spoke about entering the Tree of Life or even connecting to it.[6]

One who connects with the Tree of Life connects with stability, as the Light is a constant and is entirely positive energy. One who connects with the Tree of Knowledge of Good and Evil, on the other hand, connects with an illusion of instability and uncertainty, a world where one day is good and the next bad. Negativity only befalls when a vessel has not been properly prepared to contain the Light, which, by definition, wants to be revealed—that is the purpose of Creation. With this, the definition of free choice may be rephrased as our choice between the Tree of Life and the Tree of Knowledge of Good and Evil.

One additional term that should be pointed out is what is referred to as "seeing" and "hearing." Remember that Kabbalah defines "reality" as the totality of all that can be perceived through our five senses (i.e., all that is of a physical nature) and all that is of a spiritual nature, which we may not readily perceive. Thus seeing and hearing are not only to physical sights and sounds, but beyond them to truths within the spiritual realm.

REWARD OR PUNISHMENT

It often looks like some people have a lot more than their share of good luck, while others seem to be hit with an overdose of bad luck. But if God or the system were to work by favoritism, there would

---

6. Two examples are the Ari's (via his student and scribe, Rabbi Khayim Vital) book *The Tree of Life* and Rabbi Ashlag's book called *An Entrance to the Tree of Life* (both put out by the Kabbalah Centre).

be no room for free will.[7] With this in mind, we can emphatically say that reward and punishment as we know of them are illusions, since what and how much we receive constitutes "merely the consequence of an individual's action in exercise of free will" (Berg's *Reincarnation*, p. 46).

What this means is that in accordance with the laws of nature and paranature or physics and metaphysics, which all go together, if one sticks his finger in an electric socket, whether he be a malicious criminal or a saint, he will inevitably get a shock. That is neither reward nor punishment. Put in more technical terms:

> The law of karma [*tikune*] decrees that for every action there must be an equal corresponding reaction so that ultimately we all will receive exactly what we have solicited (ibid., p. 91).

Of course, the parallel of this on the physical level is: "For every action there is an equal and opposite reaction" (Newton's second law of physics).

With this in mind, we can also understand the proverb: "Cast thy bread upon the waters for thou shalt find it after many days" (Ecclesiastics 11:1). "It means simply that the practice of goodness and kindness will be rewarded unexpectedly after a long interval. It means that whatever one plants, that is what he will reap" (Berg's *Reincarnation*, p. 91).

> [T]he immediate application of knowledge of reincarnation lies in the area of problem solving. In the face of any affliction . . . it will take its practitioner below the level of consciousness where the cause of visible effects lie buried. To approach such problems without making that journey is like trying to fight crabgrass with a lawnmower (ibid., p. 112).

What this should mean for anyone interested in elevating his level of consciousness to transcend the illusion of "reward" and "punishment," is that when things happen, we merely need to look at them as signs for us to learn from.

---

7. Also, see the discussion on Free Choice from the last chapter.

This, however, is not given to be interpreted fatalistically. After all:

> We cannot escape the results of past actions, but we may change the results by what we do now. If the soul becomes aware of its defects [*haḵarat hara*] and brings itself into alignment with the forces of the universe and the cosmic truths of unity, pain and suffering can be modified. This is not to say that if we encounter a person deep in suffering that we should ignore his cry for help on grounds that he is merely working off his *tiḵune*. It is not our duty to interfere with the process, but we can look upon the sufferer in a different light and help him bear his burden without trying to bear it for him. . . . When we speak of the laws of *tiḵune*, we must understand that there is a cosmic energy that can help us turn or remove the misfortune that has overcome us (ibid., pp. 99–100).

Moreover, it is also important for us to remember that it is not our role to "assign" *Tiḵḵun* to anyone—the "system" takes care of that. Bob Larson recounts a discussion about a particular branch of witchcraft:

> The Frosts insist their branch of wicca is non-threatening, undergirded by the maxim, "Eight words the Wiccan Rede fulfill. If it harm none, do what you will." . . . But when [Larson] debated the Frosts on *Larry King Live*, they admitted that it is all right to inflict physical harm on an enemy if by doing so a witch may be able to *educate that person's soul*. They even acknowledged that on the way to the television show they had put a hex on a taxi driver who irritated them (*Satanism*, p. 165, emphasis added).

It is our societal obligation to educate the vessel (body and mental apparatus) of others to act ethically and morally. But no mortal, of whatever psychic level, has the right or real capacity to educate, judge, or adjudge another's soul. The body inevitably educates the soul within its confines; that is the function of the body.

The destiny line that we get ourselves into is what defines the nature of our life or incarnation; but we can change this, even in a single incarnation. Today, the souls that define our existence are composed of so many different sparks that our souls are like salads of energy. This helps explain the different facets of our personality and why some days we are like a "different person."

But to all this we need to incorporate and emphasize the aspect of free will which defines new directions or destiny lines. After all, as Rabbi Ashlag reminds us, "Every situation is the result of causes which precede it and it changes with successive events" (p. 120). Therefore, two directions or frameworks of time are involved: the past to the present and the present to the future.

We have already noted a number of times that since time, space, and motion do not exist in the Endless—in the "real" world—they are rendered *illusions*. However, it may be helpful to explain the source and purpose of time, especially when we discuss time's directions and frameworks with regard to the *Tikkun* process.

THE NECESSITY OF TIME

The Talmud tells us that initially God thought to create the world with *Midat HaDeen*, Strict Judgment. "Judgment" denotes immediacy between cause and effect. For example, as the biblical law teaches: "an eye for an eye . . ." (Exodus 21:24 and Leviticus 24:20). This does not mean that if A pokes out B's eye, intentionally or not, that A's eye be then poked out, too. Instead, what the Bible offers us is insight into the workings of the universe: A natural order of balance exists in the cosmos. If the energy lost is not restored, then circumstances will arise that effect a repayment equivalent to the energy of an eye or even an eye itself.

Crime: A person who steals $100 creates an imbalance in the universe of $100 (whatever that means). The system will provide that the energy of $100 be restored to recreate balance. The thief may then find himself "somehow" losing $100. Willingly or not, the system (the cosmic system) will make sure that that thief repays the $100 plus whatever energy sum is incurred from generating negative energy per the imbalance created by the stealing. Kabbalah also teaches us that when something—anything—is stolen, the thief only acquires the physical property of the loot, never the spiritual essence, which would translate here as the buying power of the stolen object—the Light in the object.

Similarly, we might offer a translation of the energy exchange of another crime, of which the Ten Commandments specifically warns us. Its warning is merely an immediate indication that a tremendous imbalance can result, primarily to the doer's disadvantage. Typical of his skittish yet prompting manner, Rabbi Berg challenges:

> Without conscience or morality, to kill a competitor in business, for example, might make perfectly good sense. After all, if one kills his competitor, he will be in a position to gain more energy, in the form of money or profit, will he not?
>
> The flaw in that logic is not a point of conscience or morality, however. Kabbalisticly speaking, there can be no such thing as murder for gain, simply because gain can never result from murder. . . . [W]henever one kills, he is taking another's energy without first creating a vessel in which to hold it. The only way in which he can create such a vessel is to reject murder. Without a vessel, he can never hold what the act of murder might bring to him. The energy thus taken remains with him until, in the current, or a future lifetime, an appropriate vessel is created to contain it and relieve him of his burden.
>
> Even money inherited from birth falls under these precepts. Without charity—without creation of a vessel by means of rejection [i.e., Restriction]—its internal energy cannot be held (*Reincarnation*, pp. 87–88).

In short, what Rabbi Berg is saying is that the only means of preparing a vessel in order to take another's life is by *resisting* that urge to murder, that is, by not murdering. If one does murder, he will eventually lose his own vessel (body) to compensate for the lack of vessel he had when he murdered: The killer may be murdered, or he will somehow lose his own life in a similar manner that he took his victim's.

Moreover, the term *Ten Commandments*, as Rabbi Berg says, is a corruption of the actual term, which is "10 *HaDibrot*," which literally translates back as the Ten Utterances, from the root *D-B-R*. The idea of God "commanding" us to do anything is antithetical to the very Thought of Creation: Unquestioned submission to a commandment negates the function and necessity of free will in this world.[8] It is for this reason that Rabbi Berg has stated a number of times that worship or adherence to any form of commandment borders on idolatry, which is acting against the Thought of Creation. An utterance should be understood as a form of suggestion—a divine piece of advice.

PREPARING A VESSEL

The issue of not creating or preparing a sufficient vessel is important. In this world, raw, naked energy—physical and metaphysical—is dangerous, if not deadly. Think of a live electric wire. Electricity is beneficial, but only when it is contained within a closed circuit (vessel) and when the wires directing the current are enclosed in proper wiring material, too. If this is so of physical energy, how much more so is it true of spiritual, metaphysical energy! What the murderer is left with after his act of murder is a tremendous amount of raw, naked, metaphysical energy: all of the energy of the murdered victim.

One might also note, with this in mind, that according to Kabbalah, adhering to the advice of the Ten Utterances[9] is only for the individual's, the doer's, benefit. It just is not worth it to steal or murder! We need to bear in mind the quantum physics principle, which explains that everything I do effects the entire world, just as what happens anywhere in the world, by anybody, effects me, too. Therefore, what is or isn't "worth it" to the individual is equally so for the rest of society and the world.

As the significance of the vessel in the physical world is seen in a new light, we can also understand why the Bible is encoded. Each word conveys Light and is, therefore, covered by a vessel so that we can reveal it and benefit from it. If the Light of the Bible were not covered, It would be like that live electric wire. If an individual had not prepared a sufficient vessel to receive this Light— had not sufficiently prepared himself spiritually—he would inevitably "burn."

Reading the Bible on its literal, physical, level requires physical effort, to a greater or lesser degree (eye strain, concentration,

---

8. E.g. his lecture on Passover, 1992.
9. Popularly known as the 10 Commandments; see above.

and so on); but truly *seeing* the Bible, beyond its physical level, requires spiritual effort. And spiritual effort, as we have defined, equates with Resistance. Here, what needs to be restricted or resisted is our immediate impulse to take in what is read on a literal level. That would be like mistaking the body for the soul; or like (how apropos!) judging a book by its cover. With this we can also understand Rabbi Lipschitz's seemingly cryptic words when he says:

> God "wished to hide the precious light of eternal life and to obscure it in darkness so that man will not clearly apprehend the mode of this life [which ends in death]. This was [done] in order not to infringe on man's free will, for that is the purpose of the creation of man in the world; through his [exercise of] free will he will succeed."[10]

NAKED ENERGIES

We can now understand what the Bible means when it says that Adam and Eve "were both naked, the man and his wife, and were not ashamed" (Genesis 3:25). Adam and Eve, before the Fall were pure energy intelligences.[11] At their level, there were no Husks or Curtains, no covering or concealment. Adam and Eve were "man and wife," meaning they were combined positive and negative poles. And they were "naked" not in the sense that they did not have clothes on their bodies, because before the Fall they did not have the physical bodies that we have today. Rather, they were naked in the sense that they were not concealed. At their spiritual level, they were raw, naked energies, like the live wire; but at their spiritual level they could handle it.

Parenthetically, it is interesting to point out that the word/root used to describe Adam and Eve's being naked, *Arumim* (Genesis 2:25), is the same word/root used to describe the snake. In Genesis 3:1, the English translation reads, "Now the serpent was more subtle than any beast of the field. . . ." The actual word for

---

10. Rabbi Lipschitz's sermon as translated and taken from Rabbi Aryeh Kaplan's book, *Immortality, Resurrection and the Age of the Universe*, p. 80.

11. Of the level of *Ze'ir Anpin*, as we will learn in the next chapter.

"subtle" in the Hebrew original is *Arum*, the singular of *Arumim* and literally translates back as *naked*. From this, we get a little insight into the real meaning of *snake* in Genesis: It is a raw *naked* energy—"the most naked beast of the field," to be specific.[12]

Kabbalah also explains that before the Fall, Adam and Eve were made of pure nail (like the material of our finger and toenails). We all retain a remnant of man in his perfection in our finger and toenails. We connect to this state of perfection at the end of *Shabbat* during *Havdalah* when we observe the reflection of light on our fingernails. Nail is transparent, meaning that light or the Light can pass straight or purely through it. After the Fall, man's body was taken from the ground ("for dust thou art" Genesis 3:19); "God made unto Adam and to his wife coats of skins, and clothed them" (Genesis 3:21), the earth connoting the Desire to Receive as opposed to being a channel, as they were before the Fall.

Today, our bodies are covered in skin. While it also enclothes and conceals the insides of the body, skin is also a transmissive substance. However, because it can only conduct Light to the *Klipot*, it needs to be covered.[13] This is why we enclothe our bodies, literally, with clothes. Our clothes serve as the vessel for the body and its skin. Many pagan religions, like Wiccan or witchcraft, and satanism, perform rituals naked, or as they call it, "sky clad." But drawing metaphysical energy while naked is a double whammy of Direct Light, because the Light of the body via the

---

12. We will touch on the significance of the snake more in chapter 8, when we discuss Satan.

13. In the next chapter we will discuss *Sefirot* and the issue of Husks resulting from Original Sin. But, in short, for the purpose of our discussion here, after Adam sinned, his body, which had been completely Light, fell to the *Klipot* (the Husks). Per Halakha, our bodies today are supposed to be covered from the neck down, because the body below the neck corresponds with the lower *Sefirot* of *Ze'ir Anpin* and *Malkhut* (except for that part of the arm from and including the hand to the elbow, which is considered a direct 'working tool' with the physical world), which were affected by the Fall. We cover the body to hide the *Klipot*, because, although the body can draw Light, as being of the *Klipot*, it can only do so deeper into the *Klipot*. The only time we reveal the body is for the sake of doing *Tikkun*, performing a *Mitzvah*, for example going to the *Mikveh* or *Zivug* (sexual intercourse within the sacred framework of Torah). The cults and religions that perform rituals naked, do so to draw Light directly into the *Klipot*—the epitome of a short circuit—which is the main goal of those practices of the System of the Vessel (to be discussed in chapter 8).

skin is not contained. The fact that nudity is generally not accepted socially or professionally is incidental to the spiritual–metaphysical significance (the root cause) of why we clothe our bodies.

Under the system of Strict Judgment [*Deen*], right after A pokes out B's eye, A would automatically lose his eye. There would be no time or second chances given to repair the damage and eliminate the negativity generated. This system, however, denied the Vessel the free will necessary to eliminate Bread of Shame. Therefore, God decided to create the world with *Midat HaRakhamim*, *Rakhamim* meaning "mercy." And mercy translates as time. The Talmudic discussion of *Midat HaDeen* and *Midat HaRakhamim* is *not* to infer that God was fickle and actually changed His mind. The discussion is based on the pair of the word *Et* that appears in the original Hebrew in the very first verse of Genesis. In English, this could be represented as: "In the beginning God created *Et* the heavens and *Et* the earth." The discussion, therefore, involves, not drafts of Creation, but rather the *process* of Creation.[14]

The illusion of time was provided to enable the Vessel to tender payment and rectify the cause before the effect became implemented. Time, however, also causes us to forget what we have done (the cause) to engender such effects. Time may permit years, if not lifetimes, before payment is demanded of an action. This is what causes the "why's" and "why me's." But time is necessary for the existence of free choice.

This system, with the illusion of time, means that we can, in essence, go back to the future and repair negative causes that we have set in motion, to eliminate the snowball effect that would necessarily boomerang on the doer.

Sound like science fiction? With regard to non-fictional physics, Dr. Stephen Hawking explains:

> The strong version of the cosmic censorship hypothesis states that in a realistic solution, the singularities [being a point in space–time[15] at which the space–time curvature becomes infinite, per p. 198] would always lie either entirely in future

14. For more on this topic, refer to Rabbi Berg's recorded lessons on Genesis (*Beresheet*).

15. Which, to a kabbalist, the concept of space–time is merely a double illusion!

(like the singularities of gravitational collapse) or entirely in
the past (like the Big Bang). It is greatly to be hoped that some
version of the censorship hypothesis holds because close to
naked singularities it may be possible to *travel into the past* (*A
Brief History of Time*, pp. 93–94, emphasis added).

After all, "the theory of relativity put an end to the idea of
absolute time!"[16] Such slate-cleaning that time travel to the past
allows, basically sums up the necessary spiritual work undertaken
(1) prior to Rosh HaShana, "the Day of Judgment," (2) during Rosh
HaShana, with the help of the *Shofar*, and (3) for the "Ten Days
of Repentance," beginning with the Jewish New Year. Hard, sincere, spiritual work is required of each individual before reaching
Yom Kippur; as the tenth day, Yom Kippur is the day in which
all causes set in motion during the previous year are "sealed" and
implemented.[17] But, fortunately, additional means are available to
weed out, or uproot negative causes that we may still have in our
cosmic account and which we will discuss.

Now we can understand where reincarnation fits into the
grand scheme of things. We said that the purpose of existence here
is to "correct" the Bread of Shame we (pieces of the Endless Vessel)
felt in the Endless. We are now working to overcome that obstacle,
so that we can achieve "final correction" and return to the Endless, to the Fourth Aspect of Creation, to complete the Thought of
Creation.

The law of *tikune*, therefore, is really the law of fair play. By
permitting a soul to sojourn in the physical world, it is given
an opportunity to correct misdeeds, performed in a previous
lifetime (Berg, *Reincarnation*, pp. 92–93).

When the illusory aspect of time came into play, the process
of this correction "slowed down" so that it appears to us to extend
over long periods of times, when in fact, in the grand scheme of
things, it is all part of the Third Aspect of Creation. This is where
we are now. For what we call *Tikkun* or Correction, the Orientals

---

16. Ibid., p. 22.
17. The tenth day corresponds to the *Sefirah* of *Malkhut*, which will be
discussed in chapter 5; but it is the level at which spiritual energy is implemented.

use the term *karma*. Sogyal Rinpoche defines karma as the "natural law of cause and effect" (*The Tibetan Book of Living and Dying*, p. 92). He even qualifies, "There are many kinds of karma: international karma, national karma, the karma of a city, and individual karma" (ibid.) This is basically synonymous with *Tikkun*; but *Tikkun*, even the word itself, describes the *process* more accurately.

In fact, Rabbi Yonassan Gershom, in his book *Beyond the Ashes*, offers a definition and comparison of *Tikkun* and karma by explaining:

> [T]he word "karma" literally means "action" in Sanskrit. The Talmud says that "all your deeds (actions) are written in a book" [as per his footnote: Talmud, Pirkei Avot 2:1]. There is really no difference between the Eastern concept of "karma" and the Jewish concept of "Divine Judgment." Both call us to account for our actions. While we can and do choose the general circumstances of our lives on earth, the sum total of our previous actions must also be taken into account. (p. 163).

Like the term karma, the *Tikkun* system also takes into account each individual's specific frame of reference, which would include such considerations as one's generation, family, etcetera. But a *Tikkun* also implies an obstacle; it is like a veil that obscures the Light. We strive to overcome our *Tikkunim* (plural for *Tikkun*) for our soul to be able to channel the Light more purely. And the fewer the impurities or obstacles, the more Light we can receive.

We fulfill *Tikkun* first of all by elevating our consciousness to where we admit that there is something to correct. Kabbalists call this process *HaKarat HaRah*, literally "Recognition of the Evil." If we remember that evil in each of us is defined as a Desire to Receive for Myself Alone, what this process basically involves is seeing where what I do fits into the grand scheme of things: seeing that there are things that I do that create negativity and that these things need to be corrected. We need to recognize that those elements of Desire to Receive for the Self Alone are what keep us from being spiritual, by definition, as they lack any element of Restriction.

"Recognition of the Evil" is somewhat like the practice of confession in Catholicism, whereby the evil is confessed to one's priest.

This practice may possibly derive from King David's petition to God to enable his nation of Israel to "be able to obtain pardon for their recurring sins."[18] So God told David:

> "Whenever Israel is afflicted for its sinfulness, let them appear before me united in prayer, confess their sins, and recite the special propitiatory prayers, the *Selichot*, and I will pardon them."[19]

But as God said, the practice is to be directly before Him. And since the unity spoken of is to be conducted on a spiritual level, the entire process is on a spiritual, rather that physical level. Thus the "recognition of the evil" is something that we do from within, to gain unity with the quantum whole.

One might even note that the above point identifies one of the chief differences between Judaism and Christianity. As we will discuss in chapter 8, Judaism defines the Messiah as the Vessel's achievement of the Fourth Aspect of Creation, which has yet to be achieved; whereas Christianity embodies this energy in a human figure, who has already existed—Jesus. Judaism is also a spiritual doctrine whose congregants, by definition of their metaphysical nature (as we will understand from chapter 6), cannot have any mediums between them and the Light. Moses, other prophets, and spiritual leaders *assist* Jews in connecting to the Light, but they do not represent, replace, or substitute for the Light.

As we will learn in chapter 5, different nations connect and correspond to different energies. From this, we can understand that, by definition, there can be no such thing as a "Christian Jew." Each component of such a phrase corresponds to a different energy, and juxtaposed together, the two words—Christian and Jew—constitute a contradiction in terms. Similarly, in his book *Satanism: The Seduction of America's Youth*, Bob Larson makes a point of just how preposterous and contradictory a term like "Christian Psychic" is (p. 186). The energy that corresponds with Christianity negates that of psychic practices (or New Age, as we will discuss in chapter 8). The two words cannot be mixed,

---

18. Yaacov Vainstein, *The Cycle of the Jewish Year: A Study of the Festivals and of Selections From the Liturgy*, p. 81.

19. Ibid., pp. 81–82.

because, by their definitions, they are either one or the other, but not both.

Along these same lines, certain other terms do not go together either. Nazism, as we have already pointed out and will discuss more in chapter 8, is a form of Satanism. Satanism is antithetical to Christianity. Thus, there can be no such thing as a "Christian Nazi" or even a "Christian skinhead." Each grouping is a contradiction in energies and thus in terms. As Larson points out, certain other concepts do not go together, like Robert DeGrimston's teachings, "Processian philosophy," which states that Jesus and Satan "have destroyed their enmity and [have] come together for the end of the world" (p. 144). Charles Manson was heavily influenced by this oxymoronic concept (ibid). This concept is an impossibility, physically and metaphysically, because Satan (as we will learn in chapter 8) is darkness. Light and darkness are unreconcilable opposites. That points to the very purpose of our existence—to get rid of the darkness, so that we can cleave, as we once did, to the Light.

"Recognition of the Evil," however, is only a means to an end and not an end in itself. It is what helps us reach our desired destination. It would be like somehow being southbound on a highway on which we wish to be traveling north. The first step would be to discern that something is wrong. Only then can we bring ourselves to get off that road and turn around. If we don't even see that something is wrong, we'll keep going in the wrong, and even opposite, direction.

Once we fulfill a *Tikkun* (and by now we all have many *Tikkunim* or Corrections, in the plural), the corrected part of us returns to the Endless and needs not return to this plane. *Tikkun* denotes the process at large, but also refers to individual obstacles that we effect that prevent us from connecting to the Light (as when kabbalists say that a bad habit they have is "a difficult *Tikkun*").

Tikkun can be fulfilled in one lifetime; it can even be fulfilled in one year. In Judaism, there are 613 precepts: 248 positive precepts (what one is advised to do) and 365 negative precepts (what one is advised not to do). The positive precepts merely show us how we can reveal positive energy, while the negative precepts show us how we can prevent revealing negative energy—for our own personal benefit.

As there are 365 negative precepts, each corresponds to the 365 days of the year. And, as a "negative" precept, it defines all the ways that Restriction or Resistance needs to be exerted. If one can succeed in that battle every single day for an entire year, and provided that in the meantime he does not generate new negativity, he will complete his *Tikkun*.

Most of us, however, cannot and do not succeed as such. For some, it takes an entire lifetime to fulfill just one *Tikkun* or obstacle. When one lifetime is not sufficient to fulfill all of the *Tikkun* that an individual has to fulfill, the process spreads over a period of many lifetimes.[20] Rabbi Ashlag, from a slightly different angle, offers a view of the time perspective involved:

> I begin with the words of our Sages regarding the chain of generations in the world. They say that although we see the physical bodies changing from generation to generation, this applies only to the body. The souls, which are the essence of the body, are not subject to change. Rather they migrate and inhabit body after body in generation after generation. Those very same souls that were present in the generation of the flood (Noah), returned again in the generation of upheaval (Tower of Babel), and then during the Egyptian exile, and

---

20. The topic of death and why we need to die in between lifetimes exceeds the scope of this particular focus of Kabbalah, although it ties in, as every aspect of Kabbalah interrelates. Suffice to say for now that when the energy intelligence of the body, which wants to receive for itself alone (–), overcomes the energy intelligence of the soul, which wants to share to fulfill *Tikkun* (+), the soul must leave that body, resulting in physical death. As Rabbi Berg explains, in his book, *Reincarnation*:

> It is the soul's desire to remain in a pure state of consciousness, never having to resort to the physical existence that entails being placed into a body and thus suffering the limitations of the body, that resists rebirth. The soul is a metaphysical force which creates life within us. When the soul leaves the body, it creates death, because since there is no life in the body itself, physical existence ceases to have purpose. Thus soul and body are in a constant state of struggle . . . The energy of the body is of the desire to receive for itself alone, which is the root of all evil. . . . Only the soul provides the force which can integrate body energy into the whole and convert the whole to a "desire to receive for the sake of imparting," and when that occurs, the soul has fulfilled its destiny by balancing its *tikune* (pp. 78–79).

The topic of death is discussed more in depth in the Kabbalah Centre's Beginners Course, lesson number 14 and in the advanced course on reincarnation.

again with the Egyptian exodus, etc. This process continues to our generation and will continue until the world is complete [*gmar tikun*]. It proceeds in a manner that we have no new souls as we have new bodies in our world. There are a fixed number of souls which reincarnate into new shapes. That is, each time, they are enclothed in a new body in a generation (*Gift of the Bible*, p. 106).

THE PURPOSE OF REINCARNATION

Rabbi Berg sums up the reasons for this process when he states:

> The entire physical process of reproduction and birth is designed to supply the soul with a physical body that will conform to the behavior of that soul as it existed in a prior lifetime. Reincarnation also sheds light on the subject of children who are born deformed, or who die when they still are very young (*Reincarnation*, p. 58).
>
> Each incarnation is but a continuation of the preceding one. Thus, even a short life serves a purpose—be that purpose a lesson the soul of the child needs to learn or a lesson needed by the soul of the grieving parent. However tragic the circumstances may be, nothing is ever lost and nothing is ever forgotten. No matter how short or how tragic a life may be, it either adds something of value to the memory of the soul or it permits payment of a debt (ibid., p. 62).

> Thus *Tabula Rasa* is an illusion.
>
> As Kabbalah explains, the soul reincarnates into the very state (or *Tikkun*) that it left off in its last incarnation.[21] This is why people are born into different socio-economic conditions, with various fears, addictions, talents, aspirations, and so on. This also explains the phenomenon of child prodigies. One's soul is directed by the *Tikkun* it needs to fulfill, and one's life will usually be defined or consumed by the very *Tikkun(im)* that person has. The soul will pull the blind body that does not see nor understand where it is going to exactly what the soul needs.

---

21. This point will be qualified in chapter 7.

For some people, their *Tikkunim* involve sex. We have already indicated how the energy drawn from sex can cause one to "burn" from Direct Light. We will also discuss harsher *Tikkunim*, such as homosexuality and even bestiality in chapter 7. For others, *Tikkun* lies primarily in the need for power. Desire is natural; it is, in fact, what motivates the world. But a Desire to Receive at the expense of others—power over people, ego, and various similar forms— connects with the energy of Satan, as will be discussed in chapter 8. In sum, all we, the collective Endless Vessel, really want is Light: the feeling of fulfillment that the Light Force gives. The soul wants to return to the Endless.

CLUES OF PAST LIVES

We are discovering more and more that everything about us reveals our inner being and exposes even what we try to hide. With regard to our health and well-being, reflexology says all is shown on one's foot. As Michio Kushi writes on Oriental diagnosis, "The principle tool of Oriental diagnosis is physiognomy. . . . The basic premise of Oriental physiognomy is that each individual represents a walking history of his or her development (p. vii).[22]

Thus our "clues" are exposed from our very countenance.

Graphology (or Grapho analysis) says our handwriting offers an accurate picture of our nature, personality, and "secrets." Palmistry says our destiny is spelled out on our palms. Our very outward behavior, body language, and spoken words, not to mention our inner fears and dreams, all reveal one's inner essence, which may be a dark mystery even to that individual himself.

In short, everything we need to know is readily accessible. We just need to learn how to read it. And this is true about everything regarding this life and past lives. Everything that happens to us or is a part of us constitutes a sign of what we need to work on to fulfill *Tikkun*. The totality of everything around and about us serves as the givens we need to solve for the question about our mission in life. If, for example, a relationship sours or ends, or circumstances at work or at home pushes one out, it is the system's way of get-

---

22. Michio Kushi, *An Introduction to Oriental Diagnosis: Your Face Never Lies*.

ting that individual where he needs to go. Thus pain and discomfort are not always bad—they merely constitute signs of where *Tikkun* is needed.

> In the higher worlds, the soul experiences both the beneficence of the *En Sof* and the feeling of shame that is a result of the inability to impart anything to the all-inclusive Infinite. Thus the soul descends to this world in order to erase the feeling of shame and thereby achieves fulfillment. However, in passing into this world the soul forgets its purpose in coming here, due to the influence of the Evil Inclination [the Desire to Receive for Oneself Alone], and becomes distracted by the earthly delights of this mundane existence (Berg's *Layman*, I, p. 90).

Just because we do not seem to be able to recall past lives does not mean that they do not exist, nor does it mean that we cannot discover them.

> According to the *Zohar*, the mind, or the physical brain if you will, never forgets anything. There is no disappearance in any matter concerning metaphysics or the spirit (per *Zohar*, II, p. 99a as quoted in Berg's *Reincarnation*, p. 69).
>
> We have all known the Endless One. We have experienced unity with the Force of Creation. We have tasted of the sweet fruit of perfection. Why do we not remember? The answer is we do. Only our minds have forgotten. The rest of us remembers, our blood, our genes, our bones. The memory lingers in our soul. . . . The Force is a part of us, but the Curtain and the *Tsimtsum* prevent us from remembering. It must be so. Otherwise, we would have no opportunity for correction, no way of absolving Bread of Shame (Berg's *Layman*, II, p. 137).

As discussed in the Introduction, signs exist all around us. If our internal headlights are off, then these signs will whip right by us without our being aware of them. But the signs are there to help us; so when they go by—or rather when we let them go by—things appear to exist by chance and even illogically.

Red hair or left-handedness, examples that we noted in the

last chapter, are signs that the red-haired or left-handed individual has some kind of a *Tikkun* with the Left Column. Each redhead or "lefty" will have to determine exactly how that translates to his or her individual life. The same sign in different people means something specifically different for each. A *Tikkun* with the Left Column could mean that the individual has a problem with receiving—quantitatively receiving—as it could mean that the individual does not know how to receive qualitatively. This is what Rabbi Ashlag means when he says, "Every person is obligated to reach the root of his soul" (*Gift of the Bible*, p. 143). First we need to "Recognize the Evil," and then we must work to overcome that *Tikkun*.

> Our lives abound with clues as to what has gone before [this life] and one of the most telling of those clues is fear. Almost all of us are plagued by one or more irrational, unfounded fears (Berg's *Reincarnation*, p. 71).

Simply put: Reincarnation helps "explain why we behave as we do" (ibid., p. 29).

Vis-à-vis the Mental Sciences: Sometimes the signs become so illogical that they force one to reevaluate his or her state of consciousness. This was the case for two prominent physicians, Brian Weiss, M.D., and Raymond Moody, M.D. Dr. Weiss had an Ivy League education, "a good stable marriage, two young children, and a flourishing career" (p. 9) in psychiatry. He headed the psychopharmacology division of the University of Miami and was then chief of psychiatry at a large university-affiliated hospital in Miami. He had been very conservative as a scientist and physician, until he encountered a patient named Catherine. It took Dr. Weiss four years just to muster up the courage to "take the professional risk of revealing [the] unorthodox information" (p. 12) he records in his book, *Many Lives, Many Masters*, from his sessions with Catherine. And in another book, *Life After Life: The Investigation of a Phenomenon—Survival of Bodily Death*, Dr. Raymond Moody depicts the testimony of over a hundred people who experienced "clinical death" and who were revived. Despite their wide range of backgrounds, patients offered similar, vivid descriptions of their experiences.

In his book *Beyond the Ashes: Cases of Reincarnation from the Holocaust*, Rabbi Yonassan Gershom offers "an anecdotal collec-

tion of personal stories" that were told to him over a period of
ten years "by people who believe that they died in the Holocaust
and have reincarnated" (p. xv). Parenthetical to this point of discussion, but important to note is that Rabbi Gershom (and Dr.
Moody and Dr. Weiss to a greater or lesser extent as well) observed that through his patients' opening up and telling their
deep hidden secrets and fears, most found relief from their haunt-
ing burden.

What is interesting for the purpose of this discussion is how
there are people, as Rabbi Gershom puts it,

> with strange phobias and emotional reactions that seem to
> come from nowhere. For some people, ordinary objects in-
> voke a terror that has no logical explanation in this life. But
> when put into the context of reincarnation [or past incarna-
> tions], these fears suddenly begin to make sense (*Beyond the
> Ashes*, p. 131).

For example, Rabbi Gershom tells how "one Lutheran house-
wife described a desire to light candles on Friday night, a compul-
sion which had no basis in Lutheranism and meant nothing to her
or her family" (ibid., p. 12). In the framework of a Jewish life, the
lighting of Sabbath candles on Friday at sundown would be a normal and common practice. The author then goes on to tell how

> [a]nother non-Jewish caller told [him] that when his young
> son was first learning to eat by himself, he refused to drink
> milk if there was meat on the table. If the parents insisted, he
> would dump the milk on the floor. This behavior was exas-
> perating to the boy's parents, who had no idea why he did this
> with milk but never with water or juice (ibid., p. 12).

In a Jewish household, this would be understood, since "one
of the fundamentals of the Jewish dietary laws is that meat and
milk are never under any circumstances eaten at the same meal.
On the other hand, it is perfectly kosher to eat meat with water or
juice" (ibid.).

One additional account that Rabbi Gershom relates is how
one woman discovered only in adulthood that her mother was
Jewish. This woman, as a child had strangely

insisted on sprinkling salt on her bread, a custom at the Jewish Sabbath table but generally unknown elsewhere. And when playing house, she would often wind string down her arm "like a snake"—could this have been a memory of the *tefillin* [phylacteries] straps worn on the arm by Jewish men during prayer? (p. 26).

Psychologists and psychiatrists will agree that the line between what is normal and not normal, or even pathological, is a very fine one. The study of reincarnation may offer insight not only into defining that line better but also into the cure of various mental maladies. But for those mental health physicians concerned for their jobs, Rabbi Gershom even quips:

Many people report that once they have recognized the source of the problem as coming from another life, the phobias and other symptoms disappear. This should not be taken as a prescription to stop regular medication. But if one is plagued by chronic symptoms that seem to have no organic cause, it might be worthwhile to investigate reincarnation as a possibility *in addition* to following your doctor's advice (ibid., p. 135, italics in original).

If nothing else, the doctrine of reincarnation offers insight into the root cause of various maladies, which alone may help lead to their cure. For example, as it was explained to Rabbi Gershom, "'[S]chizophrenics are people who are not fully incarnated on the earth plane'" (ibid., p. 119). Kabbalists have expressed other psychiatric phenomena in kabbalistic terms, such as two souls that, despite their many chances in numerous lifetimes, fail to reconcile their differences; they then may reincarnate into one body where they will have no escaping their *Tikkun*. We call such a phenomenon *split personalities*.

Dreams: Clues of past incarnations may also come in the form of dreams. When we sleep, we disconnect ourselves from the limitations of the physical world and our soul is free to wander in the unlimited spiritual world. In that "next world," which is not subject to time, space or motion, the soul may draw on certain memories from other incarnations. Someone we work with, for example may appear as our father, mother, sibling, or spouse, which many times gives an accurate account of our (real) relationship to that person and why we feel toward him or her the way we do. It is important to remember, though, that dream recall is important only in so far that it helps us with our *Tikkun*. Dream recall for its own sake may be fun, but when we forget that it is only a means to an end and not an end in itself, we lose the perspective of the system at large; the system may then begin to offer faulty insights as a result of one's abuse or misuse of this powerful tool.[23]

PARENTS

It is also important to note that the soul, before it descends to this plane,*chooses* to which parents and to which family it will descend. Parents, as well, *choose* what kind of children they will bring to this world: The parents' thoughts at the moment of conception[24] determine the type of soul that they will draw as their child.[25] The soul chooses the specific unit or vessel that will enable it to fulfill its *Tikkun*. The parents and family serve as tools, which the soul needs, to accomplish what it sets out to accomplish in a particular lifetime.

Thus sometimes parents serve as positive role models that help their child become like them. And sometimes parents serve as negative role models of what the child does*not* want to become, but needs to experience to learn from. If, for example, in one life an individual abuses and ignores his children, sometimes the only way for that soul to, first of all, pay back its karmic debt to his children, and secondly, to learn not to abuse and ignore, is to be an abused and ignored child himself. So parents in one lifetime may be the children in the next or previous lifetime.

---

23. For more on dreams, consult lesson, "Dreams, Death . . ." of the Kabbalah Centre's Kabbalah Beginners Course and the Kabbalah's advanced course on reincarnation.

24. Conception is the kabbalistic euphemism for the moment of the male's ejaculation.

25. The Ari goes into great detail about this point in his book *Gate of Reincarnation*. For more on this point, the reader is directed to Rabbi Berg's book, *Reincarnation* (in particular, chapter 9 on the "Power of the Mind") and to The Kabbalah Centre's advanced course on reincarnation.

This by no means gives legitimacy to parents to abuse or ignore their children; it merely explains why such phenomena exist. We are all endowed with free will. Abuse of any nature entails a karmic debt of an equal if not greater degree; it would be a child abuser's spiritual obligation to exert free will to resist his desires of negativity, so as not to generate negative energy nor perpetuate the destructive cycle of harsh tikkun.

It is for this reason that God tells us, through the Ten Commandments, "Honor thy father and mother" (Exodus 20:12). It does not say to "love," because love denotes Similarity of Form. Children whose parents serve as positive role models may love their parents, because they want and need to be like them—that is Similarity of Form. But the child of a negative role model should not strive for Similarity of Form with his parent(s), because his very *Tikkun* in that particular lifetime is to learn *not* to be like them.

But regardless of whether a child's parent(s) is a positive or negative role model(s), that child's soul *chose* its parents. Those parents, for whatever purpose the soul chose, *assisted* that soul in its tikkun. And it is for this reason that it is important to *honor* one's parents.

SUICIDE

It is also important to note that everyone gets the *Tikkun* he needs and the *Tikkun* he can bear. Some people have a very high threshold, whereas others have a very low threshold for *Tikkun*. Whatever that level of threshold, one's *Tikkun* will usually go to the very brink of that threshold, but it won't go beyond. This is important to note, because it explains why suicide is an anathema to Judeo–Christian doctrine.

Suicide causes a disruption to the balance in nature; that is, it goes against the cosmic flow. When negativity happens to a person, and he says "I can't take it," he is going against the cosmic flow because there is order in the universe. He is denying the principle of cause and effect. Moreover, suicide denies the very purpose of our existence: to exert Restriction to eliminate Bread of Shame and to reconnect to the Endless. After a suicide, the soul is not only still burdened by the same *Tikkun*, which it will inevitably face in the next incarnation, but it is added the burden of the *Tikkun* of murder—as suicide is murder of the self.

Tikkun is never easy. Rabbi Berg explains:

As a metaphysical entity . . . the soul . . . has no inherent desire to dwell in the body's linear, mundane world and, once there, inevitably wishes to depart. Psychiatrists have a label for this phenomenon, shared to greater or lesser degree by all of us. They call it "the death wish" (*Reincarnation*, pp. 79–80).

This is normal. However:

Nervous or mental breakdowns, in the Kabbalistic view, are but manifestations of the constant battle between the body's desire to receive and the soul's yearning to impart. When the body overwhelms the soul, it shuts off the flow of positive energy without which the soul cannot survive. Usually the last words of a suicide are, "I can't take it" (p. 80).

The body can no longer "take" the flow of metaphysical energy that the soul draws and needs.

With this, we might add to our definition that "being spiritual" means taking responsibility for everything we do, say and think, that is, taking responsibility for our fate and life. Being spiritual means being willing to accept responsibility when something goes "wrong" in life.

Nothing happens by chance. Per the doctrine of *Tikkun* and reincarnation, what happens to me is a direct result of my *Tikkun*. Thus, the other, or any outside force, is not the cause; external phenomena are merely effects of my *Tikkun*—agents that enable me to see and overcome my *Tikkun*. Being spiritual, then, means not pointing fingers at anyone or anything else, to thumb off responsibility when something happens. Being spiritual requires effort and Restriction. Thus being spiritual is, without a doubt, a tough order to fill!

WAYS TO DEAL WITH HARSH TIKKUN

When one feels his destiny line does not match his soul, evident by various expressions of energy imbalance, it means it is time to change "direction." Pressure, stress and anxiety[26] are merely expressions of the Light's wish to be revealed. When the vessel is insufficient for the amount of Light that is trying to be revealed, this translates as stress or anxiety. It is, therefore, a sign that a bigger, more sufficient vessel is needed to contain this greater amount of Light. And this, in turn, effects a new destiny line for that individual.

The issue of "building" or "preparing vessels" to contain the Light constitutes the very essence of Kabbalah. *Kabbalah*, as we have already said, means the *Doctrine of Receiving*. It teaches us how to receive—receive Light. And the way to prepare vessels, as we discussed in chapter 3, is by exerting Resistance/Restriction.

In getting 'what we really want,' we might allude to the duality of question and answer. A question is a type or an expression of a vessel. An answer is an expression of the Light, as It fulfills the vessel (the question). In law, as in mathematics, for instance, sometimes the hardest thing to do is to define the issue, the problem, or, in kabbalistic terms, the vessel. If one asks the wrong question, or simply defines it off slightly, one does not get the Light that he really desired. This is not because the Light does not want to fulfill, but rather because the individual did not prepare the appropriate vessel.

We get answers in different ways. We may receive express, explicit messages from people around us. Or we may pick up messages from various means of mass communication, like books, films, or TV. People are fascinated by other people's stories, fictional or nonfictional: The stories either offer suggestions as to how to handle one's own *Tikkun* (by seeing various possible outcomes of a particular *Tikkun*) or else they enable us to vicariously experience others' *Tikkunim*, whether similar to our own *Tikkunim* or significantly different.

We can receive all this stimulus and more; yet if we do not have an appropriate vessel, the answers we receive elude us. Thus, the phenomenon of Light, in whatever form It expresses Itself, goes in one end and out the other. That is, without a vessel, Light cannot be contained.

---

26. Rabbi Berg discusses these symptoms in his book *To the Power of One* (particularly in chapter 5).

NEW SOULS IN A SINGLE LIFETIME

When a person moves residences, it is said that he or she acquires a new incarnation. Or when one is involved in a near-death experience, one goes through a reincarnation process. Survivors of what would ordinarily be a fatal car accident, for example, are said to evolve into a new life. This also accounts for clinical-death experiences. Kabbalah explains that in such situations, a change of soul takes place so that the same person does not occupy the body after life is revived.

There are also what Kabbalah defines as "additions" to the soul or "an additional soul." When boys reach the age of thirteen and girls the age of twelve, they acquire an addition to their soul, which provides them with the ability to receive in order to give, that is, the potential of Central Column energy. It is for this reason that boys perform a bar-mitzvah at thirteen and girls a bat-mitzvah at twelve, as an initiation of that new energy inside them. The participation in the community prayer offers the boys the opportunity to use that new energy and share,[27] and thus implement the potential of the addition to the soul in the physical world.

The acquisition of this new energy to the soul is not always easy, especially to one who does not understand what is happening. The additional soul entails new responsibility—of sharing and of demonstrating concern for others. The body, which is a Desire to Receive energy intelligence, definitely does not like this addition. And it is for this reason that adolescence is stamped with rebellion and struggle. The struggle is between the energy intelligence of the body and the new soul. In fact, the Hebrew word for youth (adolescence) is *Ne'urim* from the root *Na'er*, meaning to "shake off." With the acquisition of the addition to the soul, the body tries to shake off its new responsibility.

On the Sabbath (*Shabbat*) we also have the ability to acquire an addition to our soul. One sign that the sages of old used to employ to discern the level of one's soul was by reading one's forehead. In the Ari's book on Reincarnation, Rabbi Haim Vital, the Ari's scribe, tells of one such reading that the Ari did of him.

---

27. As we will learn in chapters 5 and 7, girls or women are naturally or innately more "connected" than men and therefore do not need to perform as many precepts to connect to the Light.

This is translated and told in Rabbi Berg's book *Kabbalah for the Layman I*:

> One Shabbat, the Ari noticed the following text on Haim Vital's forehead: "They prepared a chair for Hezkiahu, King of Judah."[28] He understood immediately that a part of the soul of Hezkiahu had joined that of Haim Vital through the mystery of *Tosfat Shabbat*, whereby one acquires on Shabbat parts of other souls which may remain for a longer or shorter time, depending on the actions of the recipient. During that Shabbat, Vital became angry with a member of his family, and the additional soul consequently left him (Berg's *Kabbalah for the Layman I*, pp. 38–39).

IBURIM *AND* DIBBUKIM

If someone really wants something and truly works hard to achieve it, Kabbalah explains that he will be assisted in his endeavors, whatever they may be. That is, we have the ability to achieve whatever we want—if we really want and work hard enough to achieve it. Sometimes the only assistance needed is the feeling of having succeeded in exerting a particular form of Restriction. After all, if we have never experienced or felt the actual *doing* of a particular act of Restriction, how will we know if and when we do succeed in restricting? The assistance we can get comes in one of two kinds: *Iburim* and *Dibbukim*.

If the energy we want to reveal is positive, per the nature of the goal we are trying to achieve, then we may acquire an *Ibur*. An *Ibur* is usually the soul of a righteous person that attaches itself to the soul of the individual. The *Ibur* will assist the individual by providing the feeling of what it is like to achieve the positive goal and what it takes to get there. The *Tossefet Shabbat* (the additional soul acquired on *Shabbat*) is an example of an *Ibur*.

If, however, the energy we aspire for is negative (Desire to Receive for the Self Alone), then we run the risk of contracting a *Dibbuk*, which is a negative soul that attaches itself to the soul of a person who wants to be evil; the *Dibbuk* will assist the individual

---

28. Per the Ari's Gate of Reincarnation, p. 138.

to be even more evil. Unlike an *Ibur*, which one needs to work hard to acquire and which is easy to lose, a *Dibbuk* is relatively easy to acquire and difficult to get rid of. In fact, the word *Dibbuk* comes from the root/word *D-B-K*, which means glue or to stick; *Ibur* means conception or gestation.

Actually, the word *work* as used above refers to the concept per the Language of the Branches: work=exerting Resistance. *Iburim* and *Dibbukim* do not just happen; we need to draw them to us—or at least open ourselves up to them. With regard to *Dibbukim*, one can acquire a *Dibbuk* by exhibiting extreme forms of anger, as when objects are thrown.

Food and drink are other means that enable a *Dibbuk* to enter us. Kabbalah explains that one of the functions of saying the appropriate prayer or code before eating or drinking is to enable us to connect to only the positive aspect of whatever we are consuming. Such a connection protects us from any negativity that may try to enter. One is also susceptible to *Dibbukim* when one voluntarily lets down his spiritual protective shield, for example, when engaging in seances or other forms of "occult fun." Moreover, kabbalists attribute most severe mental illnesses to possessions of *Dibbukim*.[29]

We protect ourselves from negativity by surrounding ourselves with positive energy.

SIGNS OF BALANCING

Therefore, anyone who suffers some form of injury or illness should immediately ask himself whether it is the result of a *tikune* [*Tikkun*] condition from a past incarnation or the result of some flaw in the present lifetime. The illness might be nothing more than the result of eating or drinking or smoking too much, but the need some people feel to overindulge invariably has its origin in *tikune* (Berg's *Reincarnation*, p. 99).

---

29. For more on this subject, the reader can consult the Kabbalah Centre's advanced course on reincarnation (also available on audio cassette) and Gedalyah Nigal's book *Magic, Mysticism, and Hasidism*.

Sometimes the expression of a *Tikkun* from one life takes the form of the opposite extreme in the next. To illustrate, someone who was really hungry in one life, for example, may cause him to feel the need to overcompensate on eating in the next life. Or, someone who abused knowledge or power in one life may become mentally retarded in the next. Or, someone who abused the body, in whatever way, may be physically impaired in the next.

So sometimes, *Tikkun* causes a reversal of roles: In one generation or incarnation, one may be a hunter or persecutor while in the next life he is the hunted or the persecuted. One who wreaks bodily harm on others in one life may be responsible for sewing up physical wounds, as a doctor or surgeon, or mental and emotional wounds, as a psychologist or psychiatrist, in the next life. Someone who causes another to go blind in one life may be a Seeing Eye dog in the next. There are an infinite number of possibilities.

Similarly, in reviewing the principle of "an eye for an eye" from a slightly different angle, Rabbi Gershom explains:

> [I]t is not necessary for the victim to kill the perpetrator in the next life, which would only perpetuate the cycle in future lives. It can also happen that the murderer in one life gives birth to the victim in the next incarnation, thus replacing the body that was destroyed. . . .

Such would be "a perfect example of karma-stopping without tit-for-tat" (*Beyond the Ashes*, p. 158).

MEASURE OF PROGRESS

With this in mind, Rabbi Gershom offers another example of overcoming a negative *Tikkun* cycle:

> Dr. Usharbud Aryah, noted Sanskrit scholar and disciple of Swami Rama, was once asked the following question:
> "Mahatma Gandhi forgave his assassin; what is the karma in that?" Aryah's answer was that Gandhi would not be karmically tied to the assassin because he had forgiven him,

but that the assassin, unless he himself repented, would still be responsible for his own karma concerning the murder (p. 154).

Forgiving, though, is not exactly synonymous with *Tikkun*. While forgiving may be a means to the end (being *Tikkun*), the kabbalist primarily strives to (1) neutralize the negativity he has engendered, and (2) acknowledge a trying time as an opportunity to exert Resistance and fulfill *Tikkun*.

Regardless, though, not all of us are as self-disciplined as Mahatma Gandhi and fulfill *Tikkun* so gracefully even under such trying circumstances. But as the cosmos functions under a system of balance, when people act in manners that are polar opposites to that of Gandhi, their actions disrupt the universe; of course, the system, in turn, takes care to reestablish balance whether those people involved like it or not. According to the Ari's *Gate of Reincarnation*, as translated and quoted in Rabbi Berg's book, *Reincarnation*:

> [A] soul can return at a lower level than the one it left in a previous life. Indeed, if the weight of *tikun* (correction) is sufficiently heavy, a human soul may find itself reincarnated into the body of an animal, a plant, or even a stone[30] . . . [W]hat is a more metaphysically logical fate for the soul of a mass-murderer, for example, than to be locked in a stone? . . . The act of taking lives is the very manifestation of the individual's desire to receive. . . . [I]t is possible that such a soul may return to this plane . . . as an inanimate object in which the Desire to Receive is a bare minimum. In such a hell of total confinement, a soul would be able to shed the *klipot*—the evil husks of negative energy—that have covered it (Berg, pp. 49–50).

Vis-à-vis Biology: There is, however, one last observation that deserves consideration as a sign of the existence of reincarnation, and that actually relates to the field of biology or botany. Rabbi Berg discusses the following report. In 1958, Semyon and Valenina

---

30. Per the Ari, pp. 58–59.

Kirilian, two Soviet scientists, used a photographic technique to capture on film

> an impression of the biological field that constitutes the human aura. The process, called electrophotography, also makes it possible to examine the pattern of luminescence around dozens of materials. . . . The Kirilians found that the structural details of emanations were different for each item tested and photographed; but the most significant result of their penetrating study was the discovery that living things have patterns that are totally different from those emanated by inanimate objects (ibid., p. 38).

The most interesting observation from this account relates to the study the two scientists conducted on leaves from various plants: "They knew that each species has its own unique energy pattern" (ibid.). But the photos of twin leaves

> differed sharply from each other. . . . Suddenly, in a world in which paranormal, metaphysical phenomena are seen to exist, and in which even the aura of an individual entity can prove to be different from even its twin, our five senses have become pathetic guides indeed [Oshtrand and Schroder wrote about the Kirilians in "Behind the Iron Curtain" from the Kirilain Report, as quoted in Berg's *Reincarnation*, p. 39].

As far as plants are concerned, the existence and significance of reincarnation is not all that important, especially since plants lack any free will to do anything about it. But for us human beings, such an observation bears tremendous significance. First of all it reinforces the point that the physical body is an illusion, and a deceiving one. This would provide insight and understanding into the differences between twins, for example, even identical ones.

In addition, this report also illustrates that all things, animate and inanimate, have an internal essence or energy, which is the soul. Moreover, it may shed some light on the mystery of what some people call hauntings.[31] The "strange feelings" people get about certain things may not be so irrational!

---

31. Rabbi Berg touches on this in his chapter on "Incarnations at Lower Levels" in his book, *Reincarnation*.

SUMMARY OF THE FUNCTION OF TIKKUN

In short, we can say that the *Tikkun* process functions as:

1. a means to correct negativity generated in a present or past lifetime; this may take the form of a disability or a negative trait; and/or
3. a path definer: like the tracks on the railroad, it is there to steer us in a particular direction. Any attempt to deviate from those parameters may result in some effect that forces us back on to the path that we need to be on. In this case, the system functions as a preparatory means toward something in the future (and, of course, of something we chose on a spiritual level) and not just as a reaction to something in the past.

The *Tikkun* system really functions just to help all the scattered sparks of the Endless Vessel return to the Endless. The seeming complexity of the cosmic system, involving all of the billions of people of this globe, works toward this "simple" goal. In fact, the global population growth does not mean that there are more souls. There are no new souls today. Instead, there are many souls which have so much *Tikkun* to fulfill that the soul has been dispersed among a number of bodies, each to fulfill a different portion of the *Tikkun*. As we progress in the Age of Aquarius, the cosmic energy becomes stronger and stronger. Because of this, many souls are fragmenting themselves more and more, so that each body will be able to tolerate the energy it receives. There is even a saying in Hebrew that "the generation continues to dwindle." This refers to the concentration of the soul in the body, because each soul is contained today in so many bodies.

Moreover, in between the soul's sojourns on this plane, it returns to its source, as Rabbi Berg explains:

Upon death of the physical body, the soul immediately travels to Hebron [Israel] where Adam is and that it does so by means of a long tunnel.[32] This almost universally common experience, reported by Jews, Christians, agnostics and a

---

32. Per *Zohar I*, p. 127a.

broad cross section of other persuasions at the moment of clinical death, [therefore] can scarcely be the product of a particular culture or religious bias (*Reincarnation*, p. 56).

This, incidentally, is the tunnel that Dr. Moody's patients report in *Life After Life*.

But while on this plane we need to keep the big picture in mind and even heed to Rabbi Gershom's reminder:

Genuine *tikkun olam* [completing all *Tikkun*]—repairing the world—is a slow and difficult process. . . . Nevertheless, we must never become discouraged. "It is not for you to complete the work [by yourself]," said Rabbi Tarfon 2,000 years ago, "but neither are you free to quit"[33] (p. 261).

TIKKUN *AND EATING*

To fulfil *Tikkun*, we must reveal Light. To reveal Light, we must restrict. Restriction means benefiting others—"Love thy neighbor as thyself." Thus everything we do must somehow benefit others. *Everything* we do can be converted from Direct Light (for one's self) to Returning Light (for others). Everything.

Eating and drinking, for example, are usually regarded as natural, animalistic needs for survival. For some, this may be so. Eating, according to Kabbalah, is 1 percent to sustain our physical self and 99 percent to nourish our metaphysical self. Likewise, only 1 percent of the food we eat is physical substance; 99 percent is metaphysical energy. Thus, if one eats just for the body, he has nourished only the body (the 1 percent) and has (most likely) done so just for the self.

Adam and Eve, before the Fall, did not have digestive systems. They did not need the 1-percent aspect of physical nourishment. They merely *looked* at their food and by such were nourished through its metaphysical energy. After the Fall, corruption set in during the generations that followed. During these generations until Noah, which includes Atlantis, people began abusing metaphysical knowledge, creating tremendous short circuits, in-

---

33. Per Talmud, *Pirkei Avot* 2:16.

cluding copulating and experimenting with animals. Since man, by virtue of his free will, can affect the cosmos, the totality of negativity generated by those generations distorted the entire cosmic balance. It is said that even the animals began to grow in twisted and unnatural ways, as did the lower kingdoms. As Rabbi Glazerson puts it:

> During the flood the entire system of creation—the stars, the earth, and its inhabitants—went beyond the limits of natural laws and upset the natural order. All this came about because of man's corruption, which sent out extensive reverberations that undermined the whole network of creation (*From Hinduism to Judaism*, p. 85).

Ten generations after Adam, God brought the Flood, which totally destroyed the physical world save Noah, his family, and the animals on his ark. The Vessel had fallen so low into negativity, it needed to start over. However, even though the postdiluviun generations obtained new bodies and a fresh start, they still had to correct the negativity generated prior to the Flood. After all, metaphysical energy is never lost or created out of nothing: The souls or metaphysical energy of the prediluvian generations continue to reincarnate—to date—for the purpose of *Tikkun*.

These souls, that need *Tikkun* from the negativity before the Flood, exist in all levels of being. And this is the cosmological catch: because only the speaking—human beings—has free will, only humans can fulfill *Tikkun*. What that means is that the lower three levels have to rely on the speaking level to do *Tikkun for* them.

After the Flood, we humans were given two ways to fulfill *Tikkun* for those of lower levels of being, which cannot fulfill *Tikkun* on their own. The how to's of the first method are elaborately explained in the Bible under the topic of sacrifices (of members of all of the levels of being *except* speaking, for which sacrifice is forbidden, because each member of the speaking level can do his or her own *Tikkun*) in the since-destroyed Temple of Jerusalem. The Temple was the medium through which this spiritual activity was performed. However, since the Temple has been destroyed, this method has become obsolete, leaving only the second method, which is eating.

What is meant by "eating" as a method for *Tikkun* is that after ingesting a mineral, plant, or animal into ourselves, when we then act spiritually to fulfill our own *Tikkun*, we pull the internal energy or souls of everything that is a part of us up with us (after all, as they say: You are what you eat!). Only then does the act of eating become spiritual, because we are using the energy of the food to enable us to physically and spiritually perform positive actions.

More specifically, according to Kabbalah, eating is a form of communication to the internal energy or essence of the food. There are two purposes for the speaking level in eating: one is to sustain the body (which as we said earlier, comprises at best only 1 percent of our being); while the other is to sustain the soul (which comprises the bulk of our being). The soul is nourished by releasing the internal energy of the food it eats and absorbing it into itself.

We might note that everything in nature releases energy. For example, the growing level pulls minerals up from the inanimate level to the growing level by utilizing them. An animal can then pull the minerals *and* the plant up to its level of the animate by eating the plant and thus using them as energy in activities of the animate level.

In the last chapter, we mentioned the various signs that the Bible clues us into regarding which animals are and are not kosher. Put differently, the Bible tells us on which animals humans are capable of fulfilling *Tikkun*. What determines whether a particular animal is "ready" to have that final, fulfilling step of *Tikkun* done for it is that animal's level of evolvement. The animals that are most evolved metaphysically, that no longer need to return or reincarnate, are called pure, clean, or holy—all qualifiers used interchangeably. *Pure* and *clean* thus refer to the degree of evolvement of these animal's soul and not their body. *Holy* denotes the possession of the (potential) energy of circuitry, connected to the Endless. This distinction was established when God told Aaron, in juxtaposition form, to "differentiate between the holy and the common, and the unclean and the clean" (Leviticus 10:10). And the clean animals, for which humans can fulfill *Tikkun*, are enumerated specifically in the Bible in Leviticus chapter 11.

It is interesting that while many animals are not "clean," probably the all-time favorite stereotype of the nonkosher animal is the pig. As nothing is by chance, neither is this. The Hebrew word for pig is *Khazir* (or in Yiddish *Khazer* or *Chazer*). *Khazir* comes from the root *Kh-Z-R*, which means [to] return. Thus, an exact translation of *Khazir*, with its particular Hebrew noun structure would be "one who is to return." Once a kosher animal is properly "koshered," eaten, and its energy released, its soul is elevated to the Endless, requiring no more reincarnation or *return* to this plane for *Tikkun*. The pig, however, by definition, is not ready for the Endless, and thus it is not kosher.

There are a number of requirements for meat to be kosher. As we have said, the first is that the animal from which the meat is taken be of the "clean" animals. It must then be slaughtered in a very specific way, with a special knife that has a sharp, blemish-free blade, so as to cause the *least* amount of pain possible, causing the animal to die instantly. One way to check this is by checking the lungs of the animal after it is slaughtered. If the lungs are smooth, the meat can be declared *Glatt Kosher*—*Glatt* being Yiddish for "smooth." If the lungs are smooth, the animal was okay at the moment it was slaughtered; but if the lungs have even one hole, the meat is rendered not kosher.

Another main requirement for meat to be kosher is that it be completely free of blood. Thus an entire salting process is performed. Blood is the filament that links the body and the soul— the *Nefesh*, the lowest level of the soul and the body. Blood contains the "I" of the being. Thus the blood of an animal also contains that animal's physical nature and traits, which we are not interested in connecting to. We want to connect only to the higher levels of the animal's soul, which are what reconnect it to the Endless.

The Bible specifically prohibits the consumption of blood (per Leviticus chapter 17). In simple terms, as mortal beings, we simply have not a sufficient vessel to contain it. From a *Tikkun* perspective, blood (the filament or link between the body and soul) does not need *Tikkun*. We only eat what we can perform *Tikkun* on. Incidentally, it is because of this principle that Judaism prohibits cannibalism. Human beings, by virtue of their endowed free will, are capable and responsible for their own *Tikkun*. No one can do *Tikkun* for another human being.

This warrants expansion: Meat, per se, as we have defined it, is negative energy—it is red and lacks continuity. Yet when we eat meat for the purpose of elevating the soul of that animal and releasing it, we convert the negativity, Left Column, into Central

Column energy, which is the Desire to Receive For the Sake of Sharing or "Love thy neighbor as thyself." Here we eat for the sake of the food we are eating, because it cannot fulfill its own *Tikkun*.

With this in mind, kabbalists advocate eating only according to one's level of spirituality. This means refraining from eating of such a high level as that of the animate, if one is not spiritual and aware of the spiritual purpose. Without this consciousness, one would only waste that animal by sabotaging its means to *Tikkun*. In fact, the killing of an animal *not* for these spiritual purposes, is regarded as murder.

This is also why many spiritual doctrines advise refraining from eating milk and milk products (Right Column energy) and from meat (Left Column energy) and eating only a vegetarian diet (Central Column energy). Eating only a vegetarian diet is taking the "safe" route. But Right and Left Column energies are needed to create circuitry. And after all, if the whole world were to turn vegetarian, we would never fulfil the *Tikkun* of the world, because no one would be revealing the internal energy of all those of the *animate* level of being![34]

---

34. For more on kabbalistic nutrition, consult lesson/cassette No. 19 of the Kabbalah Centre's "Kabbalah Beginners Course."

III

Wiring to the Light

5

Hebrew, The Sefirot and the Names of God

Up until now we have discussed how to elevate our consciousness to where we can begin to recognize our *Tikkun* and with it, exert Resistance. These are our means of activating the Light from within us. This would be like putting together the best satellite dish or telephone that we can. Now comes the time to hook in the wiring. After all, the telephone itself can only help us when we have the proper wiring to communicate with our addressee.

Our addressee here is the Light, and our wiring is constructed of (1) the Hebrew letters, and (2) the Sefirot and the names of God (the Light).

HEBREW

Hebrew is not merely another language used in our world to communicate among one another. Hebrew is the only language that did not evolve, since it existed before the creation of the physical world. In fact it was the power of the twenty-two letters[1] of the Hebrew letters that created the world. What that means is that each of the twenty-two letters as we read them is only the physical ex-

---

1. Twelve letters created the 12 signs of the zodiac and the other 10 created the 10 *Sefirot*, to be discussed shortly.

pression or representation of a metaphysical energy. The energy is not in the physical shape of the letters per se, but rather in their internal essence. What we read is the body of these forces; but what we connect to is their soul.

THE HEBREW ALPHABET

Here are the characters [that] comprise the Hebrew alphabet: there are no capitals. The left-hand column shows the printed characters, and the right-hand column is the pronunciation.

א	alef
ב	bet
ג	gimel
ד	dalet
ה	he
ו	vav
ז	zain
ח	het
ט	tet
י	yod
כ	kaf
ל	lamed
מ, ם	mem
נ, ן	nun
ס	samekh
ע	ain
פ	pe
צ, ץ	tzadi
ק	kof
ר	resh
ש	shin
ת	tav

While the letters of other alphabets are random vis-à-vis their sound and physical representation, nothing about the Hebrew letters is random.[2] The Hebrew letters' sound and physical structure

---

2. For a more in-depth, kabbalistic study of the Hebrew letters, refer to Rabbi Berg's *Power of Aleph Beth*, vols. I and II.

or symbol represent distinct metaphysical energies or frequencies; the Hebrew letters serve as a kind of metaphysical DNA. According to Kabbalah, the function of Hebrew, while also being a means of human communication, is its ability to connect us to the inner aspect of the world and thus to the Light.

The people who built the Tower of Babel (in Genesis, chapter 11) were said to have had Jewish souls, and they built the tower through the power of the Hebrew letters (which enabled the spiritual communication they sought). Thus also the means that the system used to destroy their evil efforts was to "confound there their language, that they may not understand one another's speech" (Genesis 11:7). And with this, many different forms of physical communication—languages—came into being. What was confounded was not only their physical means of communication but, more importantly, their means of metaphysical communication.

Hebrew is the means that we connect to the Ten *Sefirot* and to the Names of God. This can be perceived by the very word for Hebrew in Hebrew, which is *Ivrit. Ivrit* comes from the root *Avar*, meaning to transfer or convey. Thus, by its very name and definition, Hebrew serves to transfer or convey energy; it is a channel for the Light. This is why Hebrew is referred to as the Holy language, as we have already learned that "holy" denotes a channel or conduit of metaphysical energy. Kabbalists will even say that Hebrew is not so much "holy" as it is "wholly," since by its very definition it serves to create a complete circuitry of energy.

It is also for this reason that whenever we wish to discern the internal essence of an entity, we look to its corresponding Hebrew name or word. Just as we discerned the internal essence of "Hebrew" from its Hebrew word, we can also, for example, understand what a "name" is. The word for *soul* in Hebrew is *neshamah*[3] or *N-SH-M-H*, since the Hebrew vowels are not part of the word itself. The word for *name* is *Shem*, or *SH-M*. As we can visually see, *SH-M* is at the very center of *N-SH-M-H*.

Therefore, a name constitutes the vessel that defines the internal essence of the entity it represents. A person's first name is

---

3. Actually, as we noted in the last chapter, the Ari in his *Gate of Reincarnation* defines five levels of the internal essence of man. *Neshamah* is the third of these levels, after *Nefesh* and *Ruakh*. However, these words are not translatable, so we will merely translate *neshamah* as soul.

thus the physical representation of that person's soul. Put differently—to define the metaphysical function of a name—a person's first name is his cosmic "telephone number."

It is for this reason that the Bible goes to such lengths to tell us all the names of various people and their children and of places. It does this for spiritual reasons, so that we know how to connect to various energies. The biblical names revealed to us are also the largest and most powerful vessels a person can have. And for this reason, kabbalists take only names that are from the Bible.

It is also in this context that we can understand the following verse: "And the man [Adam] gave names to all cattle, and to the fowl of the heaven, to every beast of the field" (Genesis 2:20). The verse in Hebrew begins, "*VaYikrah haAdam Shemot . . .*" *HaAdam* means "the man," *Shemot* means "names," and *VaYikrah* literally translates as "And He Drew." Adam did not just pick names out of a hat, as an afternoon activity having nothing better to do, as in "Okay, you, I think I'll call you "Rabbit" from now on." The key word is "draw," meaning that Adam, who was of an extremely high level of consciousness, could draw to him the internal energy intelligence of each creature and identify its corresponding vessel, or name. The tremendous spiritual work that Adam did, as per that verse, is what enables us today to discover the internal essence of all entities in our existence.

With this understanding of the function and meaning of a name, we can now also understand one of the key phrases used in Jewish liturgy and that is the prayer for when "He and His Name are one." He is the Light; His "Name" is the complete and Endless Vessel. Therefore the connection is to the Fourth Aspect of Creation, when the Vessel and Light are united again as one, the Light with the *Shekhina*.

We can now also understand why God or rather the Light Force that emanates from God has so many names. Since a name per se is a vessel, each of the Light's names serves as a conduit for a particular aspect or expression of the Light. The Light Itself is one and uniform. To some extent the Light can be likened to a generator that can find expression of its energy through a television set, a microwave, a computer, an electric can opener, a stereo system, etc. Similarly, the different names of the Light serve to express different ways that we can utilize the energy of the Light, just as it expresses the various ways that the Light transacts with our physical world. What is important to note is that the Light does not need these names. The names exist solely for *our* use and benefit. Without them we could not communicate with the Light, or we would burn from contact with the unfunneled Light.

The 72 Names: Somewhat as a computer command code works, different combinations of Hebrew letters hook us up to different aspects of the Light. The *Zohar* defines for us the seventy-two names of God that Moses revealed and which he used to part the Red Sea. These names are revealed in the book of *Shemot*, which in English is called *Exodus* but which literally translates back as (the book of) *Names*. These seventy-two names are no less than what controls the entire forces of the universe. Observing some of these seventy-two, we can see from where certain spiritual doctrines and sects have evolved. One of the seventy-two names, for example, is *H-R-Y*, from which the Hari Krishna sect evolved. Another name, *M-H-SH*, begot the Indian Maharishi Mahesh Yogi (who introduced Transcendental Meditation to the United States). And *O-H-M* is one of, if not *the* key mantra in Buddhist meditation.[4]

MIRACLES

Since we mentioned Moses' splitting of the Red Sea, it might be helpful to note the following about "miracles." Miracles, in the conventional, figurative or colloquial sense of the word, do not exist. The word for miracle in Hebrew is *Ness*, from the root *Nooss*, which means to escape or flee. When one is connected to the realm or consciousness level of the Tree of Knowledge of Good and Evil, one is subject to the laws of nature only. However, once an individual transcends to the level of consciousness of the Tree of Life, he has "fled" from the limitations of the physical realm and thus of nature.

---

4. Sogyal Rinpoche, in writing *The Tibetan Book of Living and Dying*, writes out the two most famous mantras in Tibet: (1) the mantra of Padmasambhava (the father of Tibetan Buddhism), called the Vajra Guru Mantra; and (2) the mantra of Avalokiteshvara, the Buddha of Compassion. Both beginning with *OM*.

When people attain the level of consciousness of the Tree of Life, things just start to "happen"—and mind you, Kabbalah emphatically states that there is no such thing as chance or a coincidence. In fact, Kabbalah defines *coincidence* as exactly that: two incidences that happen simultaneously, and they do so for a reason. But there are no accidents.

Moses knew what he was doing; he knew how to utilize the power of the seventy-two names. In fact, the kabbalist would look beyond the spectacle of the miracle to understand that what Moses did was split the seed energy of the sea, so that the Right Column would be distinctly to the right and the Left Column would go to the left. With this, he established the energy so he and the Israelites could walk through the middle path—the Central Column—that was, inevitably, firm, dry, and safe.

At our level today, we may not have Moses' capabilities, per his level of consciousness, but when we connect with and begin to work with the direction of the cosmic flow, things begin to flow with and for us. But, in short, a miracle is not a divine gift; *we* make "supernatural" things happen when we flee from the level of the Tree of Knowledge of Good and Evil to that of the Tree of Life.

THE SEFIROT[5]

The Light, as we have said, is our "powerhouse" and is too strong for us to channel as it is, all at once. For this reason, we funnel the energy of the Light, as we do electrical energy from its powerhouse, to a level where we can handle it and not burn. If we were to connect, say, an electric toothbrush to the generator itself, the toothbrush would burn out—in the best case scenario!—if not burn the whole house or building down with it. Therefore, the wiring that connects the toothbrush to the generator also serves as a funnel for the electrical current, as it also serves as a conduit for the energy to be revealed or utilized in a particular way.

---

5. Rabbi Kaplan offers an analytical discussion of the *Sefirot* in his posthumous book *Innerspace*.

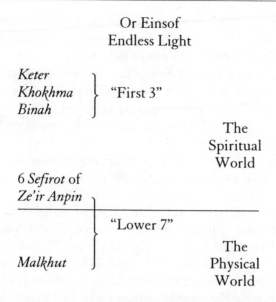

On our level, the Light appears to us via seven different vessels, since we cannot receive the Light all at once. These seven different vessels are seven means of funneling or filtering the Light to us. In Kabbalah, these seven energy structures are called the seven *Sefirot* that we can access on the physical plane. Just as there are different scales of measurement, from subatomic proportions to astrophysical proportions, seven is the scale that we use to measure our physical world. And these seven are expressed in everything that is of the physical realm: There are seven colors in the color spectrum, seven musical notes, seven days in the week, seven continents, seven atmospheric belts. Seven also expresses the seven directions that we perceive physical objects. If we look, for example, at a cube, there is up and down, the two sides, front and back, and the cube itself—seven.

The Endless Light, the Source, what we consider our powerhouse, can also be perceived as a soft drink in a glass. We want to drink the soft drink, but our only means is through a channel—a straw—which would be the system of the *Sefirot*. The straw, or *Sefirot*, per se, are empty vessels or conduits. On the other hand, our "straw" is also like the veils or "lampshades," or colored glasses, as we have called them until now. As we go through the *Sefirot* from the Endless, the Light appears to us to become dimmer as the veils become thicker. Moreover, the *Sefirots'* function may be better perceived when we understand that the *Sefirot* evolved from the *Tzimtzum*, the Endless Vessel's Restriction.

While there are seven *Sefirot* that directly correspond with and which we can access from the physical realm, there are actually five or ten *Sefirot*, depending on how you count them. The entire system of the *Sefirot* is also called (what we already know as) the Tree of Life.

Counted *as five*, the *Sefirot* are: *Keter, Khokhma, Binah, Ze'ir Anpin*, and *Malkhut*. As ten, the *Sefirah*[6] of *Ze'ir Anpin* has all six of its *Sefirot* components accounted for separately.

(1) The first *Sefirah* is called *Keter*, or translated literally, *Crown*. The *Zohar* tells us that *Keter* is composed of two segments: one that is Light and the other that is Vessel. Therefore, half of *Keter* is part of the Endless Light, and is in many cases considered still part of the Endless; yet it also contains a slight veil or aspect of the Vessel. It is the threshold between Light and Vessel. Needless to say, it is the most "transparent" *Sefirah*. What is also characteristic about *Keter* is that it radiates or influences without desire, very much like the Light. But the moment that the possibility of desire engenders in *Keter*, we come to . . .

(2) The second *Sefirah* called *Khokhma*, or Wisdom. At this level we already have the potential for desire; but it is still passive, meaning that it influences the other Sefirot but is not influenced. Connecting to *Khokhma* enables one to connect to the whole picture: to see an issue and see the whole string of consequences and results that follow. There is a saying in Hebrew that says "Who is wise? [that is, having Wisdom, or of the level of *Khokhma*] He who can see that which is born." We could take this literally and say that a wise adolescent won't play unsafe sex, because he or she can see the resulting birth of a child as a result, or some kind of VD. In this context, kabbalists also pose the riddle of what the difference is between one who is clever and one who is wise. The clever one always finds a way to get out of trouble, whereas the wise one doesn't get into trouble in the first place! So wisdom is seeing the whole process from start to finish, from above, as it were. Since at *Khokhma* there is a potential for desire, the moment *Khokhma* is ready to give, it becomes . . .

---

6. *Sefirah* is the singular form of *Sefirot*, the latter which is the plural and the term used to name the entire system of the Sefirot.

Endless Light / *Or Einsof*

Keter	Crown
Khokhma	Wisdom
Binah	Understanding

Da'at
Knowledge

Ze'ir Anpin

Small Face

Malkhut	Kingdom

Or Einsof / Endless Light

Keter	Crown
Khokhma	Wisdom
Binah	Understanding

Da'at
Knowledge

Ze'ir Anpin	Small Face

Khesed	Mercy
G'vurah	Judgment
Tiferet	Beauty
Netzakh	Victory
Hod	Glory
Yesod	Foundation

Malkhut	Kingdom

(3) The third *Sefirah*, *Binah*, or Intelligence, at which level there is already an active desire to give. For this reason, *Binah* is also called *Khafetz Khesed*, meaning Desiring or Wanting Mercy. There is movement or activity at this level, as it is already closer to physicality. *Binah*, therefore, by virtue of its activity, also contains lack. However, the minute that *Binah* actually gives (energy), she depletes herself[7] and we come to . . .

(4) The fourth *Sefirah*, *Ze'ir Anpin*, which is Aramaic for Small Face. This *Sefirah* is also called *Tiferet*; but since one of *Ze'ir Anpin*'s components is also called *Tiferet*, it is generally referred to as *Ze'ir Anpin*.

The first three *Sefirot* together are referred to as the "Upper Three," since they comprise the "Spiritual World," which, from our analogy before, is the soft drink. Put differently, the Upper Three constitute the vessels that contain the energy of the spiritual world, which for us, from our stance, is synonymous with the Endless. *Ze'ir Anpin* is the straw that connects the spiritual world with our physical world; it is our medium for drawing the energy of above to us. For this reason, Rabbi Berg refers to *Ze'ir Anpin* as "our outer-space connection."

Just as "the wire" connected to our house may actually consist of many wires, so too is *Ze'ir Anpin*, which is our wire between the spiritual world and our physical one. While *Ze'ir Anpin* from one perspective is one *Sefirah*, it is comprised of the following, each of which are themselves *Sefirot*:

1. *Khesed* — Mercy
2. *G'vurah* — Judgment
3. *Tiferet* — Beauty
4. *Netzakh* — Victory or Eternity
5. *Hod* — Glory
6. *Yesod* — Foundation

Parenthetically, in some (rare) sources, the *Sefirah* of *Khokhma* is referred to as *Gedulah,* meaning Greatness. From this we can understand one of the connections made at the beginning of

---

7. *Binah* is considered a feminine energy, not only because the word *Binah* in Hebrew is a feminine word but because she implements the energy of the *Sefirot* above her.

the Torah service[8] in the synagogue. The prayer literally reads, "*Lekha* [God's name] *HaGedulah, VeHaG'vurah, VeHaTiferet, VeHaNetzakh, VeHaHod* . . ." The prefix *ve* in Hebrew means "and," and the prefix *ha* means "the." Therefore, if we disregard the prefixes for a moment, we can see that what is being said— meaning the energy that is being drawn—is that from *Khesed* to *Hod* of *Ze'ir Anpin*.

As an aside, for us, the names of the *Sefirot*, per se, are really insignificant. The word *Khokhma*, for example, serves as our means to connect to the energy of the *Sefirah* of *Khokhma*. Its energy is drawn by its Hebrew term, as per the function of Hebrew. Thus the fact that it translates as Wisdom, and what "wisdom" means on a denotative and connotative level, is really insignificant.

However, getting back to our discussion of the *Sefirot* in their order, the last and final *Sefirah* needs to be accounted for:

(5) *Malkhut* or Kingdom. *Malkhut* is the physical, material world in which we live. At this level, the Light appears the dimmest, and consequently this level, manifests the most and strongest Desire to Receive. At this level, *all* energies need to be concealed (contained in a vessel) in order to be revealed and utilized. On this plane, one needs the body to get to the soul. And like clothing, the physical covers or conceals, but it also reveals what is within. *Malkhut* is the feminine energy of all of the ten *Sefirot*; she is what implements all of the energy from above. As *Malkhut* (Kingdom) is the name of this *Sefirah*, every time the Light funnels down to this level, the Light is referred to as "King."

Adam, before the Fall, was on the level of *Ze'ir Anpin*. At that level, Light does not need to be nor is It concealed. The Tree of Knowledge of Good and Evil is another term for *Malkhut*—our physical, corporeal world. When Adam and Eve ate from the Tree of Knowledge of Good and Evil, meaning they connected to the realm of *Malkhut*, they "fell" into the level of existence of *Malkhut*, which is below *Ze'ir Anpin*. This is the meaning of "the Fall."

The Fall constituted the shattering of the Vessel from the level of *Ze'ir Anpin*, and its shattering as fragments on the level of *Malkhut*. The Fall was from being in a pure, unified state of consciousness or spirituality to one of physicality, where each fragment

---

8. Incidentally, this exact passage is repeated at the end of the Sabbath service, at the end of the "Song of Honor," "*Shir HaKavod*," or "*Anim Zemirot*."

of the Vessel became enclothed with a lava-like covering, being the body. After the Fall, the body would need to be "deciphered" and "broken" (revealed) so as to identify and release the essence contained within it.

While Adam and Eve comprise the two poles of the same soul, in Genesis 2:22, when it says "And the Lord God formed the rib which He had taken from the man into a woman," the word *formed* is actually a mistranslation. The word for formed (which would be of the root *Y-Tz-R*) in the original is actually *vayiben*, from the root *B-N-H*. This tells us that while Adam came into being at the level of *Ze'ir Anpin*, Eve came into being at the level of *Binah*.

What happened at the Fall was that the Vessel—Adam and Eve and all the animals and so on—which had been on the level of *Ze'ir Anpin* as "naked" energies, all acquired husks (the physical bodies that cover the soul) as they reached *Malkhut*. As nothing can exist on this realm in a purely spiritual state, all of the pieces or sparks of the Vessel crumbled and became covered with physical matter that gives the appearance that each spark is a discrete and separate "body."

With this, we might summarize the key concepts that most people know: The Fall was the drop that resulted from the level of *Ze'ir Anpin* to the lowest *Sefirah* of *Malkhut*. *Sin* is defined by Kabbalah as a miss. That is, a sin occurs when one is confronted with an opportunity to exert Resistance and he or she misses that opportunity. Vis-à-vis a positive precept, one had the opportunity to reveal positive energy and the opportunity was missed; or, as regards a negative precept, one had the opportunity to resist revealing negative energy and missed that opportunity. Adam and Eve's sin was the "Original" one, because the eating from the Tree of Knowledge of Good and Evil constituted the first opportunity that the Vessel had to exert Resistance and eliminate Bread of Shame—and they missed it.[9]

The Book of Esther

Now, with regard to the concealment of all Light in the physical realm, even God is said to interact with this level of the universe,

---

9. Further discussion of the Fall will be discussed in chapter 8, when we discuss the "snake".

but only in a concealed manner. In the Book of Esther, for example, God is never expressly mentioned—not even once. But a kabbalist will point out the many times that He is referred to indirectly or in a concealed manner. One of the things this story shows is the function of human beings in implementing metaphysical energy. And the story distinctly differentiates between *the King* and *Akhashverosh*. Whenever the term "King" is used, it refers to God, or that aspect of God or the Light on the *Malkhut* level. Whenever the name "Akhashverosh" appears, it refers to the physical, living being, who was at the time of the "story," the king of the Persian Empire. Thus, when Esther is said to be "entering the King's court," the implication is to an elevated spiritual state, as opposed to merely walking into Akhashverosh's courtyard. Moreover, the root of the name Esther in Hebrew is the same for the word *concealed* in Hebrew.

There is actually one additional *Sefirah*, which is *Da'at*, or Knowledge. *Da'at* is the link between the First Three (*Keter*, *Khokhma*, and *Binah*) and the Lower Seven (the six *Sefirot* of *Ze'ir Anpin* and *Malkhut*). But for all intents and purposes, it is not enumerated in the system of the "Ten *Sefirot*."

THE *SEFIROT* ENUMERATED AS FIVE

As we said earlier, the complete system of the *Sefirot* is taken as a system of five for certain purposes and as of ten in others. It is conceived of as five when the function and energy of the individual *Sefirot* of *Ze'ir Anpin* do not need to be drawn on separately. As such, *Ze'ir Anpin* is used as a complete unit, functioning as the mediator or conductor ("straw") between the First Three and *Malkut*. One such example is the distinction of the Torah as being the "Five Books of Moses." The books are divided according to the level of energy that they serve to convey. The first book, *Beresheet* (or as it is known in Greek, Genesis) parallels the *Sefirah* of *Keter*. The second book, *Shmot* (Exodus), parallels the *Sefirah* of *Khokhma*. The third book, *VaYikra* (Leviticus), parallels *Binah*. *BaMidbar* (Numbers) parallels *Ze'ir Anpin*. And the fifth book, *Devarim* (Deuteronomy), parallels *Malkhut*.

Another such example of the system of the *Sefirot,* seen as a group of five, was the altar of the Holy Temples of Jerusalem (when they existed). The Hebrew word for altar is *Mizba'akh*. Since the vowels in Hebrew are not really part of the word, we actually have the word *M-Z-B-KH*. The word for altar is, therefore, the acronym for the four *Sefirot* from *Malkhut* through *Khokhma* (thus *M-Z-B-KH* = *Malkhut*, *Ze'ir anpin*, *Binah*, *Khokhma*), and this sheds light on the internal essence or spiritual function of the altar. In a word, the function of the altar was to serve as a conductor in the conveyance of the souls of entities lacking free will (from the inanimate to animal) from *Malkhut* to *Khokhma*.

THE TETRAGRAMMATON

One other example of the *Sefirot* grouped as five is the name or expression of the Light in its most powerful form—the Tetragrammaton. The Tetragrammaton is the most powerful vessel for drawing energy; it is the most powerful combination of the Hebrew letters, because it channels all of the Light Force at once. It is for this reason that the high priest, or *Cohen HaGadol*, meditated and said this name of God on Yom Kippur in the Holy Temple. Since the destruction of the Second Temple, however, the pronunciation of this name of God was "lost."[10] Today we meditate on this combination of Hebrew letters while we pronounce another name of God.[11]

The Tetragrammaton contains all of the five *Sefirot* and in their proper order.[12] Since *Keter* is half Light–half Vessel, for us it is completely concealed. Thus *Keter* is represented as the tip of the *Yod*. *Khokhma* is represented by the *Yod*, Binah by the first *Hey*; the *Vav* is *Ze'ir Anpin*, and the second *Hey* is *Malkhut*.

---

10. What the word *lost* actually means is that the use of the actual pronunciation of the Tetragrammaton could no longer be used. As the universe is evolving into stronger and more intense energy, its pronunciation would be too strong. The enunciation of the letters of the Tetragrammaton is not even said in passing. For purposes of study and teaching, the second and fourth letters of the Tetragrammaton, which are the Hebrew letter *Hey*, are converted into the Hebrew letter *Kuf*. *Kuf* is merely a *Hey* with the center line on the left going below the line. *Kuf* is the only letter (that is not a final letter) that goes below the line in writing, thus having the capacity to "ground" the energy of the Hey. We thus refer to the Tetragrammaton as the *Yud-Kay-Vav-Kay*. Moreover, we do not even write the letters of the Tetragrammaton without separating them, so as not to create a short circuit.

11. It is from a connection to the Tetragrammaton, being *Y-H-V-H*, that the Jehovah Witnesses come or the various pronunciations of it by the Catholic Church and other Christian denominations, in addition to various sects and cults.

12. In Hebrew, words are written and read from right to left.

THE TETRAGRAMMATON

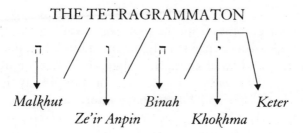

Malkhut   Binah   Keter
        Ze'ir Anpin   Khokhma

The Tetragrammaton is many times looked at in its different modes to connect to its energy. In one instance the *Yod* and first
Hey are grouped as positive energy—potential, masculine energy—while the *Vav* and second *Hey* are grouped as the negative
pole, that of feminine energy or the energy that implements the
energy of the first group. Within this structure, the letters of the
Tetragrammaton are further divided: From the first group, of *Yod*
and *Hey*, which is the positive pole, the *Yod* is called *Abba*, or father, connoting (+) within the (+) group, while the first *Hey* is called
Emma, or mother, connoting (–) within the (+) group. In the second group, which is the negative pole, the *Vav* is called *Ben* or son,
connoting (+) within the (–) group, while the second *Hey* is called
Bat, or daughter, connoting (–) within this (–) group.

$$
(+) \left\{ \begin{array}{c} \text{י} \\ \hline \text{ה} \end{array} \right.
\qquad
\begin{array}{c} — \\ — \end{array}
\qquad
\begin{array}{c} (+) \\ (-) \end{array}
$$

$$
(-) \left\{ \begin{array}{c} \text{ו} \\ \hline \text{ה} \end{array} \right.
\qquad
\begin{array}{c} — \\ — \end{array}
\qquad
\begin{array}{c} (+) \\ (-) \end{array}
$$

This tells us a number of things. First of all, it shows us just
how balanced the energy of the Tetragrammaton is. But it also
offers insight into other things. The following is one example.
There is a Sabbath hymn sung that is comprised of only five words:
"HaShomer Shabbat HaBen Im HaBat." This literally translates as
"The Sabbath-observer the son with the daughter," which at best
just sounds strange. What this actually teaches us is the cosmic state
of existence at the time of *Shabbat*, or Saturday: There is an alignment of *Ze'ir Anpin* (*Ben*, or son) with *Malkhut* (*Bat*, or daughter).

With this one might also point out, and many have already
made great ado about this, that the *Zohar* seems to be filled with
erotic allusions. Suffice to say that the *Zohar*, as do all of the works
on Kabbalah, speaks in its own nomenclature, the Language of the

Branches. The word *Zivoog*, for example, which literally translates as intercourse, comes from the root *zoog*, meaning a couple (as in "he and she are a couple") or alignment. Thus when the energies of *Khokhma* and *Binah* connect or align, the *Zohar* might say that *Khokhma* and *Binah* have intercourse, or it might say that father and mother (*Abba* and *Emma*) have intercourse. Rabbi Kaplan notes, similarly, "The prophetic experience is referred to as *Zivug* (sexual union)" (*Innerspace*, p. 169).

THE *SEFIROT* ENUMERATED AS TEN

We draw on the energy of the ten *Sefirot* when we want to connect to the entire structure of the universe. Each of these *Sefirot* correspond with each of the ten dimensions that Kabbalah explains prevail in this universe. What we perceive as dimensions of time and space are merely aspects of the dimension of *Malkhut*, the physical, corporeal world. Better yet, time, space, and motion, are defined as illusions that only exist within the realm of the Tree of Knowledge of Good and Evil. They do not exist in the realm of the Tree of Life or in the Endless and are thus illusions.

Or Einsof / Endless Light

Keter	Crown
Khokhma	Wisdom
Binah	Understanding

Ze'ir Anpin	Small Face

Khesed	Mercy
G'vurah	Judgment
Tiferet	Beauty
Netzakh	Victory
Hod	Glory
Yesod	Foundation

Malkhut	Kingdom

Since all Vessels are rooted in the spiritual realm, creating or completing a Vessel in both worlds means completing the Vessel in its entirety, from root to branch. A good example of a unit of ten directly paralleling each of the ten *Sefirot* are the Ten Commandments. The Ten Commandments were given to Moses directly from God and constitute a complete system that funnels the Light in such a way that we can utilize it and not burn from it. This is why the Ten Commandments can be direct and unconcealed (i.e., they do not need to be deciphered) without burning us: because they are balanced through their containment in all of the vessels of the ten *Sefirot*.

All other precepts discussed in the Bible are concealed, as all forms of Light exist in this realm. This concealment, the Bible's "body," can be deceiving if read literally or read its cover for its contents. For example, the laws discussed in the Bible that concern "slaves" actually refer to the karmic, cosmic law pertaining to an individual who is "enslaved" to body-material energy (the Tree of Knowledge of Good and Evil or the Desire to Receive for the Self Alone).

If read literally, if one sees only the body of the Bible and not its soul, the Bible may also appear to contain contradictions. As touched on in the Introduction, the portion that discusses death sentences in the Torah portion of *Shoftim*, is such an example. Such forms of capital punishment would seem to contradict the explicit commandment not to murder. But the *Talmud* tells us that real death was never decreed. And the *Zohar* explains that the "death sentencing" that is discussed is the annihilation of negative energy intelligence that each and every individual needs to perform from within, ridding negativity that the individual has revealed, and from one's surroundings created from others' negative activity. Thus "death sentences" refer to spiritual work that we all need to perform from within. It is this negative energy that if not attacked on a spiritual level boomerangs back and manifests on a physical level by attacking that individual. The "witnesses" the section refers to are the negative energy intelligence called Satan (which we will define in chapter 8) plus one's negative actions.[13]

Moreover, the body—of all things on this physical level—is temporal. When one reads the body of the Bible, one connects with external matters that for the most part are no longer relevant to our era; for example, oxen and tents. But when one transcends the

---

13. Rabbi Berg's recorded lecture on "*Parashat Shoftim*."

body to the soul of the Bible, one discovers timeless truth. And Cosmic Law is absolute truth.

Getting back to the discussion of ten as a reflection of the ten *Sefirot*, probably the most powerful example of the use of the complete system of the ten *Sefirot* was God's means of getting the Israelites out of ancient Egypt. Egypt at that time (over three thousand years ago) was a powerhouse of energy drawn through the System of the Vessel. For the Israelites to break free from their slavery to Egypt, this powerhouse had to be destroyed. And God did that very thing to free the Israelites by wreaking ten plagues on the Egyptians. By doing so, all the fuses of the Egyptian powerhouse were blown.

Parenthetically, it is important to differentiate between the power of Egypt and that of the Egyptians. There are Egyptians today; but they are not, energywise, the same as their ancestors. This is evidenced by the passage in the book of Exodus, chapter 14, verse 30: ". . . and Israel saw Egypt die on the shore."

The key word, which is usually erroneously translated as Egyptians, is actually Egypt; the word is *Mitzrayim* (Egypt) and not *Mitzrim* (Egyptians). The reason for this is that the verse reveals to us the knowledge that the power of ancient Egypt died and is no more. It is for this reason that mummification, for example, is no longer practiced.[14]

Minyan

Seen in more constructive terms, the ten of the ten *Sefirot* is what enables us to create a complete unit. For example, anyone can pray, but in praying, the individual is limited in the level and amount of energy that is drawn. In Judaism, there are instances when a significant amount of energy is desired to be drawn, say, for a community as a collective whole. There are certain powerful prayers whose function is to draw a large amount of energy, like the reading from the Torah (the Five Books of Moses) or on certain occasions like the Sabbath, holidays, and *Simkhot* (weddings, bar-mitzvahs, etcetera). For such occasions, a *Minyan* is needed, which denotes a congregation of at least ten men of bar-mitzvah age (i.e., thirteen years and older): ten, so that there is at least one person in relation to each of the ten *Sefirot*; men, because they are the posi-

---

14. The power of ancient Egypt will be discussed in chapter 6.

tive aspect (or energy pole), the representatives of the channels of *Ze'ir Anpin*, of humankind; and of bar-mitzvah age, because the purpose in serving in a *minyan* is to channel energy for the entire community or congregation. Before one's bar-mitzvah, the individual lacks the vessel or means of giving or conveying the energy drawn onward.

Another example of a system of ten that we build, as Rabbi Berg refers to it,[15] is the metaphysical "software program" that we set up each year at our table for Passover. This program is comprised of the ten items we place on the Seder table, each representing one of each of the ten *Sefirot*. There are the three Matzot grouped together, as they represent the "upper three" *Sefirot*;[16] there are six items placed on the Seder plate, each paralleling one of the six *Sefirot* of *Ze'ir Anpin*; and then there is the Seder plate itself, which contains or holds the representatives of *Ze'ir Anpin*. Put differently, the Seder plate makes useful the six items of *Ze'ir Anpin* or implements them, which is the power and function of *Malkhut*, the *Sefirah* that the plate represents.

THE SEVEN *SEFIROT* OF OUR WORLD

From our perspective, as beings of the level of *Malkhut*, the highest three *Sefirot*—*Keter*, *Khokhma*, and *Binah*—are so close to the Light that for all intents and purposes they are the Light; they constitute our "bank" of energy. This does not mean that they are, since the *Sefirot* per se are merely vessels; but again, they are so close to the Light that *we* can look to them as the Light. For this reason, the First Three for us are unaccessible. It is only to the Lower Seven *Sefirot* that we are able to connect—this being the six *Sefirot* of *Ze'ir Anpin* and *Malkhut*, the latter in which we live.

In the physical realm, every time we want to build a new vessel, we draw on the energy of the Lower Seven *Sefirot*. At a Jewish wedding, for example, the bride encircles her betrothed at the alter seven times. As we will discuss later on, under the topic of marriage, the function of a marriage is to fuse the souls of the

---

15. Per the five-cassette set of Rabbi Berg's recorded lectures on Passover.

16. Note: Within the framework of the entire Seder plate, the three *Matzot* refer to the first three *Sefirot*. However, as their own unit, that is, in a different frame of reference, they represent the Three-Column System of Right, Left, and Central columns.

bride and groom. To do this a new vessel needs to be built, and with such, it is done.

Another example is when there is a death in the family. The immediate family, according to Jewish Law, is to sit what is called *Shiva*, meaning "seven." And, in fact, the surviving members sit in mourning for seven days—each day relating to each of the Lower Seven *Sefirot*. With the loss of a family member, the broken vessel of the family needs to be rebuilt. This is the purpose of *Shiva*.

Seven

The number seven seems to play a significant role in many religions and practices. It is significant in Christianity, for example, with the seven sacraments and the Seven Deadly Sins. Seven is especially replete, for example, in the Book of Revelation as in the openings of the seven seals, the seven churches, the seven golden candlesticks, and the seven lamps and the "seven Spirits of God" (specifically called such in chapter 5). All these refer to the seven *Sefirot* themselves.

The number seven is important in pagan religions, too, because, by definition, paganism connects only to the forces of nature, which are governed by the seven *Sefirot*. For practitioners of voodoo, it is referred to as the "Seven Great Powers."[17] Dusty Sklar expounds on the significance of the number seven to occultists, from Freemasons (*Gods and Beasts*, p. 29) to Guido von List (ibid., p. 52).

The number seven has been used in such subtle ways, as, for instance, how the Cherokee Nation "was organized into seven clans"[18] to an outright occultist's obsession. Joseph Carr makes a point that Hitler always had an obsession with the number seven: his favorite movie, which he saw over and over, and "which was shown over and over in the *Füehrer*'s headquarters" was "Snow White and the Seven Dwarves" [sic] (*The Twisted Cross*, p. 19); and Hitler took exactly seven lumps of sugar in his tea, "never more, never less" (ibid., p. 19). Dusty Sklar also notes that Hitler's

---

17. From Larson's *Satanism*, chapter 13.

18. From Ronald Wright's *Stolen Continents: The Americas Through Indian Eyes Since 1492*, p. 99.

original membership number in the German's Workers' Party was 555, "but for some reason it was changed to 7" (*Gods and Beasts*, p. 51).

In essence, these pagan religions are connecting to the forces of nature. And it is precisely because they only connect to these forces (only the Lower Seven *Sefirot*) that they cannot explain how the energy they draw works. As Robin Skelton expresses, "Witches can practice magic successfully but cannot explain the process. . . . We know *how* magic works but we do not know *why* it works" (*The Practice of Witchcraft Today*, p. 22).

Rabbi Kaplan even goes so far as to say that the laws of nature actually "serve the purpose of concealing God's immanence in the world" (*Innerspace*, p. 146). Nature is *one* means by which the seven *Sefirot* express themselves in the physical realm. Nature is merely an effect of the metaphysical cause, which is the seven *Sefirot*. These same seven *Sefirot* express themselves in the seven planets that influence the physical plane.[19]

Systems of the Vessel versus Channel

But to connect to the forces of nature is to connect to an effect, to the vessels per se of the *Sefirot* and not to the causal Light expressed *through* them. Thus, the Language of the branches terms such practices to be of the System of the Vessel, because they connect to the *Sefirot* only in their Vessel capacity—to the vessels per se; whereas the System of the Channel connects to the *Sefirot*, not per se, but as channels for the Light. That is, it connects not to the *Sefirot* themselves, but to What is channeled through them. Moreover, Rabbi Glazerson notes:

> On the surface level, a man who lives his life respecting the laws of nature enjoys physical health . . . [But] a man who attaches the entire significance of his life to natural events, materialism and grossness, loses his spiritual essence (*From Hinduism to Judaism*, p. 9).

---

19. Only fairly recently, three additional planets to the seven that represent the seven *Sefirot*, have been discovered. Those additional three correspond to the first three, which, apropos with the energy of the Age of Aquarius or the Messianic Era, are thus surfacing.

THE SHIELD OF DAVID AND THE ATOM[20]

The Shield of David is a physical symbol that represents the meta-physical energy of *Ze'ir Anpin*: *Ze'ir Anpin* is the channel between the First Three and our physical world. Since the energy of *Ze'ir Anpin* is what governs our world, if we connect to the causal level of *Ze'ir Anpin*, we can influence a positive effect. Thus, when we connect to this energy and not merely to its physical representation (the star symbol), we gain protection from negativity.

The physical symbol of the Shield of David is a cosmic symbol and is why it has been used in Indian temples (as the Hindu Mandala), in various African tribes, by male Haitians practicing voodoo,[21] and, of course, by Jews. It is a sign of balance. The upper triad corresponds with the upper, spiritual world, and the lower triad, with the physical world. Having three points in each of the two realms (three=Central Column), it denotes balance in each. And since the two triads are linked, it connotes that the upper and lower realms are linked in harmony and balance.

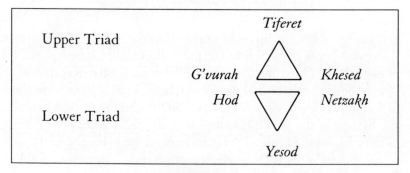

The Shield of David

---

20. Consult: Rabbi Berg's "466" ("Ten Luminous Emanations—no. 466") and the Kabbalah Beginners Course, lesson/cassette no. 8.

21. See chapter 13 of Bob Larson's *Satanism: The Seduction of America's Youth*, in which he notes that male Haitians appropriate the Shield of David symbol, while women wear the pentagram. Larson recounts witnessing a voo-

The two triads also represent potential and actual or implemented energies. The upper triad, which connects to the upper realm, corresponds with potential energy, thought energy, and energy that is beyond our immediate availability to tap. The lower triad, on the other hand, which connects to the physical world, corresponds with actual or implemented energy and that energy of the spiritual realm that we can access. The star, as a whole unit, represents the seventh *Sefirah*, which is *Malkhut*.

THE ATOM

Basically, the seven *Sefirot* of *Ze'ir Anpin* and *Malkhut* comprise the "scale" by which all in our universe can be measured. Thus, all in our universe is structured according to these seven *Sefirot*. On the smallest physical level, this structure is reflected in the very structure of the atom. There are six energy intelligences in an atom, which parallel the structure of the Shield of David.

Actually, the atom, like the nature of light (as we will shortly discuss) is very much subject to the particular frame of reference of the individual perceiving the atom. The atom may be perceived to exist as a structure of three: proton (+), electron (−) and neutron (Central Column), even though more than one of these particles may exist in a single atom. One may perceive the atom as a structure of seven, as we are demonstrating in this section. And one may perceive the atom as a structure of twelve, as science has recently discovered the top quark, in the Standard Model Theory, defining that, in addition to the subatomic particles of proton, neutron, electron, there are even smaller subatomic building blocks: six quarks and six leptons.

As a structure of seven, there are three energies, of a potential nature, of Right Column (+), Left Column (−), and Central Column (Restriction). These correspond with *Khesed, G'vurah*, and *Tiferet*. Then there are three energies, of an actual or implemented nature, that are also Right, Left and Central Columns: *Netzakh, Hod*, and *Yesod*. There is, then, the atom itself, which is *Malkhut*, the seventh *Sefirah*.

---

doo ceremony in Haiti, in which live animals were eaten. Voodoo is a practice of black magic, and is why, as Larson lightly notes, "Black magic, the ancestor of today's Satanism, is the most violent and cruel of all pagan practices" (p. 177). It is more than that: It is one of the most dangerous.

When the six energies of *Ze'ir Anpin* descend to the level of *Malkhut*, they become concealed with physical matter. Thus, when the all-pervasive structure of the *Sefirot* descends in the unit or frame of reference of an atom, we perceive quarks. That is, quarks correspond to the upper triad. The proton, electron(s), and neutron then correspond to the lower triad. This is true of all atoms, since there is only one kind of atom; it is the atom that makes up the entire universe, from solid oak tables to the air we breathe.

The moment we can sense something through our five senses, that entity must exist on the level of *Malkhut*. *Malkhut* conceals, and by doing so reveals that entity's energy. Thus, the difference between the table and the air is their respective levels of *Malkhut*. The air has less *Malkhut* and more Similarity of Form (is more akin) with the Light. The table, on the other hand, has much more *Malkhut*, meaning that much more of the table's internal essence is concealed. Thus we can put our hand through air, but we can't through a table.

Yet, even when an entity comes into *Malkhut* and becomes "physical," we need to keep proportions in proper perspective. What makes an entity physical is the nuclei of its atoms. And yet the nuclei, proportionate to the total mass or volume of the atom, is about the size of an ant in a football field. So that the majority of the atom's mass is "empty space"—the space between the nucleus and the electrons, in which the electrons rotate. It is for this reason that kabbalists throughout the ages have declared, as Rabbi Berg has, that "The denser the physical matter the greater the illusion" (*Layman*, II, p. 157).

That "empty space" only appears to be such from our physical, naked-eye perspective. That "empty space" is what Kabbalah calls the *internal intelligence* or *consciousness* of an entity. The actual "physicality" of an atom is less than one percent; ninety-nine percent of it is comprised of its corresponding essence to the six *Sefirot* of the Shield of David, that is, to *Ze'ir Anpin*. Therefore, what keeps the atom together is its *internal consciousness*, which, as we know, is balanced, since it is comprised of the three columns of both the upper and lower triads. And, therefore, what really keeps our hand from going through the solid oak table is not physical reality, but rather the ninety-nine percent of the table's internal energy. After all, what is really physical is less than the size of a pinhead!

Unity of All Theories

With this we can begin to understand how all of the theories of physics are really one and the same. The basic problem that physics has is that its theories pertaining to the large-scale structures of and in the universe do not appear to conflate with those relating to small, microscopic scales. This problem dissolves when one considers three points derived from Kabbalah.

The first point is that relativity primarily pertains to the relativity of Vessel with regard to Light. As we said, the soul, as a spark of the Endless Vessel, is the Vessel of the Light. Yet, to its enclothing body, it is Light. Physics has discussed "relativity" with only regard to the physical level of the universe. For example, according to the Theory of Relativity, "nothing can travel faster than light" (*A Brief History of Time*, p. 90). Memories, dreams, and fantasies, however, are phenomena that travel faster than light in time, space, and motion, because they are not of physical substance.

The second point is that everything in our universe, individually and collectively, is a manifested reflection of our original state in the Endless and of the *Sefirot*. Everything we desire and attain has already been contained in the Endless Vessel; we merely crave for what we once had and now feel lacking. Everything from the structure of the planets to a single atom are structured on the system of the *Sefirot*, as all parallels and reflects it. All theories must, therefore, also be one, because we all come from a unified state where "He and His Name are One" (in the First Aspect—see chapter 1). That is, all is a reflection of God: the Light is an emanation of God, the *Sefirot* are an expression of the Light, and the solar system, the human body, and the atom, are merely examples of how the *Sefirot* manifest themselves in our physical world.

Science has to a certain extent acknowledged this. Dr. Hawking states, "The whole history of science has been the gradual realization that events do not happen in an arbitrary manner, but that they reflect a certain underlying order" (*A Brief History of Time*, p. 129). The key word is "reflect": all reflects the structure of the *Sefirot*.

In many ways we can discern the unity of relativity and quantum mechanics when we perceive the unity of the Endless Light and Vessel, also reflected via body and soul. The separation of the two aspects, per *Midat HaRakhamim*, is only an illusion. Just as our soul is the Vessel of the Light, yet Light for our body, our body, that is, the Vessel of the soul, contains Light. The body is structured according to the structure of the *Sefirot* and serves as a channel for each facet of the Light.

This is also where "waves" and "particles" mesh. Every "particle" or physical body has an electromagnetic field, called an aura, which extends (for human beings) eighty-eight inches from the body.[22] Two people standing next to each other are actually standing in each other's energy field, as energy is reciprocal: It influences and is also influenced. The aura corresponds to the "waves." The same would hold true when planets align. Thus, the quantum theory works on large scales, too.

Moreover, because one's energy, say A's energy field, affects B's, which in turn affects C's, then D's and so on, in essence everything that A does affects the whole world, as does everything B, C, D and all of us do. For this reason, Kabbalah[23] has adopted the modern physics term to refer to the kabbalistic assertion that everything affects everything: the *quantum effect*.

We have, only relatively recently, discovered the quantum effect of our individual actions with regard to our physical environment. We have come to realize that each of our efforts, or lack of, affects the global state respectively. On a slightly larger scale, we have realized that, for instance, what we do to the rain forest or to marshlands affects the weather all over the world, as our individual use of aerosols affects the planetary ozone layer. What we have yet to realize and act on is the dump we have made of our *metaphysical* environment. Today we may be using nonaerosol sprays and recycling to clean up the physical environment, but we are still dumping mounds of negativity into our spiritual atmosphere, which will, as it already has begun to, inevitably come back to harm us.

In essence, the "quantum effect" is actually the basis of the doctrine of *Tikkun* and reincarnation. Everything one does affects the whole world and then, eventually, boomerangs back on that individual—the positive and negative. A person who did not care a hoot about the environment and scoffed at the idea that his little

---

22. Per Rabbi Berg's "466."
23. (in general, and Rabbi Berg in particular,)

aerosol spray was going to make a difference, may "suddenly" get skin cancer thirty years later. The very thing that was harmed due to someone's Desire to Receive For Himself Alone is the very thing that will come back to haunt that individual. The pathetic thing is that the less a person is spiritual, the less he is conscious of his actions, the more he is overcome with "why's" when the bread he has cast in the end comes back for him.

Conversely, when one internalizes the concept of the quantum effect, it is indicative of a high level of spirituality. Quantum is also at the center of Kabbalah, because what it basically boils down to is "Love thy neighbor as thyself." When one is capable of feeling for the other—any other spark of the Endless Vessel—and on the same level as one's self ("as thyself"), one has connected with the unity of the Endless. In Alice Walker's *The Color Purple*, Shug expresses this concept to Celie when she says:

> I believe God is everything. . . . Everything that is or ever was or ever will be. And when you can feel that, and be happy to feel that, you've found it. . . . [O]ne day . . . it come to me: that feeling of being part of everything, not separate at all. I knew that if I cut a tree, my arm would bleed (p. 178).

Finally, the third point that dissolves the lack of unity between the various theories of physics is that gravity is merely a reflection of the Endless Vessel, comprised of the Desire to Receive, or negative energy. Thus gravity affects the earth, the physical expression of *Malkhut*, and the individual bodies on earth, which are the physical expression of the particular soul contained in a body. Yet, with this, we can see that gravity only pertains to the physical realm, the 1 percent of reality. Neither the soul nor the Light are bound or limited by gravity.

The theory of general relativity, too, only relates to the 1 percent of reality, the physical world of *Malkhut*. What is relative, as we have said, is defined as an illusion. Thus time, space, and motion are all relative. The Endless World, with the Endless Light and Endless Vessel, is not relative. All that has evolved from the Endless is merely relative to the Endless. The reason physics, with its theory of relativity, sees light as its determining factor, is because light is the physical expression of the Light—the metaphysical Light Force of God.

The same holds true for the uncertainty principle or Pauli's exclusion principle. Change and time, space and motion, are only functions of the illusionary world. The reason observation renders an object uncertain with regard to its position or speed is because we are observing only illusionary aspects of that entity, not its internal essence, which is a constant and is thus certain.[24]

LIGHT

Most disciplines today advocate and practice fragmentation: law, medicine, science, you-name-it, everything is subject to specialization today. Fragmentation equates with end, the opposite of the whole and unified nature of the Endless (and we will expand on the topic of fragmentation in chapter 8). While we noted before that the atom can be perceived in different frames of reference— 3, 7, 12—we must bear in mind that each frame represents only a particular aspect of the atom. If we are connected to the Endless and thus connected to the atom as a whole, unified entity, then we will perceive it as a single unit that contains 3 and 7 and 12.

As Rabbi Berg explicitly explains, physical light (the physical parallel of the metaphysical Light) is a constant; thus, it has *no* movement (as movement connotes lack). The speed or movement that science perceives is merely a projection of the instruments that reveal physical light (a form of vessel) and measure its composition. Similar to the phenomenon of the Third Aspect of Creation, when the Endless Vessel restricted its receipt of Light, the Light did not stop shining or restrict Itself. No, the Light is a constant. It

---

24. Moreover, Leo Levi elaborates on this scientific concept in his essay "The Uncertainty Principle and the Wisdom of the Creator" and notes:

The uncertainty principle provides an opening through which it is possible for a totally free agent to influence the material world without violating any law of nature. The uncertainty principle allows for determinism on the macroscopic level, where it is required by the demands of the Torah; and simultaneously, for the intrusion of free volition, which takes place on the microscopic level (p. 301).

The uncertainty principle "is rather a contributory factor to a truly unified view of nature. . . . We . . . stand in reverence at . . . how, perhaps, the Creator in His wisdom has devised a principle capable of resolving the contradiction [of] the demands of free will and the reliability of nature (Carmell and Domb's *Challenge*, p. 301).

does not move or change. Movement and change exist only in and are perceptions of the Vessel, of which our instruments and eyes are apart. In fact, "light is ever present and pervades" the universe[25] yet the universe appears black only because outerspace lacks a vessel with which to reveal the light, as the moon and earth do.

Similarly, whether physical light will be perceived as waves or particles depends on the point of consciousness from which an individual (a vessel) looks at it. Physical light contains both frames of reference—particles *and* waves. Whether an individual will perceive only one or both of light's frames of reference will depend on whether the individual is connected to fragmentation (the end) or to unity (the Endless).

THE HUMAN BODY

The system of the ten *Sefirot* is the expression of Light in Its creation. In Genesis 1:27, "God created man in His image." As all of chapter I pertains to the spiritual realm and to nothing of physical nature, the "image" is the image or structure of the ten *Sefirot*. That is, the macrocosmic structure of the ten *Sefirot* is comprised, in parallel form, in the microcosmic structure of man's soul. The human body, as an expression of the soul, is thus an expression of the structure of the ten *Sefirot* as well.

The Light created the Vessel so that the latter would be able to receive endlessly, and from all of the different facets of the Light. The human body would, therefore, have to be of just the right construction to be able to tap all of these different forces. The structure of the *Sefirot* is what makes the body look the way it does. And since we are created in God's image, per the ten *Sefirot*, we are the perfect Vessel for containing all of the Light.

The First Three *Sefirot* are manifested in the human body as the head, which, accordingly, is located at the top of the body. More specifically, from the very top, or crown, (*Keter*) of the head to our eyes, is the *Sefirah* of *Keter*. As *Keter*, the energy of this part of the body—our brain—is completely concealed. From the eyes to the roof of the mouth is *Khokhma*, and from the roof of the mouth to the neck is *Binah*.

---

25. From Rabbi Berg's *The Star Connection*, p. 5.

The body from the neck down reflects the six *Sefirot* of *Ze'ir Anpin* and *Malkhut*. Interestingly, the Indians also recognize seven energy centers in the body, which they call *chakras*. The right arm parallels *Khesed*; the left arm, *G'vurah*; and the chest, *Tiferet*. The right leg is the expression of *Netzakh*; the left leg, *Hod*; and the genitals, *Yesod*. Our hands and feet are *Malkhut*.

The microcosmic reflection of the ten *Sefirot* can be seen reflected on even smaller scales, like the fact that we have ten fingers and ten toes. And then, per each hand and foot, we have five: *Keter, Khokhma, Binah, Ze'ir Anpin*, and *Malkhut*. In fact, the face, and within that, the eye alone, and the internal organs can all be observed as separate frames of reference for the expression of the structure of the ten *Sefirot*. Rabbi Berg, in his Introduction to volume I of his translation of *The Zohar: Parashat Pinhas* to English, states:

> The human body is a reflection of the vast cosmos. Human organs and limbs mirror the dynamics of the interstellar dance that is ever present within the universe (p. xxxviii).

He then goes on to give a brief summary of Kabbalistic Anatomy:

> The flesh embodies the energy-intelligence of the desire to receive for oneself alone; the skin, which extends everywhere and covers everything, is a living symbol of the upper firmament; and the veins and arteries act as chariots to link the soul with the body. Blood contains both the energy-intelligence of sharing as well as the energy-intelligence that is found in all other parts of the body, the desire to receive for oneself alone (ibid., p. xxxix).

To illustrate this reflection on a small scale, we can observe the face. Incidentally, the word for face in Hebrew is *Panim* (*P-N-M*), which has the same composition of the word *P'nim* (*P-N-M*), which means "inside" or "internal." Thus our face exposes or reflects our internal essence. *Keter*, as we said, is the brain. *Keter*, however, is beyond our capacity to connect; thus the brain too is concealed. Instead, *Khokhma* is the first *Sefirah* that offers

THE SEFIROT—RELATIONSHIP TO MAN

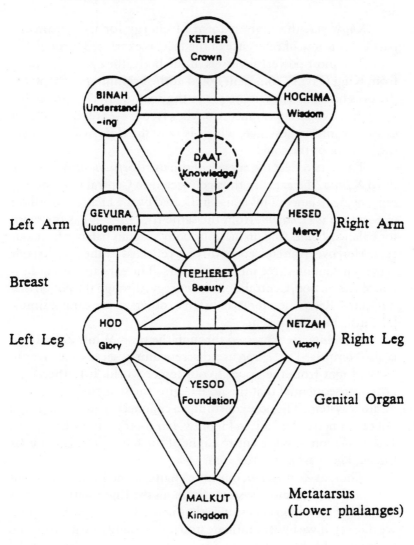

expression for us, as it is for all intents and purposes our first *Sefirah*.

Khokhma, the highest form of energy for us, within the particular frame of reference of the face, is expressed through the eyes. The most powerful vessels of the body, the eyes, as implied from King David's comment noted at the beginning of chapter 4, the eyes have the capacity to see to the root of effects—to see beyond the physical appearance. Conversely, our eyes reveal our "root cause" or internal essence, which is why the *Zohar* calls the eyes the "mirror of the soul."

The ears reflect the energy of the third *Sefirah*, *Binah*. As the third *Sefirah*, the ears are thus connected to Central Column energy, being balance. This is also indicated by the Hebrew word for ears, which is *Oznayim*, from the same root *(A-Z-N)* as the word for balance, *Ezun*. And, in fact, our body sustains balance from our ears. Moreover, the concept of three is reflected by the fact that our ears each contain three inner chambers. The ears are also indicative of Restriction, Central Column energy, through the notion that it requires Restriction for us to listen to others, as we cannot simultaneously talk and listen.

Ze'ir Anpin is expressed through the nose. While *Ze'ir Anpin* is also comprised of *Sefirot*, as a discrete unit, it serves to convey to us the Light from the upper to our lower world. It is, therefore, not inconsequential that the nose begins the structure of our respiratory system. The nose constitutes a channel to convey air in and out of our body. And air, in Hebrew *Avir* (of the letters *Aleph*, *Vav*, *Yod*, *Resh*) contains the entire Light of the ten *Sefirot*: Light is *Or* (*Aleph*, *Vav*, *Resh*); and *Yod*=ten.

Thus, as *Ze'ir Anpin*, our nose channels the Light in and out of us, as our respiratory system circulates the Light within us. It is because of air's internal essence that if we do not breath enough, we die; yet, if we hyperventillate (too much Light) we pass out. To maintain a healthy existence, we must maintain a balance of the air-Light we draw in (inhale=Desire to Receive) and resist (exhale=Desire to Give) out. It is also for this reason that so many spiritual doctrines focus on breathing as the key to successful meditation—Kabbalistic meditation included.

The mouth corresponds with *Malkhut*. The mouth is our connection with the physical world through eating and speaking. The mouth, as *Malkhut* functions, implements our thoughts into spoken words as it also reveals, through its implementation, the internal essence of the particular individual.[26]

Two more points with regard to kabbalistic anatomy warrant mention. The first is the function of hair. In brief, hair constitutes a type of antenna that draws in Light. This was, for instance, the secret of Samson's tremendous strength—his hair. However, while Samson did not cut his hair, which would be a demonstration of Restriction, he balanced the great amount of Light he drew by exerting other forms of Restriction.

Because hair is an antenna for Direct Light, many spiritual doctrines recommend some kind of covering to put over one's hair: in Judaism, the small *Kippah* or yarmulka (the Yiddish word for *Kippah*) is sufficient for men to demonstrate Resistance. Some African tribes, as does Islam (by wearing the Kafia) and many Oriental cults and sects require that the head be covered. Even the Catholic pope wears a yarmulka of some sorts. It is for the purpose of restricting the Direct Light drawn by the hair, and subsequently turning it into Returning Light, that so many spiritual doctrines have its practitioners cover their hair.[27]

The second point with regard to kabbalistic anatomy that warrants mention, relates to the *Sefirah* of *Yesod. Yesod* is the last *Sefirah* of *Ze'ir Anpin* before *Malkhut.* As the doorway between the spiritual and the physical, it is at the level of *Yesod* that *husks* (*Klipot*) appear.

As we have said, Adam before the Fall, was completely made of nail. Being of completely transparent material, he channeled all of the Light there was to receive. The Fall caused a *husk* to appear at the level of *Yesod*, to conceal the Light from *Malkhut.* And since the structure of the *Sefirot* permeates all of existence, that *husk* is represented in all things on our physical world at the level of *Yesod.* Vis-à-vis the human body, *Yesod* is the genitals. And thus man acquired a foreskin as a result of the Fall. This is also what

---

26. For more on kabbalistic anatomy, the reader is directed to lessons/ cassettes nos. 10 and 11 of the Kabbalah Centre's "Kabbalah Beginners Course" and to the recorded lectures on "Kabbalah and Medicine." With regard to kabbalistic meditation, the Kabbalah Centre offers an entire advanced course on this subject.

27. Actually, restriction over hair is only required of men, who would otherwise not attain balance. In chapter 7 we will understand why women do not need to cover their hair to attain balance.

the Torah means when it says that Adam was created circumcised: He came into existence without any *husks*.

Where there is a *husk*, there is potential for a revelation of Light. The greater the *husk*, the greater the potential of revelation. Thus the performance of circumcision is the physical removal of the foreskin from the male penis, as it is a spiritual or metaphysical removal of a large *husk*.

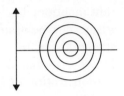

Within the frame of reference of the "speaking" level, men are the human expression of positive, potential, energy, while women are the human expression of negative energy, or the energy of implementation. That is, men correspond to *Ze'ir Anpin*, as channels for the Light, while women correspond to *Malkhut*, as the implementers of the channeled Light. And since men correspond or serve as *Ze'ir Anpin* within the human frame of reference, and *Yesod* is part of *Ze'ir Anpin*, only male children are circumcised.[28]

ADDITIONAL, MISCELLANEOUS TOOLS

While Hebrew is our key means of revealing the internal essence of all that exists in our universe, there are additional tools that aid us in deciphering that essence, even from the Hebrew word itself. One of those additional tools is the utilization of the numerical equivalent of the Hebrew word (*Gematria*); the other is by various juxtapositions of the Hebrew letters.

Gematria, or numerology, is generally dubbed Kabbalistic mathematics. While various cultures and languages utilize discrete symbols for numbers, in addition to their alphabet letters, the Hebrew letters serve both functions. Each Hebrew letter represents a specific numerical value or power. So while the alphabetical function of the Hebrew word serves to reveal the entity's internal es-

---

28. In addition to the lesson on circumcision (*Brit Milah*) in the Kabbalah Beginners Course, Rabbi Berg has a (recorded) two-part advanced lecture on *Brit Milah* (circumcision) that discusses how the proper performance of a *Brit Milah*, or the proper removal of the negativity in the foreskin, promotes a strong human immune system that helps shield us from the AIDS virus.

sence, its numerical function simultaneously serves to reveal that entity's level of energy or intensity. The word *Ekhad*, for example, literally means "one." But, Kabbalistically, "one" also connotes "unity" and a "Similiarity of Form." The word *Ekhad* also has the numerical value of thirteen: *Aleph* = 1, *Khet* = 8, *Dalet* = 4.

NUMERICAL VALUES

Alef	—	א	— 1
Bet	—	ב	— 2
Gimel	—	ג	— 3
Dalet	—	ד	— 4
Heh	—	ה	— 5
Vav	—	ו	— 6
Zayin	—	ז	— 7
Chet	—	ח	— 8
Tet	—	ט	— 9
Yod	—	י	— 10
Kaf	—	כ	— 20
Lamed	—	ל	— 30
Mem	—	מ	— 40
Nun	—	נ	— 50
Samekh	—	ס	— 60
Ayin	—	ע	— 70
Peh	—	פ	— 80
Tzadi	—	צ	— 90
Kof	—	ק	— 100
Resh	—	ר	— 200
Shin	—	ש	— 300
Tav	—	ת	— 400

Unlike conventional mathematics, in *Gematria*, a larger or bigger number does not necessarily denote greater intensity. (A mathematician might appreciate this by the Gematric statement that $x<$ is not necessarily greater than $x>$). The numerical value of the Tetragrammaton, for example, is twenty-six, which may not seem like a lot quantitatively, but qualitatively, it denotes an extremely high level of energy—high and balanced.

On the other hand, *Gematria* is similar to conventional mathematics in that what it proffers to show is that various entities, represented as mathematical expressions of equal value, share the same level of energy or intensity. For example, the Hebrew word for "love," denoting Similarity of Form, is *Ahava*. *Ahava* has the numerical value of thirteen: *Aleph*=1, *Hey*=5, *Vet/Bet*=2, *Hey*=5. Just as in conventional Mathematics, $1+2=2+1=3$, we can now see that "one" is synonymous with "love" as $1+8+4 = 1+5+2+5=13$.

Numbers, as they represent different entities' internal essence (soul), also represent entire structures of energy. Three, as we have learned, represents the Central Column or the energy structure of balance. Four (four letters, or twenty-six) is the Tetragrammaton, representing the complete structure and optimal flow of energy. Seven, as per the seven *Sefirot* of *Ze'ir Anpin* plus *Malkhut*, represents those forces that pertain to the physical realm. Ten represents the ten *Sefirot* or the entire structure of forces of the spiritual and physical worlds together. Twelve connotes the complete body of knowledge that is contained within the *Sefirah* of *Ze'ir Anpin*: twelve represents, for example, the twelve tribes of Israel, the twelve Zodiac signs and the twelve months of the year.

In an equation, whenever a (1) is added to one mathematical expression, the (1) represents the individual or his or her injection of free will to create balance and thus transcend the power of that mathematical expression's equivalent. Love and One, both thirteen, are good examples of energies that *we* have the ability to generate, by exerting our free will to transcend and overcome the power of destiny, dictated by the stars. Love=One=$12+1$, which tells us that they contain the power to transcend the force of the twelve signs of the Zodiac, through our exerting free will.

The reason the Tower of Babel got as far as it did was because, at the outset of its construction, its participants were united. So long as they were one (13), they could overcome the forces controlling the physical world (12); thus, nothing could hurt them or stop them in their endeavor. But, as the tower progressed, the people became fragmented and ceased to love their neighbor as themselves. Agadah holds that it got to where when a person died while working on the tower, the others would use the corpse as mortar towards the progress of the tower's construction. This fragmentation reduced their level of thirteen (one), so that they became subject to the forces of twelve (the zodiac/destiny), which inevitably destroyed them completely, as the cosmic system does not tolerate the imbalance begot from the negative energy of the Desire to Receive for Oneself Alone.

The energy of unity, or of "one" or of "Love thy neighbor as thyself" (they are all synonymns) is very powerful. The energy is so strong that most pagan and satanic religions or sects that connect to the forces of nature, have considered thirteen an "unlucky" number. This is because unity is stronger than the forces of nature. But thirteen for the kabbalalist is a "good" or "positive" number. In fact, Friday the thirteenth would be an extremely positive day, as it combines two balanced and very positive energies: Friday, the sixth day (6=the Shield of David and 2x3, thus the 3 of Returning Light) and thirteen is unity and love.

The number thirteen represents energy that is beyond what the pagan vessel can contain. Energy is only considered "unlucky" or "bad" when the recipient lacks a sufficient vessel with which to contain that energy. For example, water is a "positive" energy in that it is life-giving (+), life-sustaining and a stable element, chemically. If one holds an eight ounce vessel and is given eight ounces of water, the water can be contained and thus enjoyed. But if onto that same individual, with the eight ounce vessel, the entire contents of the Colorado River were poured, he would drown—not because water is bad or unlucky, but because that individual did not prepare a sufficient vessel with which to contain the energy being given him. In these terms, the energy of thirteen would be like the 8 oz.-fill to the Kabbalist, whereas to another, that same energy would be like the entire Colorado River coming down!

One additional example of this use of *Gematria* can be found in the liturgical phrase we analyzed earlier: [When] "He and His Name are One." We said that "name" means vessel. This can also be discerned through the numerical value of the Hebrew word for "His name" (*Shmo*), which is 346. The word "desire" (synonymous of Vessel, the Desire to Receive) is also 346. Thus, because numerically, His name=346=desire, the two terms can be used interchangeably.

Moreover, the Hebrew word for desire, *Ratzon* (*R-Tz-N*), contains the same letters as the word for Channel, *Tzinor* (*Tz-N-R*). This demonstrates an additional aspect of *Gematria* and that is that the equations it formulates represent only absolute numbers. *Gematria* can, thus, show us both sides of the same coin or the expression of the two opposite potential energies (positive and negative) in a particular energy.

Desire (*R-Tz-N*), meaning the Desire to Receive, can be

represented as (–346). Channel (*Tz-N-R*), on the other hand, primarily functions to convey or give energy, and can, thus, be represented as (+346). Therefore, Desire and Channel are the two sides (implementations or realizations of the potential energy of |346|.[29]

In both conventional mathematics and *Gematria*, a number represents the combination of all its equivalent mathematical expressions. In many ways, *Gematria*, though, takes this function a step further, since it represents the expressions' internal quality and not just its quantitative level. Thus, *Gematria* functions somewhat like a recipe. While the ingredients of, say, simple paste have no likeness to paste, one can perceive the process and final product if we were to state that: flour + water = paste. The formula itself may not explain what to do with the flour and water to get paste, but it shows what can result from their combination.

An example of this facet of *Gematria* is the root *A-M-N*, which gives us the words *Amen* and *Emuna* (belief). *A-M-N* has the numerical value of ninety-one. Ninety-one is the sum of the numerical value of two names of the Light: *Adonai* and the Tetragrammaton. *Adonai* corresponds with the energy level of *Malkhut*, while the Tetragrammaton, is our "outer space connection," connecting us to *Ze'ir Anpin*.

Kabbalah teaches us that it is our connection to *Ze'ir Anpin* (the energy of the Shield of David) that gains us protection and security in the cosmos. Various prayers, meditations, rituals, etc. provide us with the means to connect with *Ze'ir Anpin*. But, for that connection to actually help us, we need to draw it to our level of *Malkhut*. "Amen" is the meditation that transforms the Desire to Receive, the energy of *Malkhut*, to that of *Ze'ir Anpin*, which is the energy of sharing, and by this, unifies the two levels or *Sefirot* (*Ze'ir Anpin* + *Malkhut*).

Therefore, saying "Amen" is like pressing the "Enter" key on a computer keyboard. One person meditates on reciting a prayer. That connects him to *Ze'ir Anpin*. But at that level, the energy is only potential, as is typing in a command on the computer. A second person (at least one) is then needed to implement that potential energy. And *Malkhut* (of feminine energy or the energy of implementation) is what affects that. And the more

29. We will apply this tool in another example, when we come to the issue of Satan and Messaiah, in chapter 8.

people who serve to channel that energy of implementation (those who say Amen), the more that energy, from *Ze'ir Anpin,* can be implemented in *Malkhut*, in our physical world. Moreover, the root *A-M-N* literally means (to) train or (to) nurture, both of which are forms of implementing potential energy in the physical.

The function of the root *A-M-N* sheds light onto the key of prayer and meditation: They are not for the Light or God, but rather solely for the Vessel. The Light is whole, complete and perfect. It lacks nothing. To assume that the Light needs our prayers or our thanks implies that He is not whole without the Vessel's doing. Such an assumption can be relegated to a form of idolatry.[30]

It is only the Vessel that needs prayer and meditation, as it is only the vessel that *needs* such connections (to *Ze'ir Anpin*). Thus, it is only the Vessel who needs thanksgiving. By offering thanks (+), the Vessel creates a balance from the energy he receives (−) from the Light. That is, thanksgiving is a means for the Vessel to exert Restriction on the energy it receives. Saying thanks also assists the Vessel in internalizing his function and status in the grand scheme of things: that the Vessel exists to receive fulfillment from the Light, and that everything in this world comes from the Light—the Vessel can create nothing.[31] That is, the Vessel must remind itself that it can never be God.

The other derivative of the root *A-M-N* is the word *Emuna*, whose literal English translation, belief, is, as Rabbi Berg explains, somewhat deceiving.[32] In the Language of the Branches, when we say we "know," it means we are connecting with the Light.[33] Similarly, in its colloquial context, when we say we "know" something,

---

30. See chapter 8 regarding ego and Satan.

31. Again, see chapter 8 about the importance of the Vessel's keeping a proper perspective on his place in the universe.

32. This entire discussion on *A-M-N* is taken from Rabbi Berg's recorded lecture on the Torah portions of *Ekev* and *VaEtkhanan* ("*Zohar: Ekev— Vaetchnan*").

33. To know = to connect. Thus, when the Bible writes that "And Adam knew Eve his wife; and she conceived, and bore Cain . . ." (Genesis 4:1), *to know* implies more than just sexual intercourse, as the Bible employs many terms for the same physical act. In this context, *to know* means to engage in sexual intercourse (on the physical level) while connecting (on the spiritual or metaphysical level) to the energy of the Light that would enable conception. From the above example, we can see that Adam evidently really *knew* his stuff!

it implies that we are sure about the energy of that thing being a part of us. Conversely, though, when we say we "believe" something, it automatically implies that we do not *know* it to be true for sure, but rather that we are willing to suspend our disbelief and just accept it as so with blind faith. Such blind faith actually equates with doubt.[34]

It is for this reason that the word "belief", or at least its connotation, is problematic—it implies the very opposite of the Hebrew word it purports to translate. Belief, with the connotation of blind faith, effects no connection to *Ze'ir Anpin*. Therefore, it cannot aid the "believer." As Rabbi Berg suggests, a better translation of *Emuna* is "security," because those "believers" who subscribe to this meaning, make the proper and necessary connections. The one who subscribes to the "belief" translation is usually the one who, in retrospect of an incident in which he was not protected, asks "Where were you, God?!" And, in turn, such a question is indicative of the "believer's" level of consciousness: doubt.

The AT-BaSh Language: The other tool we mentioned that helps us decipher a Hebrew word's internal essence, is juxtaposing the Hebrew letters in their alphabetic function. There are a number of such groupings, as in taking a word and then looking at the letters that immediately proceed the letters of the word. Another form of such grouping is called the *AT-BaSh* language. In *AT-BaSh*, the twenty-two Hebrew letters are divided in half, so that the first letter equals the last letter. Thus, A(leph)=T(uf) and B(et)=Sh(in), hence *AT-BaSh*.

THE את—בש KEY

א-ת	ז-ע
ב-ש	ח-ס
ג-ר	ט-נ
ד-ק	י-מ
ה-צ	כ-ל
ו-פ	

The function of such juxtapositions is primarily to reveal various letters that denote energies of the First Three *Sefirot*, that

---

34. Doubt, as we will discuss in chapter 8, is a form of "Satanic Consciousness."

must be and are concealed in our physical realm. That is, letters representing the First Three are concealed, even in words. The juxtaposition is a form of concealment, so that the energy is not revealed, which had it been, would act like a live wire (since by itself, it lacks a vessel). One example, using the *AT-BaSh* system, is the word *Mitzvah*, the Hebrew word for "precept." We said that in Judaism there are 613 precepts, 365 negative and 248 positive precepts. The function of a precept is to ensure that we reveal only balanced energy. The Hebrew word itself explains how this is accomplished.

Grammatically, the word *Mitzvah* comes from the root (*Tz-V-T*), which means joining or (*Tzavta*) togetherness. Kabbalah explains that what is joined by the performance of a precept are the upper, spiritual, world and the lower, physical, world. The *AT-BaSh* system, together with what we learned about the Tetragrammaton, will help us understand exactly how this is effected.

As we have already learned, the Hebrew letters that make up the Tetragrammaton, represent the entire system of the *Sefirot*. The first two letters, the *Yod* and the first *Hey*, correspond to the "First Three," whereas the last two letters, the Vav and the second Hey, correspond to the Lower Seven. The First Three in our physical world exist only in a concealed manner. And so it is in the word which serves to create the energy flow of the Tetragrammaton. Per the *AT-BaSh* system: *Yod=Mem* and *Hey=Tzadik*. Thus, if we reveal the first two letters of the word *Mitzvah* (M-Tz-V-H), we get the very letters of the Tetragrammaton, in their appropriate sequence. Therefore, by performing a precept, a *Mitzvah*, we join the upper and lower worlds and implement the potential energy of the Tetragrammaton in our individual life and in the entire world.

IV

Various Applications of the Basic Principles

6

The Different Nations of the World: And What Is a Jew Anyway?

Kabbalah defines a "nation" (in Hebrew *uma*) as a group of people who have the same facet of the Light as their internal essence, or their soul. The Light is the powerhouse. From It, one channels energy through various facets to fulfill different functions. The *Zohar* even defines that in addition to that of the Jewish nation, there are seventy different kinds of souls: that is, there are seventy different facets of the Light reflected through seventy different kinds of vessels, in addition to the Jewish vessel. The people of one nation would, thus, share the same type of soul. And, with this, a particular nation would also share a particular collective *Tikkun*.[1]

---

1. A nation should not be confused with a religion or with a spiritual doctrine. For example, as Robin Skelton asserts, "A witch is a person who follows the 'Old Religion,' which he or she believes to pre-date the Judaic–Christian religion and which is nowadays called Wicca" (*The Practice of Witchcraft Today*, p. 17). The 'Old Religion' or any religion is the physical practice undertaken by a group of people. Interestingly, Larry Kahaner points out that "the name often given to modern Witchcraft [Wicca, actually] grew out of Great Britian from the writings of two people, Gerald Gardner and Alex Sanders" (*Cults That Kill*, p. 98). Bob Larson qualifies this by noting, "Though witches delight in suggesting their beliefs have been handed down from pre-existing traditions, the truth is most witches follow the [Gerald] Garderian [b.England 1884–1964, per p. 163] legacy, which combines occultism with Eastern mysticism" (*Satanism*, p. 164). Thus, the specific Wiccan spiritual doctrine (the prescribed practice and understanding of the cosmos) was formed in the nineteenth century. The Jewish spiritual doctrine, Kabbalah, predates all physical existence.

The fact that what we, or the U.N. or whoever, define as a "nation" does not necessarily mean that two groups are spiritually different. The nations of the Far East, for example, are for the most part one discrete spiritual nation. Moreover, the internal quality of a nation—its soul—reincarnates as does the individual soul. Thus wars between nations are really between two conflicting energies on the metaphysical level. The human soldiers merely implement and serve as the physical manifestation of the metaphysical conflict.

In our modern, capitalistic minds, we tend to associate *more* with *better*. As nature demonstrates, this is not always true. Robin Skelton, in discussing the practice of Witchcraft, demonstrates this through the nature of medicine:

> [O]ne must recall that in medicine it is often the case that a small dose may be effective and a larger one either ineffective or counter-productive. One cannot measure effectiveness in terms of quantity in either medicine or mechanics (*The Practice of Witchcraft*, p. 23).

Similarly, H_2O_2 (hydrogen peroxide) is not necessarily "better" than H_2O (water) by virtue of its extra oxygen; the compositions of hydrogen peroxide and water have just made them different things. In fact, here is a simple but good example of where more is actually less stable, as hydrogen peroxide (having +2 and −4) looks to interact (i.e., react) with other positive charges to attain balance, where water (having +2 and −2) is a stable and nonreactive compound.[2]

It is important to emphasize this idea of "bigger," because, as we have politically-correctedly been conditioned, we may assume a bias and pass judgment on natural states that do not read into themselves this way. A large vessel (say, a soup bowl) can hold more energy than a small vessel (say, a demitasse), but it can equally contain more emptiness and darkness, which on the spiritual level translates to negativity and evil—more so than with regard to the smaller vessel.

---

2. Joel H. Hildebrand and Richard E. Powell, PhDs. *Principles of Chemistry*, 6th edition. New York: Macmillan Co.

Kabbalists many times refer to the accompanying diagram to illustrate that a smaller vessel (represented by the smaller circle) can only go so high above the median line; but then it can only go the equal distance down. The larger vessel can achieve that much greater a spiritual high;  but when it is not spiritual, it can descend to equal depths of darkness and negativity, manifested by depression, evil, etcetera.

For each different type of soul (nation) there is an equal and corresponding spiritual doctrine tailored specifically to the needs of that group soul. In his book *The Tibetan Book of Living and Dying*, Sogyal Rinpoche says that "meditation . . . is the way to bring us back to ourselves" (p. 57); "meditation is the road to enlightenment and the greatest endeavor of this life" (p. 80). A Jew, for instance, could meditate or walk on hot coals or whatever, but it would never fulfill him completely, nor would it enable him to fulfill his spiritual function in this world. A Jew is defined as the soul type that has the greatest Desire to Receive. As such, he requires the spiritual doctrine that can provide him with the means to reveal the greatest amount of Light. As we discussed in the Introduction, that is why Abraham gave all of his spiritual knowledge to Isaac, whereas to the others he gave only fragments of that complete body of knowledge. This is also why only Kabbalah can provide an overview of the entire cosmic structure—because only in it is contained the totality of all cosmic knowledge.

Since an individual or nation is defined by its internal essence, or soul, if we were to inquire into the energy of the Jew or of the member of any other nation, the question to ask would be *"What* is a Jew?" and not *"Who* is a Jew?" Moreover, Kabbalah explains that only when Elijah the Prophet descends will we be able to know who is a Jew and who isn't. As we have seen from Rabbi Gershom's book, a non-Jew can actually be Jewish (or vice versa) due to his soul being Jewish, regardless of where his body ends up. The physical body is only a cover, a facade; it can reveal the internal essence, but it can also deceive the naked eye.

A LIGHT FOR ALL NATIONS

A Jew is a spiritual-metaphysical energy intelligence of the largest Desire to Receive. However, as we have already noted, the larger the vessel, the greater the ability to reveal Light, but equally in a positive or negative way. God channels through Isaiah that the Jewish people are to be "*LeOr Goyim*," "the Light for [all] the nations" (Isaiah 42:6 and 49:6).

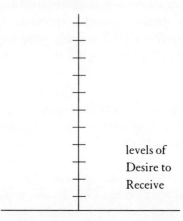

levels of Desire to Receive

But then the Talmud tells us that after the Jews at Mount Sinai received the Torah, God placed them inside the mountain and said that if they do not accept the precepts of the Torah, that under the mountain would be their burial place. This seems to contradict the basic tenet of Kabbalah and, hence, of metaphysics that there is no coercion in spirituality.

The issue here is not coercion, but rather refers to that of cause and effect: if the Jew exerts Restriction and reveals Returning Light, he brings Light to all of the lower vessels, i.e. to all of the other nations of the world. But if, on the other hand, he draws Direct Light, as the largest Desire to Receive, he creates the greatest short circuit— a short circuit that is felt by all of the other nations and thus, consequently, destroys himself and the world.

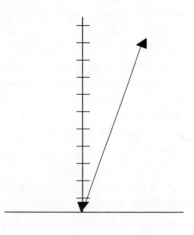

During the time that the Holy Temple of Jerusalem existed, on Yom Kippur, the high priest, the *Cohen HaGadol*, would go into the chamber of the Holy of Holies and draw on the energy of the Tetragrammaton. In doing so, he would reveal Light for the entire world. With this, the next questions we have to ask are "How do we define the function of the Jew, the function that he needs to fulfill?" and "Why was the Holy Temple Destroyed?" And while we're at it, what exactly does it mean to be the "Chosen" People?

THE CHOSEN PEOPLE

In Exodus 19:5, God tells Moses, as representative of the entire Jewish nation, "If you will hearken into My voice indeed, and keep My covenant, then shall ye be unto Me a peculiar treasure above all nations." But this is the English translation of this key verse. In Hebrew, however, the term for "peculiar treasure" is *Segulah*. The word *Segulah* has no lexical meaning in this context. Actually, the word *Segulah* is the feminine form of the word *purple*. Interestingly, *Am Segulah*, literally "the Segulah Nation," has been translated as the "Chosen Nation" or the "Chosen People."

However, using the pronunciation guide to Hebrew, we can come to define what *Segulah* is and even how this relates to purple. In Hebrew, a word is composed of only consonants; although some letters, in certain contexts, are used as vowels as well. What determines how a letter, say the *Daled* [D] is pronounced—da, di, do, du, etcetera—is which vowel is used with it. And most vowels are dots added above, though mostly below the letter. Looking at the vowel guide on the next page, we can see that one of the vowels is called *Segol* (the masculine form of *Segulah*), which is represented by the symbol ∴

Three dots: From chapter 3, the significance of three should immediately ring when three dots are represented. Three denotes the Central Column—the positive and negative poles combined to create balance: the Desire to Receive for the Sake of Sharing. From this we can understand why the above translation is actually a mistranslation of tremendous significance. The term *segulah* in its original language (Hebrew), defines the very function of the Jew: to serve as the channel of the Light for the entire world.

This is also why Jews pray three times a day: once in the morning, in relation to the Right Column, once in the afternoon for the Left Column, and once in the evening for the Central Column. Moslems pray five times a day—to connect to each of the five *Sefirot* (*Keter, Khokhma, Binah, Ze'ir Anpin,* and *Malkhut*). But, unlike Moslems (who are of Left-Column energy and can thus draw en-

VOWEL SIGNS

Vowel signs and dots occur mostly under the letter; sometimes inside or over it. They are pronounced *after* the letter
that carries the sign, for example, פָּשׁוט pashut.

The system of vowel signs is as follows:

אַ/אָ/אֲ — pronounced as the vowel sound in rut, hut
              (symbol used a)

אוּ/אֻ — pronounced as oo (symbol used u) in root

אִ   — pronounced as ee (symbol used i) in feet

אֹ/אוֹ/אָ — pronounced as o in lot, got

אֲ   — pronounced as a half-vowel; something like
              the a in machine

אֶ/אֵ/אֱ — pronounced as e in pet

"Segol"   "Tzereh"

Note: The letters א,ו,י can also function as vowels depending
on the vowel sign:

א   like a, e, o, i or u

ו   o or u

י   like i

---

ergy in such a way), Jews are of Central Column energy and thus,
above all else, need to attain balance.

Three is indicative of Central Column energy, which is balance. Three is also represented by the *Segol*. With this, we can note
that per the study of auras, when a person's aura contains purple
(in Hebrew *Segol*, the masculine form of the word, or *Segulah*, the
feminine form of the word), it means that he or she is balanced.
Parenthically as well, one can see through the visual representation of the energies, that ∵ is the opposite of ∴ the later representing the pyramids of Egypt and thus of the Desire to Receive for
the Self Alone.

Two dots: When a Jew does not exert Resistance, as per his
function and definition, as represented by ∵, he is rendered ‥.
Again, using the vowel guide, we can see that the parallel Hebrew
vowel of *Segol* is *Tzereh*, represented by two dots ‥. The word
Tzereh comes from the root Tzar, meaning narrow. This is the
metaphysical and grammatical root of *Tzarot* (troubles, or in Yiddish *Tzures*) and narrow-mindedness (*Tzarut*).

With this, we can get a preliminary insight into the internal energy of Egypt, which in Hebrew is *Mitzrayim*. In Hebrew, "Egypt" (*Mitzrayim*) is also from the root *Tzar* (narrow) or its elaborated form *Matzar* (straights, or narrows). When the Israelites in the Land of Israel were faced with a famine (material lack), they went down into Egypt (*Mitzrayim*). There they became slaves— not so much in the physical sense, but rather in the spiritual sense.[3] The Jews had reduced their spiritual level to one of a Desire to Receive for the Self Alone. And they were, thus, slaves to the material energy of Egypt.

If we remember that the Bible is a cosmic code of law and the Torah, the revealed blueprint of the universe, then we can even understand why the Jews were first slaves in Egypt and then only 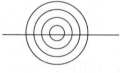 after, received the Torah. As there is no time, space or motion in the metaphysical, the internal essence of the Jew existed even before they received the Torah on Mount Sinai. But it was only by experiencing the lowest spiritual level that they could achieve and reveal the highest spiritual level, after the exodus.

BIBLICAL NAZISM[4]

The fact that the acronym for Hitler's party, the National Socialist German Workers' Party in German is "Nazi" does not explain its root source. We know by now that nothing on the physical plane can be a cause. A physical phenomenon can only be a reflection or parallel manifestation of an energy that exists on the metaphysical level. Therefore, even the name of Hitler's movement stems from above.

---

3. The Israelites' material needs were met, apparently beyond plenty, as per Exodus 12:34–39, where we learn that they left Egypt with cakes of bread baking and vessels of gold and silver and clothes. Moreover, in Numbers 11:4–5 they complain about being in the desert and reminisce about the golden days in Egypt: "And the children of Israel also wept and said, who will give us meat to eat? We remember the fish we ate in Egypt for nothing, the cucumbers and the melons, the leeks and the onions and the garlic."

4. In addition to lesson/cassette no. 6 of the Kabbalah Beginners Course, the reader is directed to Rabbi Berg's recorded lecture "Spiritual Insights Into the Rise of Neo-Nazism."

The word, or root, "Nazi" appears twice in the Bible:

1. And the Lord said unto Moses: How long yet shall this people provoke Me? and how long yet will they not believe in Me, with all the signs which I have shown in the midst of them? (Numbers 14:11).
2. Shall surely not see the land which I have sworn unto their fathers, yea all those that have provoked Me shall not see it (Numbers 14:23).

In the original (Hebrew), the word "provoked" in both cases has the root *Natzi* (which is how *Nazi* is pronounced); in verse 11 the word is *YeNa'aTZuNI*; while in verse 23 the word is *MeNa'aTZIi*. Per se, the word *nazi* in its biblical context has no meaning; the word *provoked* has been dubbed in absense of a real translation. However, after WWII, after this term's energy has surfaced and been expressed in full form, we can see what "Nazi" means—the word that was used to describe bickering Jews amoung themselves.[5]

HOW BICKERING JEWS AFFECT THE WORLD AND WHY THE HOLY TEMPLE WAS DESTROYED

Implied from the subtitle is the notion that when Jews bicker among themselves, they affect the entire world. As the *Malkhut* of all the nations, the Jew is the channel of Light for the whole world. When the Jew properly exerts Resistance, Light is revealed for all of the other nations, too; but when he draws Direct Light or causes a short circuit, the other nations remain either in lack or are affected by the short circuit, respectively.

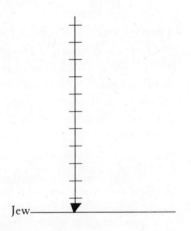

Jew

---

5. The issue of conflict and fragmentation will be expanded upon in chapter 8.

Today, a good deal of the Jewish population is completely assimilated into the general populace, to the extent that they do not know what it even means to be Jewish. Those who still retain some tie to their Jewish heritage are by and large in some way or another engaged in contributing to the fragmentation of the Jewish Nation—be it between the Liberals and the Conservatives, the secular and the religious, the different religious sects among themselves, or between the Ashkenazim and the Sefaradim. Jews even bicker about *who* is a Jew![6] "*Sinat Khinam*," "Hatred for No Reason," was the main cause of the destruction of the Holy Temple. That is, it is the fragmentation of the Jewish people, or rather the energy emanating from this fragmentation, that negatively effects the world. As the energy that we generate or sow is precisely the energy we reap, the energy of *Sinat Khinam* boomerangs back to negatively effect the Jewish nation.

Vessel = Cohen + Levite + Israelite (C.L.I.)

The complete Vessel, which in Hebrew is *Kli* or *CLI*, is comprised of the Cohens, Levites, and Israelites—the three functional divisions in Judaism. The Cohen, parallels the proton of the atom (+), the Levite the electron (−), and the Israelite the neutron (Central Column). Fragmenting or splitting this balanced unit affects on a metaphysical level what splitting the atom does on the physical level!

"And thou wilt not go aside from all the words which I command thee this day, to the right, or to the left, to go after strange gods, to serve them" (Deuteronomy 28:14).

Before we move on, there are a number of terms that warrant definition. We will discuss two—*religious* and *Sephardic*—and touch on a third. The two named terms are kabbalistic terms of art, which have no bearing on their loosely used colloquial derivatives. The word for "religious" in Hebrew is *Dotti* or *D-T-Y*. To

---

6. Unfortunately, the list of such fragmentation goes on and on, on a religious level—as the violent battles between the Hassidim and the Mitnagdim—as on a national level—as the equally violent battles between the three Jewish undergrounds in Israel before its 1948 statehood, the *Saison* and between the *Ekhud* and *MeUkhad* kibbutz movements, that even tore at the very fabric of the family unit.

understand what it means, we need to remember that Central Column is derived from the energies of the Right and Left Columns: Central Column is Right Column over Left Column to attain balance. *D-T-Y* is the acronym of the three *Sefirot* that are of Central Column energy: *Da'at*, *Tiferet*, and *Yesod*. Thus, by definition, to be *D-T-Y* or "religious," one must be balanced.

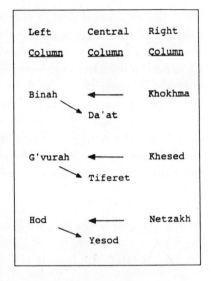

In essence, the balance requisited of being religious refers to a balance between the spiritual and physical worlds as regards one's individual life as it also refers to balance in one's relationship toward others. Thus "religious," "spiritual," "Central Column," "balance," and "Love thy neighbor as thyself" are all synonymns for the same energy. Therefore, a term like "religious fanaticism," like "holy war," is an oxymoronic contradiction in terms. If one is truly religious, then he follows the central path of balance. A fanatic, on the other hand, leans either too far to the Right or the Left Column; either way, he is off of Central Column. Parenthetically, fanaticism finds expression in both zealousy in adhering to spiritual precepts as it does in adhering to rebellion against spiritual precepts. Both cause short circuits.

The term "Sephardic" today is dubbed to refer to a Jew of Spanish, North African, or Mid Eastern origin. *Sepharad* is the Hebrew word for "Spain", as *Ashkenaz* generally refers to the area of Germany. But the actual word *Sepharad* is noted in the Bible in the 20th verse of Ovadia, thus indicating that it possesses a deeper, metaphysical denotation.

To understand what Sephardic means we need to refer to the acronym *Pardes*[7] or *P-R-D-S*, which abbreviates the four levels of

---

7. The word *Pardes* literally means "orchard". From this, various tales are told of great sages "entering the orchard." Such tales are allegories of the sages delving into all four of the levels of Torah study.

Torah study: *P('shat)*, *R(emez)*, *D(rash)*, and *S(od)*. *Sod* literally means "secret" in Hebrew and refers to the esoteric study of Torah, which is Kabbalah. If one places the *Sod* at the beginning of the levels of Torah study, of *P-R-D-S*, one gets the word *S-P-R-D*. Thus, a "SePhaRDic" Jew is one who studies Kabbalah and understands its significance with regard to the complete study of Torah.

A kabbalist, or Sepharadi, understands that the study of *Halakhah*, taught through *Remez* and *Drash*, is important, just as knowing how to fine tune one's radio dial to the exact frequency is important to receive the best reception off the air waves. In metaphysics, these "air waves" are very powerful and are not something to play with or abuse. But a kabbalist knows that understanding the reasons *why* things are done in their particular ways—what the composition of various meditations or prayers do, why and how—precedes their performance. This is because it is only with the proper meditative focus, called *kavanah*, that one can achieve the goal derived from meditation or prayer.[8]

It is also for this reason that the term *Sephardic* has no real bearing on one's physical place of origin. Spiritually speaking, one can be from the Arctic Circle or Madrid, but what determines whether one is Sephardic or not rests only in that individual's subscription to Kabbalah or lack thereof. Relegating such significance to one's physical origin is Nazi in nature, if not expressly satanic (as we will discuss in the last chapter). In the final analysis, just as the color of one's skin does not necessarily reflect the nature of his soul, the body, in general, is not to be substituted for anyone's or anything's internal essence.

On the same token, a Jew who does not study Kabbalah or who opposes its study, even by others, is called an *Ashkenazi*, regardless, too, of his or her physical place of origin.

---

8. The response of the Children of Israel to their receipt of the Torah on Mount Sinai was "All the words which the Lord hath spoken we will do/make and we will listen" (Exodus 24:7). *Na'ase*, which translates as [to] do or make is not the word for [to] perform or fulfill. Thus, what the Israelites rightfully inferred was that they will first *make* a vessel to be able to contain the Light Force of God and then they will listen to His words. An appropriate and sufficient vessel is necessary and precedes any performance of spiritual actions. Such a vessel is created via knowledge and *kavanah* (meditative focus).

Kabbalah explains that the Jews that left Egypt with Moses over thirty-two centuries ago were of two kinds:

(1) "Real" Jews, what the Bible refers to as the "Nation of Israel," or "children of Israel," and

(2) *Erev Rav*, which the Bible differentiates from the first group by merely calling them "the People." The *Erev Rav* were a number of different nations that were in Egypt with the Jews, and included Pharoah's magicians. These people, however, had Jewish souls and so decided to leave with Moses in the Exodus.

Almost every time that the Bible tells us that the Jews argued or complained to Moses in the desert, it references only "the People." In fact, it was the *Erev Rav* that succumbed to building the golden calf, which caused that entire generation to be banned from entering the Promised Land of Israel. And it was them who later contributed to the destruction of the Holy Temple.

It is important to identify the signs of the *Erev Rav*. The *Erev Rav* is the kind of individual who forgets the favors done for him in the past. He is the kind who retains hate and grudges. The "real" Jew does not retain hate or harbor grudges. The reason it is important to identify such signs of the *Erev Rav* is that there is an element of *Erev Rav* in all nations, just as all of us, individually, have a bit of *Erev Rav* in us. *Erev Rav* is a destructive energy; but without identifying it—that is, "recognizing the evil"—we cannot correct it (fulfill *Tikkun* on it).

CONVERSION

A soul is a metaphysical spark of the Endless energy intelligence of the Desire to Receive (the Endless Vessel). While the bodies that a soul inhabits throughout many lifetimes change, the soul does not change. Therefore, a Jew, as an example of the seventy-one nations, is a particular type of spiritual vessel; what a Jew is, is a type of soul, which makes the body that enclothes that soul "Jewish." A nation, as Judaism, is not a race, nor is it a religion: a race pertains only to categorizations of the body; and a religion is generally a physical institution structured over a particular spiritual doctrine, which, in turn, corresponds to a particular type of soul.

Halakhah defines that a Jew is someone who is born of a Jewish mother or who converts according to *Halakhah*. A woman is the physical expression of the feminine energy of the "speaking" or human kingdom.[9] It is, therefore, the mother who implements what can only potentially be a Jew: she implements (the *Malkhut* level) the energy type "Jew" into a physical being that, in turn, becomes a Jew.

But while the rule is that the mother determines the soul of her child, there are exceptions, per various karmic reasons of the parents and the child. As we discussed under *Tikkun* and reincarnation, we saw examples where Jewish souls apparently reincarnated into non-Jewish bodies and environments. That was evidently their particular *Tikkun*. There are also cases of non-Jewish souls reincarnating into Jewish vessels (bodies, families, and so on). And this would be true across the board for all soul types, not just Jewish souls.

Thus, technically, Kabbalah does not "believe" in conversion: A soul is what it is and cannot be changed. If a non-Jew has a Jewish soul, the Jewish conversion process will not make him or her Jewish. When done correctly, the process merely enables that individual to reveal his soul, by helping him or her prepare the proper vessel for it. If someone is not Jewish, he can go through the entire conversion process and perform all kinds of rituals, etcetera, but that will not change his internal essence.[10] Similarly, if a Jew were to decide to convert to Christianity or Islam or whatever, if his soul is Jewish, he remains Jewish regardless of what he does on a physical level. For the most part, the same holds true of all other soul types, too.

---

9. Per the four kingdoms or levels of the Vessel: Inanimate, Growing (plants), Living (animal), and Speaking (human).

10. It is most likely for this reason that, as Rabbi Gershom explains: "Most rabbis . . . will discourage people from converting to Judaism. Traditionally, a seeker must be turned away three times before being accepted as a prospective convert" (*Beyond the Ashes*, p. 104). This is because Judaism contends "that non-Jews, too, can serve God without becoming Jews . . . [and] that any Gentile can get to Heaven if he or she obeys the Seven Laws of Noah . . . so there is no need for the individual to convert to Judaism unless specifically attracted to serving God through the Covenant at Sinai.

The Seven Laws of Noah are: (1) not to worship idols, (2) not to profane the name of God, (3) not to murder, (4) not to steal, (5) not to eat blood or flesh cut from an animal while it is still alive, (6) not to commit adultery or incest, (7) not to take the law into one's own hands, but to settle disputes in courts of justice" (ibid.).

LAND AND NATIONS

The word for land in Hebrew is *Adama*. Reminiscent of *Adam*, it stem from the word for "red"—*Adom*. And red, as we have learned, is a physical expression of Left Column energy. Thus land, or Mother Earth, is an energy field of the Desire to Receive. Just as there are different levels or intensities of Desire to Receive energies in all other forms of the vessel—people, objects, etcetera—so, too, are there different levels of the Desire to Receive in different places. In fact, as there are seventy-one nations, so too are there seventy-one different energy levels of land on earth.

Different cultures have stayed in different places where they felt energy, like Peru, Mexico, and China. Each area of land has a particular level of energy that corresponds to that particular nation of the same level of Desire to Receive. In other words, there is a particular area of land that is Similar in Form to a particular nation, and only on that particular area of land will that nation— provided it reveals its internal energy—feel comfortable.

Far East

There are three energy centers of land on earth that correspond to each of the three Columns of energy. The Far East is the energy center of Right Column energy. It is, therefore, unsurprising that the Oriental spiritual doctrines advocate annihilating the self (the body, negative aspect, or the Left Column) and strive to defy bodily desires and even nature. Prolonged fasting,[11] castration, oaths of celibacy and poverty, coal-walking, levitation, and sleeping on nails are indicative of extreme Right Column energy. Parenthetically, in many ways, Christianity (or more precisely, Catholicism) seems to have evolved from Judaism as a Right Column doctrine. Oaths of celibacy and poverty and the medieval expression of public Penance by flogging oneself are indicative of strict Right Column energy.

---

11. In Hebrew, the word for fasting, *Tzom*, comes from the root of *Tzimtzum*, Restriction. Thus fasting is a form or demonstration of Restriction. Restriction creates balance. But since "excess" and "balance" are opposites by nature, excessive or prolonged demonstrations of Restriction are no longer of Central Column energy.

Egypt

Egypt is the center of Left Column energy, the energy of the Desire to Receive. As the center of Left Column energy, Egypt's energy is actually of the energy of the Desire to Receive For One's Self Alone, as we will soon see. Such energy emphasizes the body, material energy, and the self—energy which creates short circuitry. Mummification performed in ancient Egypt is a perfect example of strong Left Column energy: its focus is on preserving the body and material energy, as opposed to emphasizing the soul and spiritual, more Right Column energy.

The pyramids also served to preserve body energy and material of the physical world. The very structure of the pyramid is indicative of the Desire to Receive For the Self Alone and is why it was constructed such: the top of the structure 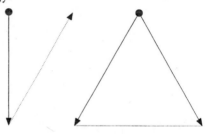 represents the part that connects with the upper, spiritual world—the point. It then has a wide bottom, representing the quantity of energy it is to draw to the physical plane. One might compare this to the energy drawn through the Shield of David, whereby (Direct) Light is drawn from the upper worlds, represented by the upper triad; but the interlocking lower triad serves to resist the flow of Light that is actually drawn, into the lower, physical world, by bringing it to a point (Returning Light). The pyramid, thus, epitomizes the Desire to Receive For One's Self Alone.

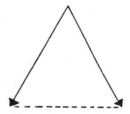
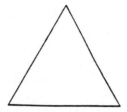

THE PYRAMID

(Continued)

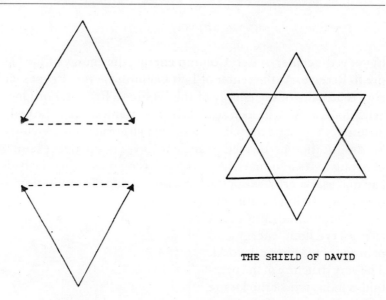

THE SHIELD OF DAVID

When the Bible tells of the famine that befell the Land of Israel, it is thus not by chance that the people of Israel, the Jews, went *down* into Egypt, as the phrase goes. Unfortunately, their level of Desire to Receive was so strong that they became *enslaved* to the Egyptian energy.

The Land of Israel

The Land of Israel is the energy center of Central Column energy, with Jerusalem its energy capital and the Temple Mount (in the Old City of Jerusalem) the core of the energy center itself. Abraham, who lived over thirty-seven centuries ago, and who was the first Jew, was told by God to leave his native land and go to the Land of Canaan (Genesis 12:1, 13:14–15). It is because the energy level of the Land of Israel corresponds to that of the Jewish nation, Central Column energy, that God told Abraham when he arrived in Canaan that "the land that you see is yours which I give to you and to your seed forever" (Genesis 13:15). This is not so much a gift from God (as the problems that have abound in that country from Jewish inhabitance can hardly be considered a gift!), as it is a direction given by God as to the area which corresponds to and will suit Abraham and his descendants' level and nature of energy.

Strangely enough, throughout history, the Jews have controlled the Land of Israel the least. Also throughout history, most of the great empires of the world, after acquiring their great empire, also felt compelled to conquer Israel. What has drawn all these other nations to conquer Israel is the fact that Israel is the energy capital of Central Column energy—the energy of balance—of the world.

However, the vessel of all these other nations, meaning their metaphysical capacity to handle the energy of the Land of Israel, has never been sufficient. And it is for this reason that all of the great empires throughout history that have conquered Israel, have "burned"—if they have not completely disappeared. The ancient Greeks, Palestinians, Phoenicians, Romans, Babylonians, Assyrians, and Persians have all disappeared. The powerful ancient Greeks or Romans and Persians of then are not in size or strength, the same Greeks or Romans (Italians) and Persians as today. Even the British empire, over whose flag the sun never set, has not the same power it had before it conquered Israel.

All things, and land included, have a particular, defined energy charge level. But that energy level, like an absolute number, exists in a potential state, to become either (+) or (−). Israel, the land and nation, bears the spiritual responsibility and function of channeling Light for the whole world. Today, however, Israel's primary export is weaponry.[12] This clash between the energy of its ultimate function and the energy generated from its present preoccupation is the main metaphysical reason that most Jews today, and even most Israelis, do not live in Israel. In fact, because Israel is the energy center of the Central Column energy, being balance, the metaphysical conflict of energies prevalent there bothers the entire world.

Ironically, though, war is what has generally created unity in Israel. And in those wars in which the people and the multi-party government were united, Israel won. What makes the Israeli soldier the great fighter that he is lies in the element of unity, too,

---

12. This is by no means to be construed as a political statement, nor as a pacifistic plea. The fact that Israel's primary involvement today relates to weaponry is merely indicative of its spiritual imbalance. After all, what exists on the physical is merely an expression of its metaphysical root. The solution to this problem is likewise to be found on a spiritual and not physical level.

engendered through Israeli combat training. This is ironic and even sad, because on a regular, nonwar, non-combat basis, Israelis eat each other alive (figuratively, of course!), and generally act with a lack of basic politesse. Leaving the obvious conclusion to the reader, it will simply be pointed out that the destruction of the Holy Temple and the subsequent exile of the Jews from Israel were caused by *Erev Rav* and *Sinat kHinam*, the latter meaning "hatred of one another for no reason."

UFOS

Malkhut, as we have stated, is the level of our physical existence. However, this needs to be qualified, since there are different levels (*Sefirot*) within each *Sefirah*. For example, if one rises from the level of *Yesod* to *Hod*, one rises through *Malkhut* of *Yesod*, then *Yesod* of *Yesod*, *Hod* of *Yesod*, to *Keter* of *Yesod*, after which one would come to *Malkhut* of *Hod*, and so on. Our level of *Malkhut* is actually comprised of eight sub-*Sefirot* from *Malkhut* of *Malkhut* to *Binah* of *Malkhut*.

In his recorded lecture "Kabbalah and UFOs,"[13] Shaul Youdkevich directs us to the exact source of knowledge regarding UFOs—the *Zohar* (vol. 17 of the *Zohar Khadash*, p. 92). Within this section on the book of Genesis is an article called "Adam and Cain and Seven Lands." Here we learn that within our galaxy are six additional "lands" or dimensions to our dimension on earth (the lowest dimension comprises both the *Malkhut* and *Yesod* levels of *Malkhut*).

The meaning of "dimension" is somewhat like a frequency. All of the frequencies or stations on the radio and television exist simultaneously. What determines which station we listen to or watch depends on to which frequency each of us individually tunes in. One person may tune in one frequency, while another tunes in another featuring a completely different kind of broadcast. Each of these frequencies or dimensions is within the level of *Malkhut*.

---

13. Available through the Kabbalah Centre.

The *Zohar* explains that there are seven dimensions, all inhabited by the descendants of Adam;[14] we, human beings, along with the animate, growing and inanimate kingdoms are what inhabit the highest dimension, that of *Binah* of *Malkhut*, also called *Tevel*. The inhabitants of these other six dimensions are what we have come to call UFOs or extraterrestrials (ETs). They inhabit the six levels below ours:

7	*Tevel*	*Binah* of *Malkhut*
6	*Tzia*	*Hesed* of *Malkhut*
5	*Neshia*	*G'vurah* of *Malkhut*
4	*Guy*	*Tiferet* of *Malkhut*
3	*Arka*	*Netzakh* of *Malkhut*
2	*Adama*	*Hod* of *Malkhut*
1	*Eretz*	*Yesod* and *Malkhut* of *Malkhut*

While it may seem as if the inhabitants of these other six dimensions have greater abilities than us, as they have the know-how of going in and out of dimensions, we human beings (the speaking kingdom) are the only ones in the entire universe that possess free will; thus, we are the highest.

The *Zohar* goes into great detail in describing the inhabitants of each of the dimensions and each of the dimensions themselves. Within the dimension of *Guy*, for example, a small strip is described as leading from *Guy* to *Tevel*, which is the entrance to Hell (*Guy-bein-hinom*, or *Gehenom*). Lacking free will, the inhabitants of the lower dimensions are preprogrammed as either positive or negative entities. Rabbi Berg, in chapter 24 of his book *Reincarnation: The Wheels of a Soul*, recounts Rabbi Nehorai the Elder's (second century *tannah*) encounter with aliens who lived at the bottom of the sea and who looked like "strange human beings of diminutive size" (p. 140)—a physical trait of the inhabitants of *Neshia*.

One last point about this expansive topic regards our human contact with these ETs. The accounts kabbalists like Rabbi Nehorai tell of such encounters are about positive entities. Moreover, like

---

14. Shaul Youdkevich offers a close reading of the Book of Genesis that explains this, and the reader is directed to his recorded lecture for more on this topic.

the above account, they are for the most part kabbalists peeking in, as it were, on the other dimensions. This also ties in our discussion in chapter 3 about the difference between proactiveness and reactiveness. The areas on earth that report the most incidents of UFO sightings, landings, or "intrusions" (i.e., human passivity/reactiveness) are areas that have engaged in black magic and sorcery for many centuries: primarily Central and South America, and even Haifa, Israel.[15] While the inhabitants of the other dimensions lack free will, they are "invited" to enter our dimension via the negative cosmic intelligences that we create by Left Column practices (like witchcraft, black magic, and sorcery) of the Desire to Receive For the Self Alone.

------

15. To date, Haifa has been a host and center in Israel for many cults and practices of negative energies. In 1 Kings chapter 18, we read of King Ahab, who imported the pagan cult of Ba'al into Israel, and about the contest held at Mt. Carmel, Haifa, between 450 Ba'al priests and Elijah the Prophet. In fact, Haifa has the same *Gematria*, 103, as the word *EGeL*, indicating at its connection with the sin of the Golden Calf. For more on UFOs and the sin of the Golden Calf, the reader is directed to the Kabbalah Centre's advanced reincarnation course (also on audiocassette) and to Shaul Youdkevich's recorded tape on Kabbalah and UFOs.

7

Personal Relations:
Male and Female

Adam, the first "man," who was the composite of all human souls, was initially created androgenous. This means that he had both the male and female aspects of his soul in him together. Eve was not created as a separate, discrete being, but was—for lack of a better-sounding word—"extracted" from Adam. Eve was the embodiment of the feminine aspect of Adam's soul, so that once Eve came into being, Adam embodied only the male aspect of his soul. This explains why, for instance, Eve was punished along with Adam for Original Sin, even though Eve was not "there" when God told Adam not to eat from the Tree of Knowledge of Good and Evil: She wasn't a separate being, but she was "there"—inside and part of Adam.

In his book on reincarnation, Rabbi Berg quotes from the *Zohar* and explains that "'all the figures of souls that are to be born stand before the Almighty in pairs.' In other words, they are divided into male and female, and eventually, after they have worked their way through the lifetime corridors of reincarnation . . . to merit each other, the Almighty mates them" (p. 101). So that Rabbi Berg defines that "soulmates are but two halves—male and female—of what began in the Endless World as a single soul . . . the male is the aspect of the Right Column, both of the body and soul, and the female is the aspect of the Left Column" (ibid., p. 102). This is what is really meant by "opposites attract."

"Opposites" refer to positive and negative, on a *metaphysical* level, not the physical. Common sense tells us that a physical or earthy difference between two people would more likely than not cause them *not* to attract, as, for example, if one were to be a smoker and his or her date not. What determines whether or not chemistry will exist between two people, like the magnet, is their internal essence.

By him- or herself, an individual can only reveal half of his soul's ability to reveal Light. Thus, for a soul to be able to reveal its full potential, it needs its opposite pole: It takes both a positive and a negative pole, together, to create circuitry. This is why individuals marry, because marriage is a physical ritual performed to fuse the souls of the two together on a metaphysical level, so that they can work as a closed, complete unit for circuitry.

The energy type of either half of a soul remains a constant. Thus the feminine (–) half of a soul is always of feminine energy and never becomes masculine (+) energy. Therefore, "technically" the female aspect should always reincarnate into a female body and the male aspect into a male body. However, for various karmic reasons, there are times when a male soul will incarnate in a female body or vice versa—a female soul will incarnate in a male body. This is what we call homosexuality.

Homosexuality is, therefore, a type of *Tikkun*. It can even be a very difficult *Tikkun*; but it is not a mistake. In a general frame of reference, the body and soul in a "normal" state are already in conflict, as the body, being a Desire to Receive, tries constantly to quash the nature of the soul, which is to share. But vis-à-vis each individual soul, each soul normally abodes in a body that is similar in form—a male soul in a male body and a female soul in a female body—so that the two aspects can work together for the soul to fulfill *Tikkun*. For example, how is a male soul to fulfill the *Tikkun* of circumcision if it incarnates into a female body? It cannot.

The struggle between body and soul, in the case of homosexuality, is magnified and usually engenders much confusion about one's identity. Since the soul is potential energy, it needs a "matching" body to implement that energy. Thus, for example, if a male soul enters a female vessel (body), that individual becomes a woman/female, because it is the mother or vessel (body) that determines how the Light will be manifested on the physical level.

In his book *Reincarnation*, Rabbi Berg notes that Rabbi Akiva's[1] father-in-law, Kalba Savu'a, was a homosexual. It is for this reason that "he returned [reincarnated] as a woman" (p. 153).

The Bible, as per Leviticus 18:22 forbids homosexual relations. This can be explained in "electrical" terms. Two males (homosexuals) engaging in personal relations create a short circuit, metaphysically, because they are combining two positive poles. Two females (lesbians) engaging in personal relations also create a metaphysical short circuit because they are combining two negative poles. Thus "holy matrimony" is only between a man and a woman, because a man and woman each represent the two opposite poles (positive and negative) needed to create metaphysical circuitry, which is what "holy" means.

Incidentally, in the next verse, Leviticus 18:23, the Bible also expressly prohibits beastiality. This is because beastiality creates another kind of metaphysical short circuit through sexual relations. Homosexuality is something like combining two of the same poles of, say, an AA battery. Beastiality would be like combining an AA and an AAA battery to draw energy. On the physical, as on the metaphysical levels, to get a balanced flow of energy, one needs the two opposite poles of the same size battery. This translates as a man and a woman of the speaking (human) form. Leviticus chapter 18 basically offers a rundown of different ways we create short circuits and thus lists sexual acts or combinations we should avoid doing.

With regard to marriage, it is interesting that the Torah only requires it of men and not of women. Of course, to fulfill this precept, men would necessarily *need* women to participate. To understand this, we need to understand the difference between the two sexes a little better.

The Ari tells us that women do not have to reincarnate any more—they have balanced their karmic account. But women volunteer now to descend to this plane to assist their male counterparts. Of course, in doing so, a woman comes down with the entire "package," including a body and part of her male counterpart's *Tikkun*. After all, a soul, a metaphysical energy, requires concealment—husks—just to survive on this plane. However, after her sojourn here, she goes through a purification process ("Hell"), to

---

1. Rabbi Akiva (15–135 C.E.) was Rabbi Shimon Bar Yokhai's teacher.

rid herself of these husks. A man, or male soul, on the other hand, leaves one incarnation and enters the next at exactly the same point, with regard to his *Tikkun*, that he left the last life.

Women have completed their *Tikkun* because they are spiritually and naturally more balanced. While they embody negative energy (Desire to Receive [–]), women are more nurturing, more giving (Desire to Give [+]) than men. And Left Column + Right Column = Central Column, which is balance. Men are also generally more firmly connected to the physical plane, while women maintain connection to the spiritual realm as well. This is why women are generally more intuitive and why more woman than men pursue spirituality. On the other hand, because women are Left Column energy, if they are not giving, but are selfish and greedy, they create a greater short circuit than if a man is selfish and greedy (energy of the Desire for the Self Alone).

Even a woman's body expresses her balance. When she acquires her additional soul, which enables free will (Bat Mitzvah), her body becomes equipped and ready to give and sustain life; thus her menstrual cycle and breasts develop. The woman's monthly cycle parallels the monthly cycle of the moon, which fills and then empties itself of the sun's light.

While, from a physical perspective, a woman's menstrual cycle seems to cause her to be unbalanced, it is, paradoxically, the very thing that gives her spiritual balance. Rabbi Kaplan, in his book on the *Mikvah* (the ritual bath), concisely defines the physical functioning of the woman's period:

> Every month, a woman releases an ovum or egg, which, if fertilized, becomes an embryo which will grow into a new human being. The lining of the uterus (endometrium) thickens to accommodate the fertilized egg. It develops an increased blood supply with which to nourish the embryo if the egg is fertilized.
>
> If the egg is not fertilized, after approximately two weeks, it is expelled. The uteral lining and its accumulated blood is also shed and the expelled material is essentially what constitutes the menstral flow. Thus, the menstrual cycle involves the construction and destruction of an enriched uteral lining (*Waters of Eden*, p. 40).

Rabbi Kaplan then goes on to point out:

This well-known fact is by no means that simple or logical. From a biological standpoint, it would be much more economical if the uteral lining would be reabsorbed instead of expelled. This would certainly be more esthetic and comfortable for the woman. She would then not have to lose a significant amount of her vital fluids each month.

Even more efficient, from a biological viewpoint, would be a situation that would allow the womb to remain in a constant state of readiness to nourish the fertilized ovum. Actually, there is no biological or medical reason why the uteral lining must be expelled and restored each month. There is no reason why the ovum has to "die" only to be replaced by another egg. Most biologists look upon this as an example of unexplained inefficiency in the human reproductive system (ibid., pp. 40–41).

Yet, nothing in our universe is either inefficient or redundant. The reason the woman's cycle is as it is, is based on two issues: (1) water, change, and renewal; and (2) activity (as opposed to passivity).

The thickening of the uteral lining and the increase in blood supply connote a filled, strong vessel. When the uteral lining and its accumulated blood are expelled, it connotes a broken vessel. The shattering of such a vessel, which was prepared to give life, is what creates the emotional and physical negativity felt by most women, as PMS, discomfort, etcetera. From the moment blood discharges from the body, the woman is in a state of what is called *Niddah*.

Niddah basically means that the woman, as a broken vessel, is like a live wire of the negative pole (as women are Left Column energy). Blood, being red and indicating the destruction of the life-giving egg, is merely a physical expression of the woman's metaphysical state. As such, as Rabbi Kaplan states, all sexual activity and physical contact with the opposite sex is forbidden (ibid., p. 40).

Sexual intercourse is a powerful means of drawing Light. The *Zohar* even defines that sex is a sixtieth of the (state of the) Garden of Eden; so imagine what the Garden of Eden must be like! But since sex is a means of drawing energy, it must be contained within a closed circuit and Restriction must be exerted. Since a woman in

Nidah is, energywise, like a live wire, a closed circuit is not possible; drawn energy cannot be contained. And since, as we said in chapter 3, there is no filament between blood (red, negative energy) and the sperm (white, positive energy), a separation of the man and woman is necessary.

Incidentally, this separation is claimed by many (if not most) observant couples of this precept to be the preventative antidote to waning passion. Aside from its metaphysical function, Rabbi Kaplan points out:

> The monthly separation tends to renew the sexual relationship and thus stabilize the marriage bond. It is interesting to note that among families who observe the *Niddah* laws, infidelity is virtually unknown, and the divorce rate is significantly below the normal level. In a pragmatic sense, we can say that the structure of the *Niddah* laws is a system that actually works (ibid., p. 45).

Once there is no more appearance of blood, the woman is still *Niddah* for seven more days. As seven stands for the seven *Sefirot* of *Ze'ir Anpin* and *Malkhut*, during these seven days, the woman is (metaphysically) building a new vessel. However, since negative energy (as all metaphysical energy) cannot be destroyed, but rather can only be displaced, the woman must actively rid this negativity from her body. This, incidentally, is part of the biological reason that the body cannot reabsorb the uteral lining or blood, since the shattering of this vessel is what creates the excess negativity. The physical aspect of this negativity must be rid of before the metaphysical aspect can be dealt with. If the body were to keep reabsorbing the physical effects of a broken vessel, not only would a woman never have the ability to rid herself of negative energy, but the negativity would accumulate with each month.

Once the physical aspect of the negativity (the blood) is displaced and a new vessel has been built, for the metaphysical aspect of the negativity to be displaced, the woman immerses herself in a *Mikvah*, a ritual bath. After an initial immersion, the procedure is to totally immerse the body under water in a fetal position so that one's feet do not touch the floor and one's hair is completely submerged. This is done seven times for each of the seven *Sefirot*. This removes the husks from the Lower Seven, which are the *Sefirot* onto which husks accumulate, and by doing so one creates a new, purified and complete vessel.

Water

The key to this purification process of husks is water. As Rabbi Kaplan explains:

> Water is the primary connection that we have with the Garden of Eden. The Talmud tells us that all the water in the world ultimately has its root in the river that emerged from Eden [per *Bechoros* 55a. See Malbim on Genesis 2:10, per p. 84] . . . Thus, when a person immerses in the waters of the *Mikvah*, he is also reestablishing a link with man's perfected state (ibid., p. 35).

There are a number of *Halakhic* requirements in building and maintaining the *Mikvah*.

> This also explains why the *Mikvah* must be linked to natural water. Water must come to the *Mikvah* from its natural state, and must not come in contact with man in his state of spiritual exile [i.e., the "exile" of the Vessel from the Endless] (ibid., pp. 35–36).

Change

The main spiritual concept of water is that of change and development (ibid., p. 66).

According to many authorities, the 'water' mentioned in the first days of creation refers to the fluid state of the universe [per *Yerushalmi, Chagigah* 2:1 (8b), *Mechilta* to Exodus 15:11, *Berashis Rabbah* 4:1, 5:2, *Sh'mos Rabbah* 15:22, *Midrash Tehillim* 104:7, from Psalm 104:3. Cf. Job 28:20, per p. 88]. Before creation, change did not exist (ibid., p. 63).

As the Midrash teaches us, man is a combination of "dust and water," permanence and change [per *Yerushalmi Shabbos* 2:6 (p. 20a), *Berashis Rabbah* 14:1, *Sh'mos Rabbah* 30:13, per p. 89]. As long as man is alive, this "water" is a most essential part of his being (ibid., p. 66).

Activity

In addition to the aspect of change, there is also the aspect of activity. From the *Tzimtzum*, the Endless Vessel mandated that we be active in our receipt of Light and initiate Its flow. In fact, in electricity, while the positive pole is that which gives off energy, the negative pole initiates the flow. This was determined by the Vessel. For the womb to remain in a "constant state of readiness" would connote passivity.

Moreover, in our linear realm there is no such thing as a spiritual level of suspended animation: One either progresses spiritually or one regresses. Progress is a function of fulfilling *Tikkun*. Thus progress entails a constant state of change, in which the individual actively works to eliminate Bread of Shame. As Rabbi Kaplan states:

> Man's ego represents the element of his permanence, and therefore, when he is totally immersed in the concept of change, his ego is nullified. Thus, when he emerges from the *Mikvah*, he is in a total state of renewal and rebirth (ibid., pp. 66–67).

This is especially important, since, as we will discuss in chapter 8, ego is connected with "Satanic Consciousness."

It is this continual cycle of change and renewal, in addition to a woman's natural nurturing tendency, that naturally keeps her in a spiritual state of balance. It is for this reason that women are exempt from most of the precepts defined by Torah—women simply do not need them! Precepts are a means of attaining balance, and since women are already naturally balanced, for them to perform precepts anyway would be like lighting a candle during the day, on a Los Angeles beach, in the middle of July to get light—quite unnecessary.

Men need all the precepts defined for them, just to attain the balance women already have. Thus, while women need to immerse themselves in a *Mikvah* once a month, men need to do so at least every three days. And thus all men, of all ages, need to cover their head, while women, until they are married, do not.

The reason married women cover their hair, however, is *not* to exert Resistance to attain balance as men; rather, the reason pertains to the function of marriage. In short, the function of marriage is to enable two individuals to work together spiritually to fulfill *Tikkun*. When each serves as a support and mirror for the other, the marriage succeeds and all of the wonderful appertanences of marriage come naturally: love, children, happiness, and so on.

A wedding, as we have already said, is a procedure we perform that engenders a metaphysical fusion of the souls of the bride and groom into one. This can be understood better with the help of an allusion to a cart and horse. Let's say the cart represents the soul and the horse, the body. The horse is merely the vehicle for the cart—the means—and it is from the cart level that the horse is guided. Before marriage, the man and woman are each a cart and horse. After marriage, they are one bigger cart with two horses. It is, therefore, very important for the husband and wife to work together, because should each horse go off in opposite directions, they would tear at the cart.

Let's switch the allusion to that of a TV set. Each individual comes into this world equipped, per the very structure of his body (as we discussed in chapter 5), to receive Light. We can say that each individual functions as an antenna and TV set together: The first part channels the energy and the latter receives the waves and implements them into a picture. Now, if a married couple is functioning as a single unit, that means there is one antenna and one TV set, not two of each working separately as the couple does before the wedding. Man, as we have said, functions as the *Ze'ir Anpin* or the channel (of the speaking kingdom), and thus he assumes the role of "antenna"; the woman, who functions as the *Malkhut* of the speaking kingdom, assumes the role of the TV set.

In this context we might also note that the Hebrew word for *husband* is *ba'al*, which literally translates back as "owner." The souls of the bride and groom are fused, per the wedding ceremony. Upon the consummation of the marriage, a part of the groom's soul enters the bride and she undergoes a total, metaphysical transformation. The man, then, becomes the owner of the Light for that couple. The woman no longer channels Light for herself.[2]

---

2. This author assumes that the source of history's corrupted notion that a married woman is her husband's "property" comes from a misunderstanding of the above Hebrew term: It is a reversal or reversed understanding of the

Hair, we know (from chapter 5), functions as an antenna for the body to draw Light. Thus men need to exert Restriction on their hair. For this reason, they don a head covering. A married woman, on the other hand, by marrying, turns over the entire role of antenna to her husband. She, therefore, covers all of her hair. It is for this reason that observant, married women either cover their hair with a scarf or wear a wig.

SOUL MATES

When one connects to the Endless, he necessarily connects to his soul mate, because he is connecting to wholeness, completion. And one's soul mate is the completion of one's soul. The energy of "soul mate" can be manifested by our "connecting" to live in just the right place or to work in just the right job, with just the right people, etcetera—the energy of totality, not just one aspect of our lives. When we break down the barriers that keep us from the Endless, we merit the Endless, which includes our soul mate.

The *Zohar* explains that it is specifically up to *men* to balance their karmic debts and achieve the level of consciousness to merit their soul mates. That is, it is up to the male to elevate himself spiritually to the level of his female counterpart. However, once a man has earned his right to be united with his soul mate, he almost literally draws her to him from wherever she is on the face of the globe and from whatever she is doing. This is what happened to two staff members of the Kabbalah Centre now located at the Centre's L. A. branch: Batya and Chaim.[3]

Batya had been interested in various spiritual doctrines for many years. A hairdresser from New York, she eventually began taking classes in Kabbalah, given by the Kabbalah Centre in Man-

---

physical aspect of the individual and his or her metaphysical essence. Human beings are not, or at least should not (let themselves) be "property" of others. According to Kabbalah, that the woman/wife should be property is anything but true. She is the one who implements her husband's energy or Light, while he is the one who channels It. The reader is directed to The Kabbalah Centre's advanced course on "Reincarnation" for more on the topic of marriage.

3. Express permission has been given to use the real, personal names of the people mentioned, for the purpose of this essay.

hattan. Chaim, her husband-to-be, began studying Kabbalah for a number of years and finally joined and began teaching Kabbalah at the Centre. Chaim had been sent by the Centre to Brazil for a while; but only a few weeks after returning to the United States and resuming his teaching in New York, Batya showed up in one of his classes as a student. As expected, a romance began, and about a year later they were married.

There are a number of telltale signs of a soulmate union. Sometimes soul mates resemble one another: They may look like they are related or have similar features about their countenance. Rabbi Berg notes another telltale sign of a soul mate union in his book *Reincarnation*: "[A] marriage where the participants simply cannot bear to be without each other *all* of the time is an exemplification of soulmates in the highest degree" (p. 162).

There is usually some final, physical obstacle or husk that challenges the connection to the Endless and thus to the two soul mate parties; but in the end, the obstacle is usually overcome, enabling the union. The possibilities of what this obstacle could be are countless; but it is basically anything that keeps the real essence of one or both of the partners from shining through so that they can "recognize" one another.

Such a barrier may be geographical distance or the fact that one is not yet in the profession that truly suits and brings out the attributes from which the person can be recognized by the soul mate. Or the obstacle might even be that one party is going through a "phase" or is in the middle of a relationship that is not the right match. A good example of this is the true story of the soul mate union between Leslie Parrish-Bach and Richard Bach, as told in Richard's heartwarming book *The Bridge Across Forever*.

Another example of an obstacle may be some kind of trait or habit that hides or prevents the other soul mate from being revealed to the other. A wonderful example of this was demonstrated by two other staff members of the Kabbalah Centre. Believe it or not, the obstacle that kept the now husband and wife from uniting was her name. If we recall from chapter 5, an individual's first name is his cosmic telephone number: it constitutes the code of that person's internal essence. When Nitza first started working at the Kabbalah Centre, she was single. She worked with a colleague named Abraham. They got along well, but there was no "chemistry" between the two for anything serious or intimate.

Now, many times Kabbalists come to a point in their life when they feel that they have, spiritually, changed so significantly that they no longer fit their given name from birth. When this happens, many go through a ritual of changing their Hebrew name. Such changes, though done usually once or at the most twice in a lifetime, are common among Kabbalists.

In the case of Nitzah, she had come to such a point in her life, and at the time of her renaming she and her colleagues did the proper meditations to connect her with her new name, Sarah, and with her namesake, Sarah the Matriarch. Strangely enough, not too long after this metaphysical change took place, a romance began to develop between the "new" Sarah and her old friend Abraham. What became clear was that this was a soul mate relationship. And for the real-life fairy-tale ending, they were subsequently married.

It might be pointed out that while it was Nitzah who needed to change her name, Kabbalah says that the change is only caused by the man's spiritual work: If Abraham had not progressed spiritually, the two could work together as colleagues or live right next door until the cows came home and they would never have known that they were soul mates. His progress caused her to change her name.

Sometimes one or both parties are not revealing their true selves, even if they do so unintentionally. But once a change is made to overcome this obstacle, the two are mated. Other times, however, the chronologically converse is the case: The man and woman are given the opportunity to meet each other, but a spiritual change must still take place for the union to succeed so they can be wed. One example of this may be conceived through the fictional union of Dmitri and Grushenka in Dostoyevsky's *The Brothers Karamazov*. Dmitri and Grushenka undergo tremendous spiritual growth immediately preceding and following their culminating meeting (when Dmitri goes to her at her old lover's home), in which they declare their love for one another; both engage in much soul-searching and taking stock of their lives, which signifies their regeneration and striving for redemption.

Soul mates also tend to feel some kind of psychic energy between themselves. This may be demonstrated by sensing when the other is physically close or somewhere particular. Many examples of such phenomena between soul mates have been dramatized during gothic or romantic periods in history through art. Two examples of this are found in Charlotte Brontë's *Jane Eyre*, between Jane Eyre and Mr. Rochester, and in the author's sister Emily Brontë's, *Wuthering Heights*, between Cathy and Heathcliff.

One other sign that two people are soul mates may be that they have complimentary zodiac signs. Complimentary zodiac signs are those directly opposite one another on the zodiac wheel, such as Cancer and Capricorn or Taurus and Scorpio or Virgo and Pisces and so on. Kabbalistic Astrology explains this "chemistry" of the dualities as based on the nature of the four elements and their relationships to one another. Earth signs, for example, corresponds best with and are enhanced by water signs, as fire signs corresponds best with and are enhanced by air signs.[4]

While corresponding zodiac signs may at times be a good indication of a soul mate relationship, it is less so now than in the past. Our souls today are very far along in their evolution, and there are no more new souls on this earth. Due to our individual karmic debts, our soul mate may not have a corresponding zodiac sign. And this lack of correlation may very well be the final obstacle needed to be overcome to enable the soul mate union. What this means is that one may possess a particular trait (*Tikkun*), dictated by that person's zodiac sign, but that is a hindrance to the workings of the soul mate relationship. That undesirable trait would need to be worked out for the relationship to succeed.

The ultimate purpose of the union of soul mates is for spiritual reasons: to assist each other fulfill *Tikkun* and to reveal more Light in the world. The energy that can be generated from the union of soul mates is tremendous—it is the sense of power people feel when they are "whole" and fulfilled. This completion of the self and the circuitry of energy that is set in motion enables the two, as a couple, to do and achieve great, spiritual heights. One manifestation of this tremendous energy (of the union) is how the union brings out the best of the two—the highest self of each partner.

---

4. For more on Kabbalistic Astrology, the reader is directed to Rabbi Berg's *Astrology: The Star Connection* and *Time Zones*. The Kabbalah Centre also offers an entire advanced course on Kabbalistic Astrology.

However, if soul mates do not strive to fulfill this spiritual objective and purpose, their union will inevitably fail. The classic dramatized example of such a failed soul mate union is the relationship of Cathy and Heathcliff in Emily Brontë's enduring novel, *Wuthering Heights*. This couple, as noted before, demonstrates many of the typical tell-tale signs of soul mates; but to the heartbreak of their readers, they never actually unite in marriage. This is because they use their energies—the tremendous energy brought on by such a union—in a negative way: They work to avenge and purposely destroy the lives of other people. Of course, as the author shows us, the forces of good outdo those of evil, as the avengees in the end happily fulfill their lives and inadvertently avenge the avengers.

On the other hand, a classic example of a successful soul mate union, the antithesis of the fictional tale told in *Wuthering Heights*, is a coupling recounted in *Jane Eyre* by Emily's sister, Charlotte Brontë. In this novel, Mr. Rochester and Jane also demonstrate many of the tell-tale signs of being soul mates, and to the reader's delight, they do marry and live happily ever after. This is because the two characters utilize their individual energies and the powerful energy generated from being united as soul mates in a very positive and spiritual way. In this instance, the energy generated by the soul mate union is shown to be so strong that it shatters the almost-incapacitating obstacles that stand in their way.

It is important to remember that soul mates are mirror images of each other. If the couple conscientiously works together to grow spiritually, then this can truly be a match made in heaven, ensuring a happy and successful marriage. Rabbi Berg defines marriage as "the opportunity for two imperfect individuals to help each other discharge their respective *tikune* [karmic] debts and advance their spiritual understanding" (Berg's *Reincarnation*, p. 101).

But a lack of this consciousness can make it seem like a match made in hell. Imagine someone who has a whole slew of hang-ups and actually wants to meet someone who is stable, clearheaded and strong. Someone who is a mirror image would most likely make that person miserable. One's soul mate may also be preoccupied with the difficulties of balancing karmic debts, which is especially trying when one is dragged through them without the spiritual consciousness of *why* they exist. In such a case, it is probably far preferable to link up with someone with whom one has good chemistry and get along. That is, sometimes "close but no cigar" may actually be better than the cigar itself!

In fact, as Kabbalah explains, if one is already married, then the person that one is married to is the *most suitable* partner for his current correction (*Tikkun*) purposes; even one's own soul mate would not be more suitable. It is mainly for this reason that Kabbalists do not advocate impetuously filing for divorce if one is already married, just to rush off in search of the "real" soul mate. Based on the cosmic laws of karma and reincarnation, Rabbi Berg points out that "no marriage is a result of chance and no marriage is begun on a clean slate. Every marriage is but an episode in a series of stories begun long ago in which the parties have been related to each other in previous lives" (ibid., p. 101).

Moreover, couples who are not soul mates may have a karmic chemistry very close to that of soul mates. And such a relationship can also reach tremendous heights. However, regardless of what kind of relationship one is in—soul mate or not—the success of the relationship depends to a great extent on how the couple grows together. In fact, if the couple works to connect to the Endless, then they, together as a couple, will be metaphysically connected to their soul mates. Therefore, it would be preferable for a couple who are not soul mates, but who consciously and conscientiously strive to grow together and who use their union in a positive way, to unite than for a union of a soul mate couple who does not strive for growth or for positivity. The first would be successful and fulfilling, while the latter would inevitably fail. For some people in the first group, the search is less one for the soul mate than it is for a means to enhance an already good union.

Our generation today is the same generation as that of the Golden Calf episode. When the Israelites were waiting for Moses to descend from Mount Sinai, they were already feeling the fulfillment of the Light. This generation is known as *Dor haDe'ah*, "the Generation of Knowledge." And knowledge denotes connection to the Light. The men, who were channeling the Light, knew they needed to implement the Light they were receiving. But instead of exerting Resistance and waiting for Moses to come down, they decided to create a physical vessel that would implement their energy. Thus the Golden Calf.

It is explained that the men ran and willingly gave up their gold[5] for the purpose of the idol; but the women did not. The women refused to give up their gold, but were forced to do so by the men—who are said to have even ripped gold off the women's bodies. The women, therefore, were not involved in creating this tremendous short circuit—a (negative) short circuit as big as the revelation of all of the Light through the Torah was on a positive level.

This is how kabbalists explain the (relatively) recent rise of the feminist movement. These are the women's souls that are returning from the *Dor haDe'ah* and who are still angry at their male counterparts for not fulfilling their spiritual function. It is from a feeling of frustration that they are not receiving their due Light from their men, who are supposed to channel It to them.[6]

Within this context, Rabbi Berg notes:

> When women return, karmic debt balanced, it is usually to aid a man who is struggling to balance his [per the Ari's *Gate of Reincarnation*, p. 35]. The aid is not always gentle. A man who has repeatedly failed to achieve soul correction may be given a woman who will make his life anything but pleasant. This would imply that when divorce and remarriage—often several times—occur, none of those unions are wasted. Every one of them was meant to be for the sake of whatever virtue a man must learn if it be one he will learn only through marriage [per ibid., pp. 32–33] (Rabbi Berg's *Reincarnation*, pp. 60–61).

As such, women are taking a firmer grip of the reins today in all areas of life; they are doing so to push their male counterparts to achieve *Tikkun*.

---

5. There is a lot of discussion in the Bible about metals, especially with regard to building the Holy Ark. Suffice it to say, for the purpose of this discussion, that gold is the metal that corresponds to the Left Column. Thus gold has the ability to draw and contain energy.

6. Refer to The Kabbalah Centre's casssette/lesson no. 12 of the Kabbalah Beginners Course and to the recorded lecture "The Woman's Place in Kabbalah."

8

Satan and the Messiah

This book began by saying, "Life seems to have become increasingly complex and difficult." The key word here is *seems*. Light is a constant; It does not change, and thus It does not "become" anything. Only the Vessel changes. Since the revelation of Light in our realm depends solely on the Vessel, it is, therefore, the *Vessel* that has made things appear complex and difficult, even painful.

Darkness, as we have said, is not an entity in itself; darkness is merely a lack of Light. But what is lacking is not Light (again, since Light is a constant), but rather a *sufficient Vessel* is lacking with which to contain the Light. Crime and violence, war and hatred, sickness and disease, and depression and anxiety are all physical expressions of metaphysical darkness. They express a lack of fulfillment, which comes from the Light.

More specifically, darkness was the product of the Endless Vessel's Restriction in the Third Aspect of Creation. The Light enabled an empty space (in eternal timelessness and spacelessness), because it is this energy of lack that gives the Vessel free will. And it is only through free will that the Thought of Creation can be implemented.

In the Language of the Branches, this darkness is called Satan. Satan is not a businessman who has the capacity or inclination to draw up written contracts or pacts with human beings. Satan is a state or level of consciousness. Thus, there are those, like self-proclaimed satanists, who intentionally draw on this energy. But there are also those who fall into its trap inadvertently.

To be sure, Dr. Faustus is a very intriguing and mysterious figure, who arouses our imagination and inner, gothic, fascination. But such a figure does not exist. Satan is a purely metaphysical energy. However, it can and does express itself, as do all metaphysical energies in our physical world in various ways. As such, Satan basically comes in two main flavors: doubt and ego.

DOUBT

The epitome of the *opposite* of doubt is Nakhshon, the head of the tribe of Judah. According to the Talmud, when the Israelites were at the shore of the Red Sea with the Egyptians approaching fast from behind, there was a hiatus between when Moses had established the metaphysical forces to part the sea and when the sea actually parted. To the individual who is connected to the Tree of Life, once something is established metaphysically, the physical is rendered a total illusion. Moses declared that the sea was split; but the Israelites, who were connected to the illusory realm, only saw the water and hesitated. Nakhshon, on the other hand, jumped right into the sea and landed safely on dry ground.

Doubt is connected to the effect of metaphysical processes, as opposed to their causal level. If one were to totally destroy the roots of, say, a large ominous tree, the trunk and branches could remain upright for some time, but the individual would no longer be affected by what was apparent above ground, because the roots are what determine the tree's existence. The causal level is always concealed— as are the roots of a tree. The individual "connected" to the truth of the roots' state, would not fear the tree. The tree may *appear* to be well and strong, but it would only be a matter of time before the whole thing toppled over. And what is time but an illusion!

With regard to the biblical passage on Jacob's ladder (Genesis chapter 28, section 7), Rabbi Lawrence Kushner tells that

> Rabbi Shmuel bar Nachmani taught that the Holy One showed Jacob the prince of Babylonia ascending seventy rungs [years]; the prince of Persia ascending fifty-two rungs; the prince of Greece ascending one-hundred-and-eight

rungs; and the prince of Rome ascending more than Jacob could count. When he saw this, Jacob became frightened and asked: "Is it possible that Rome will never come down?"

The Holy One replied by quoting Scripture, "Don't be afraid, O Jacob, My servant, for even if he ascends all the way to the top and sits besides Me, I will bring him down from there. . . ."

Rabbi Meir, a contemporary of Nachmani, also taught that the Holy One quoted the same verse to Jacob, "Don't be afraid, O Jacob, My servant, if you ascend the ladder, you will never go down." But Jacob did not believe God and did not ascend. Whereupon the Holy One said to him: "If only you had believed and come up, you never would have come down. Now, however, since you did not believe and did not come up, your children will be enslaved by these four empires" (*God was in this Place and I, i did not know*, pp. 108–109).

AMaLeK = 240 = Doubt (SaFeK)

In Exodus chapter 17 we get a prime example of doubt. Here Moses names a certain place in the desert "Massah and Meribah,[1] because of the quarreling of the children of Israel, and because they tried the Lord, saying: Is the Lord among us, or not?" (Exodus 17:7). In the very next verse we are told that "Then came *Amalek*, and fought with Israel" (Exodus 17:8). *Amalek*, in Kabbalah, is less a name than it is a concept. *Amalek* means doubt—doubt of God.

A very peculiar military tactic then seems to unfold in the above passage:

And it came to pass, when Moses held up his hand, that Israel prevailed: and when he let down his hand that *Amalek* prevailed (Exodus 17:11).

If Moses' hand were the causative factor of Israel's win or loss, wouldn't it be logical for him to keep his hand up, instead of what he appears to be doing—playing? One can be sure that Moses was not teasing or getting his kicks at the expense of his people. The issue is really one of cause and effect.

_____

1. Which literally means *Trying and Quarrel* in Hebrew.

Moses' hand, holding "the staff of God" (Exodus 17:9), served as a kind of metaphysical barometer. His hand merely indicated the effect of the Israelites' spiritual level as they battled with doubt. When the Jews raised their consciousness level to that of the Tree of Life, the *upper* realm, Moses' hand went up. When the Jews' consciousness fell to the level of the Tree of Knowledge of Good and Evil, the *lower* realm and into doubt of God, Moses' hand went down. Thus is the destructive effect of doubt when *we let it prevail*.

Kabbalah explains that *Amalek*, the energy of doubt, has been embodied by various nations or their representatives throughout history until this very day, from the Persian Haman of the Book of Esther to Adolf Hitler to Saddam Hussein. The uncertainty of God (the Light) that we harbor inside ourselves is what Rabbi Berg defines as "Satanic Consciousness."[2] It is this energy that Jews work (spiritually) to destroy from within themselves on the holiday (which Kabbalah defines holiday as a "cosmic event") of Purim. Satanic consciousness is robotic consciousness: it means we have opted to connect to the Tree of Knowledge of Good and Evil level, to be swayed like a pawn by destiny.

Doubt is also accompanied by worry. It is one thing to be concerned; but it is another to worry. People only worry when they do not believe in the Light, or however they wish to call It. If one does the best that he can, and things work out—it was meant to be. But if one does the best job possible and things still do not work out—it was not meant to be. Concern without worry means we accept that the Light really knows what is best. Worry implies that we believe we are the ones ultimately in control. But, as vessels, we can never be the source of Light. Moreover, our generation has also learned the hard way the tremendous toll entailed from worry: the mental and physical effects of worry, literally, create for the worrier an existence of Hell.

EGO

The other tempting flavor of Satan actually comes in a number of luscious varieties. Ego is one. Ego is very much like doubt.

---

2. "How To Bring Moshiach To Our Lives." (recorded lecture) The Kabbalah Centre. NY

Ego says, "What happens to me is not due or thanks to the Light, but rather all thanks to my tremendous I.Q. or because I am so great." Ego means that the individual has become so engrossed in himself, that proportions as they really are on the macro level, are distorted. To a certain extent, Rabbi Kushner defines ego when he writes:

> It is taught in the name of Menachem Mendl: "The great hazard is that one will be filled with himself or herself, with conceit, with self-satisfaction, feelings which are nothing less than idol-worship. . . ." The first idol, and the one that makes us all idolaters, is not a statue, but the ego. I am not referring to that imaginary dimension of the psyche postulated by Freud, also called ego, but rather to a way of acting that says, "I judge us [myself and the other] both, and I am more important than you." Ego is not thinking you're a talented or a good person. That is only self-confidence, or, in extreme cases, ordinary conceit. Ego is arrogance. It is thinking that you are better than someone else. It is making yourself big in the presence, and at the expense, of someone else (*God was in this Place and I, i did not know*, p. 46).

Rabbi Kushner simulates a discussion between Jacob the Patriarch and Menachem Mendl of Kotzk [Polish Hassidic thinker, 1787–1859]. Jacob finally realizes his ego problem and tells the Kotzker: "'God was here all along, and the reason I didn't know it is because I was too busy paying attention to myself'" (p. 48). That is, the Vessel "forgets" that all it is is an empty Desire to Receive. He can receive Light, but only if he earns it. And even then, it is still—and always—the Light Who is dishing, never the Vessel.

It is for this reason, as Rabbi Kaplan explains, that in kabbalistic meditation, "[o]ne of the purposes of meditation is to help banish the ego. This is often difficult in the modern world" (*Jewish Meditation*, p. 96). Although one may perceive that this would be counterproductive in the modern world, as Rabbi Kaplan continues:

> The method of conversing with God does not have this drawback. It is true that, like other forms of meditation, this method can help a person overcome the ego. Nevertheless,

this is a method that replaces the ego with something stronger [i.e., God]. . . . Therefore, the goal is to attain and maintain a balance (ibid., pp. 96–97).

An inflated ego is more than just a social annoyance. It is deadly. The behavior, and thus the energy, of the owner of an inflated ego, is just the opposite of "Love thy neighbor as thyself." The effect is inevitably a short circuit. And that energy, per the quantum theory, generates out into the entire cosmos. As we have seen from the Desire to Receive for the Self Alone of the generation of Noah and Atlantis, egoism generates negativity to such an extent that it *literally* destroys the world. As Sogyal Rinpoche writes in his book *The Tibetan Book of Living and Dying,*

> Our society is dedicated almost entirely to the celebration of ego, with all its sad fantasies about success and power, and it celebrates those very forces of greed and ignorance that are destroying the planet (p. 128).

Thus the prophet Michah offers sound metaphysical advice when he says: "Oh, man, God has told what is good and what God demands of you—only that you act justly, love goodness and walk humbly with your God" (Michah 6:8).[3] Humility is merely the Vessel acknowledging its actual function and proportion in the universe.

One aspect of ego, which is another expression of the negative energy of Satan, is reversal. An inflated ego perceives a reversal of Light and Vessel. Ego says, "It's *me*, wonderful *me*, and all thanks to *my* doing," reversing, or ignoring, the Light's prime function in the cosmos and the individual's own reason for existing in the first place. But, again, the Vessel, in and of itself, has no Light. So that instead of facing toward the Light, when one faces the opposite direction, into the Light's shadow, where there is a lack of Light, one can only get darkness. In fact, "what occultists use to write their personal prayers and incantations to summon the demons" is literally called a "Book of Shadows."[4]

---

3. Dennis Prager regards this verse as the sum of Ethical Monotheism, and as such, he has named his organization "The Michah Center."

4. Taken from Larry Kahaner's *Cults That Kill*, p. 24. Bob Larson, on the other hand, in his book *Satanism: The Seduction of America's Youth*, defines

Satanism, and to a certain extent, pagan occult practices in general, basically strive to keep the individual from attaining the level of consciousness of the Tree of Life. It either does this by connecting one to doubt, Satan's first flavor, or it reverses the "signs" the individual receives so that the direction the individual takes misleadingly goes in the very opposite direction of what is beneficial to him. This is why satanists write words and prayers backward.

> Satanism advocates practising a modification of the Golden Rule. Our interpretation of this rule is: 'Do unto others as they do unto you.' This comment from *The Satanic Bible* by Anton Szandor LaVey, founder of the Church of Satan in San Francisco, neatly illustrates the principle on which Satanism is based. Things which are backwards, upside down, the wrong way round, are symbolically connected with the Devil (*Man, Myth & Magic*, p. 2477).

The most obvious demonstration of reversal on a large scale was performed by Adolf Hitler through his Nazi doctrine. Dusty Sklar and Joseph Carr both show how Hitler and some of his top Nazis were occult enthusiasts well before Hitler rose to power. Hitler acted to reverse the Catholic ideas by which he was raised. "Hitler parodied Jesus . . . Hitler said: 'Whoever proclaims his allegience to *me* is by this very proclamation and by the manner in which it is made, one of the chosen'" (*Gods and Beasts*, p. 55). In fact, ringing a similar tune as George Orwell's *1984*:

> In many households, one's offspring became one's worst enemy. It was not at all uncommon for children to denounce their parents as traitors to the state. . . . *Children worshipped the Fuhrer as a god* (*Gods and Beasts*, p. 111, emphasis added).

Joseph Carr notes, "After his ascension to power in 1933, Hitler required German school children to recite a prayer that gave Hitler [Jesus'] place;"[5] "The Ministry of Propaganda and Enlightment . . .

"Book of Shadows" as simply a book of "rituals hand-copied by each individual witch" (p. 168).

5. Per Robert G. L. Waite's *The Psychopathic God—Adolf Hitler*. New York: Basic Books, 1977.

explicitly taught German school children that Adolf Hitler was on a parallel with Jesus" (*The Twisted Cross*, p. 38); and "The Nazis . . . perverted the Christian message with an obscene paraphrase of the Lord's Prayer" [but to Hitler] (ibid., p. 39).

Hitler's swastika is another major demonstration of satanic reversal. As Carr explains in his book, many cultures held the sinistrogyrate swastika as a symbol of goodness, for example by the American Indians and the Baal worship (*The Twisted Cross*, p. 101); it is also "related to the concept of *Tao* from China," as it was attached to "gnostic-Christian alchemists of the Middle Ages" (ibid., p. 102).

Most cultures favored the leftward rotating sinistrogyrate[6] swastika because . . . it rotates with the motions of the sun; hence the concepts of goodness and rightness are associated with the symbol. The dextrogyrate swastika used by the Nazis, on the other hand, almost universally represents evil and a condition of being out of harmony with the laws of the universe. . . . Almost as soon as he became leader of the Nazi party (1920) Hitler demanded that the group have a special symbol, and a flag with recognition power and appeal. A number of designs were presented to him, but all were initially rejected. Finally, one design was successful. . . . Doctor Friedrich Krohn produced a design that featured the sinistrogyrate swastika circumscribed with a white circle resting on a blood-red background. The swastika used by Krohn symbolized goodness, rightness with nature and oneness with the forces of good. Hitler accepted the design, but he *reversed the swastika to the evil dextrogyrate form*. Hitler intentionally reversed the swastika to the form that represents evil, darkness and black magic (ibid., pp. 102–103 [italics in original]).

The satanic essence of Nazism reversed the celebration of life, so characteristic of Judaism or Judeo–Christian doctrine, to that of death. This demonstration of reversal is indicative in their practice of human sacrifice. One need only look throughout history to

---

6. That is, rotating so that right is over left or the Desire to Share dominates the Desire to Receive.

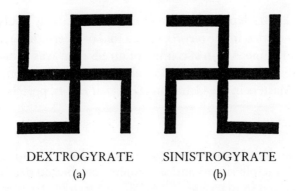

DEXTROGYRATE   SINISTROGYRATE
(a)   (b)

see that, as a metaphysical rule, where human sacrifices have been performed, there has always been an extreme imbalance of energy—so much so that it many times completely destoys or burns out its practitioners.

Carr inquires:

Why was Hitler so gleeful over the deaths of thousands of loyal men of the *SS-Liebstandarte Adolf Hitler* [in Russia, by the Russian forces]? . . . [Because] it was a *ritual sacrifice*! Satanic rituals are supposedly most effective when a human sacrifice is involved, and Hitler had the power to offer thousands of human sacrifices to his "god" (ibid., pp. 85–86).

This "god," as Carr explains, was Woton, the old teutonic god of destruction (ibid., p. 71). This explains, as Carr points out, Hitler's seemingly irrational exclamation at the "news that the *SS-Liebstandarte Adolf Hitler* was being decimated" of: "'Good! Casualties can never be too high!'" (ibid., p. 83). In short:

The satanic nature of the Holocaust is seen in the single fact that the slaughtering of Jews took precedence over everything else . . . most pressing needs of the war came second (ibid., pp. 14–15).

And thus the only industry a regime of death could build, as they did in fact build, would be a death industry.

Dusty Sklar informs us that a professor friend of C. Scott Littleton, a professor of anthropology at Occidental College in California, claims he saw original Nazi depositions taken for the Nuremberg Trials, but never included in the record, which told of a periodic sacrifice wherein a fine Aryan specimen of an SS man was beheaded and the severed head made a vehicle for communion with Secret Masters in the Caucasus (*Gods and Beasts*, pp. 99–100).

In fact

Hitler and his Nazis were never very good at celebrating life. Their principle rituals and sacraments celebrated death and dying. Even in marriage . . . Adolf and Eva Hitler consummated their marriage with cyanide (p. 54).

Moreover, Hitler

had arranged his affairs so that even his suicide should be a sacrificial tribute to the Powers of Darkness. April 30 . . . is perhaps the most important date in the whole calendar of Satanism (Sklar's *Gods and Beasts*, p. 81).

Sardonically, though, it seems that there was one cosmic law the Nazis would not deny nor defy:

The waiting SS officers were making a fatal selection: those who were sent to the *right* would live a little while longer as slaves in one of Auschwitz' factories or work camps; those who were sent to the *left* were condemned to die immediately in one of Auschwitz's gas chambers. To the *right* meant life, to the *left* meant death (*The Twisted Cross*, p. 175, emphasis added).

To the followers of Hitler's Nazism, "[t]he idea of war itself had become beautiful. It was to give people back their lives. 'Peace,' as someone pointed out, 'had become insupportable'" (Sklar, p. 6). This is yet a further indication of satanic essence: War and peace are reversed and so is one's sense of free will. When Sklar points out that "[t]he state, assuming more and more control, seemed bent on crushing individuality" (p. 8), this excedes the "normal" evil nature of virulent Nationalism.[7]

---

7. Dennis Prager points out, in his essay "The Case For Ethical Monotheism," that Fascism, Nazism, and Communism, where "the state became an end

"As one young Nazi put it just before World War II, 'We Germans are so happy. We are free of freedom'" (*Gods and Beasts*, p. 152).

> Hitler's antidote to democracy: the restoration of insurmountable barriers between two breeds of people, as he presumed to have existed in ancient great civilizations. Only Germans would have rights. Hitler had come to free them from "the dirty and degrading chimera called conscience and morality, and from the demands of a freedom and personal independence which only a very few can bear." They would be beyond good and evil. He would liberate them from "*the burden of free will.*" He opposed . . . the significance "of the individual soul and of personal responsibility." Judging from Hitler's popularity, the suffering masses apparently found relief in this message (ibid., p. 58, emphasis added).

Every individual is responsible for his own spiritual work. No one can do it for him. Moses could not do it for the Israelites over three thousand years ago, and no religious, spiritual, or political leader can do it for us today. The only means that we have to complete our *Tikkun* and eliminate Bread of Shame is to exert our own individual free will.

It is only when one deliberately relinquishes his free will that he can commit so destructive a short circuit, for the very sake of causing a short circuit: evil for evil's sake.

> A British soldier, writing home [about Nazism], remarked: "It is not even organized terrorism, but cruelty and bestiality practised *for its own sake*, the worst offenders being German boys between the ages of 16 and 18" (ibid., p. 112, emphasis added).

In fact,

> Hitler had promised . . . that Germany would never surrender again. If she could not conquer her enemies, she would drag them down to destruction with her. Once Hitler was

---

in itself" (p. 15), is an example of when values "become ends in themselves" and thus "divert people's attention from good and evil, and then allow evil" (p. 11).

convinced that Germany could not be saved, he made good his promise. When the American and Russian troops were outside of Berlin, Hitler ordered all food and clothing stores, all bridges and dams, all military, industrial, transportation, and communication facilities in the whole country destroyed. Any Germans who stood in the way were to be killed (ibid., p. 80).

Interestingly, Herman Melville offers profound insight into Hitler's national suicide when he writes in *Moby Dick*, at the end of the story, as the Pequod is almost sunk:

A sky-hawk that tauntingly had followed the main-trunk downwards from its natural home among the stars, pecking at the flag . . . this bird now chanced to intercept its broad fluttering wing between the hammer and the wood; and simultaneously feeling that etherial thrill, the submerged savage beneath, in his death-gasp, kept his hammer frozen there; and so *the bird of heaven*, with archangelic shrieks, and his imperial beak thrust upwards, and his whole captive form folded in the flag of Ahab, went down with his ship, which, *like Satan, would not sink to hell till she had dragged a living part of heaven along with her*, and helmeted herself with it (pp. 821–822, emphasis added).

Of course, the two main, absurd reversals that the Nazis thrived on were the (or *their*) concepts of holy and racism. The main contributors to Hitler's doctrine were the teachings of "[t]wo Austrain occultists, Jorg Lanz von Liebenfels and Guido von List" (Sklar, p. 5). List studied

the origins of Jewish mysticism [that] had taught him the importance of imbuing a people with a Messianic hope. . . . List gave the Germans, in effect, an opportunity to become competitors of the Jews for the honor of "chosen people" (ibid., p. 13).

Sklar also gives evidence that Hitler was influenced by Lanz's Ariosophy by quoting a passage from *Mein Kampf*, in which Hitler writes:

"By defending myself against the Jew, I am fighting for the handiwork of the Lord. . . . This Jewification of our spiritual life . . . will sooner or later destroy our entire offspring. . . ." (ibid., p. 21).

As Sklar sums up, the Nazis were at "a holy war against the enemies: Freemasons, liberals, and Jews" (p. 108). The Nazi reversal became so reversed in itself that they persecuted the Jew because they regarded him as "Satan in disguise" (Sklar, p. 95), while the Nazis themselves were satanists!

Moreover, as Joseph Carr points out, "To the Nazi, the prime capital crime of the Jewish people was 'race defilement,' which meant intermingling of blood lines" (p. 44). Blood, race, the body. What the Nazis reversed was the significance of the body vis-à-vis the soul. It is hard to believe that groups espousing white supremacy still exist, which are determined to wipe out what they call the "mud races." This notion is erroneous for two main reasons: (1) race refers to the body and not to the real essence of a person, which is always his soul; and (2) with regard to the word "mud," per Genesis 3:19, all men go from dust to dust: "for dust art [man], and unto dust shalt [man] return."

All of our bodies, being a Desire to Receive and of the physical realm, come from and return to the element of the Desire to Receive, Mother Earth. But Satan tries to reverse our consciousness so that we connect to the energy intelligence of the body— the Desire for the Self Alone, Evil—and not to the soul. In fact, the Nazis' version of this reversal became so ridiculous that, as Sklar points out:

To the discerning eye, [Heinrich Himmler] insisted, the uninterrupted script of the Northmen of the Dark Ages resembled Japanese ideograms. This was evidence that the Japanese, too, were Aryans (*Gods and Beasts*, p. 89).

But *all* forms of racism are satanic.

And yet, racism is only one form of such (satanic) reversal of body and soul. Any practice that raises the material and the body over the importance of the soul or the spiritual, is destructive. On the grand level, such a reversal constitutes idolatry of ancient Greek proportions. And idolatry is a form of fragmentation (soon to be discussed): fragmentation of the totality and unity of the Light. Healthy care and maintenance of the body is important—it is our soul's vessel; yet, idolatry is rendered when any focus on the body is overdone. Diet and exercise are examples of practices that, for all intents and purposes, have become "idolatrous religions" in our modern society.

Probably the worse problem with playing with Satan is that Satan is a double agent. Satan is an energy which is the opposite of positivity. Thus Satan shares with no one.

It soon became apparent to Hitler that the satanic "providence" that he had followed most of his adult life was now toying with him like a cat toys with a mouse before the kill. Perhaps he finally realized that his "providence" was not God, but Satan. It was only seventeen days after hearing of Roosevelt's death that Hitler ended his own life (*The Twisted Cross*, p. 67).

Try as he might, the satanist can not relinquish his place in God's Thought of Creation. One might look at one Nazi's death-bed confession as proof that the abuser of the cosmic system eventually pays (or begins to!) for his abuse:

Albrecht Haushofer participated in a coup d'etat against Hitler on July 20, 1944. The Fuhrer escaped death. Karl Haushofer was sent to Dachau, Albrecht to Moabite prison. Before his execution, Albrecht composed eighty sonnets. . . . Sonnet 39 is called 'Guilt':
"I should have seen my duty sooner and should have dared with louder voice to name as evil the thing my judgment knew as evil but held too long unspoken . . . I deceived my own conscience. I lied to myself and others. I early understood the whole sequence of the misery to come' (Sklar's *Gods and Beasts*, pp. 71–72).

In fact, to date, no occult group that has focused only on it-self and has generated negativity to such an extent has ever flour-ished, or even survived. The negativity eventually burns out the Direct Light drawer. On the large scale, there are the generations before the Deluge, including Atlantis, that completely destroyed themselves to the point of zero continuity. And there are those whose continuity was rendered close to nil, as were the powers of ancient Egypt. One might even lump into the last category the civilizations of ancient Rome, the Aztecs, the Mayans, and the Native Americans.[8]

On the smaller scale, we can look at occult leaders in the near history to see just what all their "powers" got them. Aleister Crowley, for example (born in England in 1875), "became the most infamous black magician of all time. . . . [He] believed quite literally that he was the Beast of Revelation and declared open revolt against God. . . . He was eventually expelled from the Hermetic Order [of the Golden Dawn] after gaining a reputation for breaking every moral law—from fornication to murder" (Larson's *Satanism*, p. 151). "Toward the end of his life, Crowley was unable to communicate coherently. He died a poverty-stricken drug addict in 1947 (ibid., p. 153).

With regard to Madame Helena Petrovna Blavatsky, "a Russian expatriate countess who organized The Theosophical Society in New York in 1875" (Sklar, p. 11),

Eventually the prestigious Society of Psychical Research in Britain investigated Blavatsky's claims and found them wanting. She was accused of being a magician, hypnotist, and charlatan. Helena Petrovna Blavatsky died in disgrace as a lonely, obese, miserably sick woman (Larson, p. 155).

We might even look at the former Soviet Union, which, in its ardent endeavor to win the Cold War, engaged in a systematic and "scientific" abuse of metaphysical forces. Like all other individuals or nations who have ever played with black magic, the Soviets eventually burned and self-destroyed. One of the richest countries in natural resources could no longer even

---

8. These groups would be more of the "close to nil" category, despite Ronald Wright's insistance, as he purports in his book, *Stolen Continents: The Americas Through Indian Eyes Since 1492*, that the civilizations of the Mayans, Aztecs, Incas, and Native Americans are on the up-and-up and will yet see a full rebirth.

reed its own people. When the laws of nature are violated, nature prosecutes.

There can be no fulfillment from the shadow or from darkness—only the temporary illusion of fulfillment, as darkness itself is an illusion.

Is it any wonder, then, that in satanic groups "[f]ollowers are held in the group by drugs, mind control, intimidation, and the cult of confession" (Kahaner's *Cults That Kill*, p. 89). Or, as Larson puts it, Satanic cults hold "[h]orrifying ceremonies designed to instill terror, guilt, and silence" (*Satanism*, p. 23).

> Drugs and Satanism have been uniquely joined for centuries. Archaeologists note that pre-Columbian cultures forged a link between sadism, terrorism, and human sacrifice by taking drugs. The Meso-American folk religions of the Mayas and Aztecs required human sacrifices and used drugs to induce apathy in the victims. . . . Drugs render the devil's devotees addictively dependent and less likely to abandon their allegiance to Satan. Mind-altering substances, combined with the charismatic control of an influencial cult leader, trap Satanists, leaving them no way out. Ironically, the cult leader seldom uses drugs. . . . By staying sober, he can better manipulate the group (Larson, pp. 87–88).

But what destroys the satanist is not the drugs—what kills them is Satan himself. In his lesson on the Torah portion of *Shoftim* (Judges), Rabbi Berg explains that we all have Satan in us. Satan is the accumulation of all of our own negative energy intelligence in the form of *thoughts* that subsequently become manifest. And it is Satan who takes us to court—the "court" discussed in this portion of the Bible is of the upper realm—and testifies against us.

The real matter in court is not decided on the physical level. When things happen on the physical level, they actually began long before when our thoughts determined our actions. Therefore, when our matters on the upper, causal level are straightened out, our matters on the lower, corporeal level are necessarily straightened out as well. To our society, which has become ridiculously litigious, this sounds an important message.

FRAGMENTATION

The other dangerously delicious variety of Satan is fragmentation. Satan is the result of what is called *Makhloket LeShem Shamayim*, "Dispute In the Name of Heaven."[9] When one thinks that only he is right and the other, or all others are wrong, this is Satan, and thus the individual, regardless of what he has to say, is wrong.

In the book of Numbers chapter 16, the Bible tells of a guy named Korakh. Korakh basically accosts Moses and Aaron (Moses' brother) and says that he, Korakh, wants to be the high priest instead of Aaron and basically accuses Moses of nepotism. The chapter begins: "And Korakh, the son of Yitzher, the son of Kehat, the son of Levi, took; and Datan and Aviram, the son of Eliav and On, the son of Pelet, the son of Reuven: And they rose up before Moses" (Numbers 16:1–2). The *Zohar* points out that the first verse lacks proper grammatical sense. The word "took" (in Hebrew as in English) is a "transitive verb," meaning that it "requires an object to complete its meaning."[10]

The first verse, which basically begins "And Korakh . . . took," lacks a necessary object. For this reason, many translations read "Now Korakh . . . took [a bold step], together with Datan . . ." (sic), or "And Korakh . . . took men . . ." But this is not how the original text reads. The *Zohar* then explains what it questions that what Korakh took was "his bad advice to himself." That is, Korakh took his own point of view. And anyone that agreed with him was right in his eyes, and anyone that disagreed with him, according to him, was wrong.

Moses then tries to talk to Korakh and his followers to negotiate and to try to resolve the dispute. But Korakh refuses to reconcile his differences. God then tells Moses and Aaron to "separate [them]selves from the midst of [Korakh]'s congregation" (Numbers 16:21). With this, a nominal or symbolic separation of the camps is made, because, as God is basically telling Moses and Aaron, Korakh, with his negative energy of fragmentation, is inevitably going to cause an earthquake. And, in fact,

---

9. Rabbi Berg discusses this at length in his recorded lesson on the portion of "*Korach-Chukat*."

10. *Harbrace College Handbook*, 10th ed., p. 526.

it came to pass . . . that the ground that was under [Korakh and his followers] was cloven asunder: And the earth opened her mouth, and swallowed them up, and their houses, and all the men that appertained unto Korakh, and all their belongings (Numbers 16:31–32).[11]

From this we learn, as Rabbi Berg tells us, that there is no such thing as a "natural disaster" or an "act of God," despite what our insurance policies may tell us. *We* create these disasters by generating too much negativity. The negativity that Korakh created was fragmentation. But by virtue of his possessing free will, he was responsible for the energy he produced, as are all of us for our own doings.

The word *Makhloket*, in English *dispute*, comes from the root *Kh-L-K*, meaning [to] separate. The Torah teaches that those who *kholek all shalom*, "those who dispute (or separate) peace," *kholek all shmo HaKadosh*, "dispute (or separate) His holy name." The Light, as we have learned, has many names. Each name is a channel of a different intensity level. But all of the names of the Light together represent *shalom*—peace—because *shalom* comes from the same root, *Sh-L-M*, meaning *whole* (*Shalem*). Thus, all of the Light's names comprise a unified whole. In the same way, all of the different nations of the world are part of the same unified whole: We are all the sparks of the one Endless Vessel. Each nation may be different; but each is different only in terms of its channeling nature or capacity of the Light. All of these different expressions of the Vessel add up to one unified whole: *shalem* (wholeness), and thus *shalom* (peace). As Rabbi Kaplan expresses it:

[N]o matter how many different ways we experience the Divine, they are all One and all have one source. We recognize that there is a basic Oneness in the universe and beyond, and in our search for the transcendental, it is precisely this Oneness that we are seeking. We see in God the most absolute Unity imaginable, the Oneness that unifies all creation (*Jewish Meditation*, p. 126).

---

11. Refer to Rabbi Berg's recorded lectures: "How to Bring Moshiach In to Our Lives" and "*Korach-Chukat*."

"No one has to agree with everyone," explains Rabbi Berg. "However, the fact that we are not completely alike, should not be, says the *Zohar*, a reason for *Makhloket*, for disagreement." How can two opposites be part of the same whole? Just look at the bulb, which wonderously creates light. The fact that the bulb contains two poles that are opposites is no reflection on separation.

BEIT HILLEL AND BEIT SHAMMAI

There were even two schools of Jewish thought—two schools that explained the Oral Torah and established rules of *Halakhah* (1st century B.C.E.–2nd century C.E.). The first, *"Beit Hillel"* ("The House of Hillel"), was more compassionate and permissive, whereas the second, *"Beit Shammai"* ("The House of Shammai") was more restrictive and severe. The first would decree that an action was permitted, while the second would say that it is forbidden. According to the *Zohar*, Hillel and Shammai were each coming from their own frame of reference or level of consciousness: Hillel was from the Right Column and Shammai was from the Left Column. But since the two schools were not in conflict, it was declared that *both* were right. So, even while the first would answer "yes" to a *Halakhic* question and the second "no," the Torah says that *both* are the word of God and both are correct answers.[12]

Thus, according to the Torah, if a dispute is raised "in the name of Heaven" and it is a dispute, like the bulb, to create harmony and a unified whole—both parties are declared right. However, if a dispute of differences is initiated "in the name of Heaven" that brings the parties apart, it not only brings in the name of God (Who is wholeness and thus peace), but it also brings in Satan.

The internal energy of Satan is division, fragmentation, and lack of peace. In this instance, says the Torah, both parties are wrong. This is why such "holy wars" as the medieval Christian Crusades, *"Holy* Inquisition," or the Moslem Jihads are wrong: They are not, by definition, "in the name of God." They may draw in the name of God, but their focus of fragmentation operates only Satan.

---

12. Refer to Rabbi Berg's recorded lecture on "Relationships."

Hitler's method of managing the men appointed to carry out the "final solution" proffers a prime example of fragmentation. As Joseph Carr records, Hitler "carefully calculated" his method to keep his men

> squabbling with each other so much that they could never combine against him to stage a *coup*. Toward this end, he intentionally issued vague orders and created overlapping jurisdictions (*The Twisted Cross*, p. 125).

Irrespective of one's position, if the position is that "only *my* position is the correct one and the other's is wrong," like Korakh, the world cannot exist—its balance is disrupted. Such a position immediately shuts out the Light, which is our Life Force. And, therefore, divisions that we see in the form of war or Holocaust are only the *result* of man's negative actions. If man's head is not on *shalom*, on peace and wholeness, what follows is Satan.

Thus Satan is not the enemy. Satan is merely the *result* of our short circuitness. Satan always goes where there is *Makhloket*, dispute, and not a condition of one unified whole. Satan goes where two people or two groups cannot live along side one another.[13]

In his book *The Twisted Cross*, Joseph Carr notes, "In a twisted and demonic way the church abetted Hitler's slaughter of the Jewish people" (p. 197). As a Christian, Carr rightfully bemoans the fact that

> The church the world over is split into denominations, factions and splinter groups that rarely have anything to do with each other, except to throw mud. Doctrinal, liturgical and mere procedural disputes have caused antagonism among Christians that comforts only Satan. Sometimes, our differences are so acute that no communication at all is possible. It can be said that it is so difficult to hear the voice of the shepherd over the constant bleating of the sheep. Such was true of the church in Europe prior to World War II (ibid., p. 199).

---

13. Taken from Rabbi Berg's "*Korach-Chukat*" recorded lesson.

And, unfortunately, such is just as true of Judaism before World War II as it is today. It also accounts for the state of most nations today in the world—fragmentation.

THE SNAKE

The third chapter of Genesis tells of another form or expression of Satan—the snake. As we discussed in chapter 4, the snake refers to an energy—the energy, or angel, of death. The *Zohar* defines the snake as the "Evil Inclination"—the Desire to Receive for the Self Alone.

The snake tells Eve about the "fruit" of the Tree of Knowledge of Good and Evil:

> Ye will surely not die. For God doth know, that, on the day ye eat thereof, your eyes will be opened, and ye will be as God, knowing good and evil (Genesis 3:4–5).

To "die" in the Language of the Branches means to sever oneself from the Tree of Life.[14] Before the Fall, Adam and Eve, who were either halves of the complete Vessel, were connected to the level of consciousness of the Tree of Life and, thus, were not connected to any lack, evil or darkness. The level of the Tree of Knowledge of Good and Evil, which is of *Malkhut*, already existed—but was below Adam and Eve, who were at the level of *Ze'ir Anpin*. The snake, however, was of the bottom of the level of *Malkhut*. Therefore, Adam and Eve knew the snake was really speaking the truth: they knew death (via *Malkhut*) was right before them in potential, and they had the power to transcend its power of evil (Desire to Receive for the Self Alone), which is its effect of death.

The snake is not quite the "trickster" that Carl Jung would have us believe.[15] Both Adam and Eve knew that what the snake was in essence telling them was that the very reason for the cre-

---

14. Conversely, "the Resurrection of the Dead" means a reconnection to The Tree of Life. Physical life and death are effected by spiritual life and death, respectively.

15. C. G. Jung, *Four Archetypes: Mother, Rebirth, Spirit, Trickster*.

ation of the Vessel (per the Thought of Creation) and why Adam and Eve were in the Garden of Eden in the first place, was in fact to "eat" from the Tree of Knowledge of Good and Evil. The only way *Tikkun* could be completely fulfilled, so that the totality of the Light could be revealed as it had been in the Endless, would be when the Vessel (Adam and Eve) would take the greatest Desire to Receive, and would then convert it into the Desire to Receive for the Sake of Sharing.

In short, Adam's and Eve's very purpose of being in the Garden of Eden was precisely to eat from (connect to) the Tree of Knowledge of Good and Evil. There is nothing of the Tree of Life to correct (on which to fulfill *Tikkun*). *Tikkun* can only be accomplished at the level of the Tree of Knowledge of Good and Evil, where there is, by definition, Good and Evil. And this is accomplished only when one connects to the lower level, resists the Evil aspect (the Desire to Receive for the Self Alone) and takes only the Good aspect (Right Column, sharing): to take the Good and resist the Evil.

While the snake was actually speaking truth, he was speaking only a half truth, which is why he is said to have deceived Adam and Eve. The snake "seduced" Eve in to connecting to the level of the Tree of Knowledge of Good and Evil on Friday afternoon,[16] the time of day when Left Column energy (negativity) is predominant. If Adam and Eve had only waited six more hours, until *Shabbat*, the energy around them, of the Sabbath, would have helped, as opposed to hindering them to make the proper connection and to complete *Tikkun*.

Moreover, the *Zohar* reveals to us that there were two bites that Adam and Eve took of the Tree of Knowledge of Good and Evil. The first bite was okay: it was taken with the intention of exerting Resistance, by rejecting the evil. With the first bite they succeeded. It was the second bite that caused the Fall.

After having successfully exerted Restriction on the first bite, as per the laws of the cosmos, the Light became fully revealed. But Adam and Eve enjoyed It so much that they took the

---

16. The three energy states or periods of the day are discussed in lesson no. 9 of the Kabbalah Beginners Course, under the topic of the "Binding of Isaac."

second bite. By the second time it was no longer for the sake of exerting Restriction to complete *Tikkun*, but rather to feel more of that good and warm Light. That is, the second bite was taken out of a Desire to Receive for the Self Alone. They succumbed to the evil aspect of The Tree of Knowledge of Good and Evil. Thus the Fall.

Just as the Third Aspect of Creation[17] was intended and part of the Thought of Creation, so too was Original Sin and the Fall. The name "Adam" comes from the root *A-D-M*, which is that of the color red, *Adom*. Thus Adam was the Desire to Receive, the Vessel. The name Eve, in Hebrew *Khavah*, comes from the root *Kh-V-H*, which means [to] experience.[18] That is, while they were at the level of *Ze'ir Anpin*—before the Fall—Adam and Eve only perceived of evil, and thus of death, on a potential basis.

To complete the Thought of Creation, Adam and Eve would need to *experience* evil/death, so that they would "crave" the Light and desire to connect back to the Tree of Life. They would have to experience the painful level of the Tree of Knowledge of Good and Evil, which entails trial and error, good and evil, and ups and downs, to eventually, sincerely appreciate the level of the Tree of Life, where there is only Life—a constant energy of positivity. And thus, evil, via Satan and the snake, have a function in the Thought of Creation: to enable the Vessel free choice (free will).[19] As Rabbi Kaplan puts it:

> The purpose of evil is to tempt us and allow us to have free choice. Without the existence of evil, we would have no other choice but to do good and there would be no virtue in the good we do (*Jewish Meditation*, p. 123).

Once one realizes that evil plays a highly important role in God's plan, evil is no longer a threat (ibid.).

---

17. See chapter 1.

18. Many writers, especially non-Hebrew-speaking fiction writers, have evidently confused the Hebrew root *Kh-V-H*, [to] experience, with the root *Kh-Y-H*, [to] live. But this is a mistake: Eve in Hebrew is *Khavah*, not *Khayah*.

19. For more on this subject of the Garden of Eden, consult lesson no. 18 of the Kabbalah Beginners Course.

THE MESSIAH

I will put My law in their inward parts, and in their heart will I write it . . . and they shall teach no more every man his neighbor, and every man his brother, saying: "Know the Lord; for they shall all know Me, from the least of them unto the greatest of them" (Jeremiah 31:32–33).

Kabbalah explains that the ninth day of the Hebrew month of *Av* (*Tisha B'Av*) is the date of a cosmic event in which a particular energy came into being. This energy, like an absolute number, needed definition. If it, being of the energy intensity of $|359|$, is revealed as its negative side (–359), it is called "Satan": as in Hebrew, the letters *Seen* = 300; *Tet* = 9; *Noon* = 50, equal 359. If, however, we insert into this energy our free will (+1), then the energy is revealed as (+358 +1), which is "Messiah": *Mem* = 40; *Shin* = 300; *Yud* = 10; *Khet* = 8, equaling 358. Thus, Satan and Messiah are energies that are opposite sides of the same coin.[20]

Therefore, according to Judaism, the Messiah is not an individual, but rather an energy—a global state of consciousness. Messiah is a state in which the Vessel (all of us collectively) is at the level of the Tree of Life.

The *Zohar*, written in the Language of the Branches, defines that the Messiah "will ride upon a white donkey." This requires deciphering. The word *donkey* in Hebrew is *Khamor*. *Khamor* (*Kh-M-R*) has the same letters as the word for *material*, which is *Khomer* (*Kh-M-R*). Thus, references to donkeys in the Bible are actually code terms for material, or the material, physical realm of the Tree of Knowledge of Good and Evil.

The physical realm is of a Desire to Receive energy (red, negative pole). White, as we have learned, indicates positive energy. Therefore, a "white donkey" connotes a contradiction, indicating a transcendence from the physical (red, negative) realm to that of the level of the Tree of Life. Thus, the total consciousness state,

---

20. See chapter 5 for the discussion on *Gematria*. Incidentally, the word for snake in Hebrew, *Nakhash*, has the exact same *Gematria* (358) as *Mashiakh* (Messiah). Thus, they too, as we have already discovered, are opposites of the same coin: the snake brings the Vessel to the Tree of Knowledge of Good and Evil, whereas the Messiah brings it to the Tree of Life.

called Messiah, will exist when the physical realm has transcended to the level of the Tree of Life, which is *Ze'ir Anpin*, and, therefore, no longer of physical matter.

While Messiah transcends the physical realm—that is, goes from a Desire to Receive to a Desire to Impart—Satan is called a "fallen angel." *Angel*, as we know, denotes a channel for a specific intensity or unit of energy, and *fallen* means descending in consciousness levels from a Desire to Receive to a Desire to Receive for the Self Alone, or Evil (*Rah*). We also say one goes down to Hell, because he refuses to *rise* above his natural inclination, which is a Desire to Receive for the Self Alone.

THE ULTIMATE WAR: THE PHYSICAL VERSUS THE METAPHYSICAL

As we continue to go about our everyday lives, some have this notion that someday, some wonderful figure will appear and save us from this increasingly complex and difficult existence that we have created for ourselves. And, as Rabbi Berg expresses in his recorded lecture "How to Bring *Moshiach* [Messiah] Into Our Lives," these same people are also disillusioned by the idea that the world will be thrilled to pieces and will accept the Messiah with open arms. Not so says the *Zohar*.

The *Zohar*, under the portion of *Shmot* (Exodus), tells us that "in that day, that the Messiah will come out, the whole world will become angry." And then "all of the children of the world will hide," meaning from the Messiah. As we are now in the "Messianic Era," the ultimate war between the consciousness states of the Tree of Knowledge of Good and Evil and of the Tree of Life has already begun. It is a war that we may not be able to see with the naked eye (that is, if we are connected to the Tree of Knowledge of Good and Evil); although it may also manifest itself on the physical via warplanes and firearms. It is a war between the physical and the metaphysical. In Hebrew, this war is called *Gog U'Magog*—in English, *Armageddon*. But regardless of how one calls it, it is already well underway.

If one choses to cling to the physical side of this war, he will inevitably perish. The "physical" comes in a variety of colors and flavors—for example, medicine and law enforcement. Both of these examples may help us; but if we look to them as gods to ultimately save us, we will lose the battle. We can get all the shots and take all the vitamins the doctor prescribes, jog and watch our weight, but as we have seen, a new disease or epidemic can arise and stump all those worshippers of such a false god as medicine, or even of the human body.

Rabbi Kaplan points out that

according to many important Jewish thinkers, the Messianic Age will not be a time of miracles, and no laws of nature will be changed. This is particularly true in the teachings of Maimonides, who states that prophecies that appear to predict miracles actually refer to technological rather than literal miracles [per Commentary on Sanhedrin 10:1. Cf. Melakhim 11:3] (*Immortality, Resurrection, and the Age of the Universe*, p. 23).

So medicine and technology can only constitute a means, if we are already on the right side of the war and prepare an appropriate vessel for this means.

Science, technology and the various security and law enforcement forces are merely *means* by which the Light expresses Itself. As sophisticated as our technology has become, we still have not gotten the upper hand on crime; in fact, the streets are more dangerous today than they have ever been. If it were only a function of money, we could buy the best security system, mace, etcetera, and be set and safe. But, then, a new form of crime—as carjacking did—would just pop up and catch us off guard without the right security paraphernalia. *That* is reality—the reality of the Tree of Knowledge of Good and Evil.

Money, status, university degrees, connections, or good looks will not help the one who clings to the physical to help protect him. As Californians can attest, even the very earth beneath our feet can no longer be trusted to always be "firma." Not the air we breathe. Not the water we drink. And this is just the beginning of Armaggedon. As Kabbalah explains, the greatest revelation of Light follows the greatest darkness. That is why the darkest period of the night is just before dawn.

The cosmic system will continue to pull the rug out from under those who adamantly hold tight to the robotic consciousness of the Tree of Knowledge of Good and Evil. These people will deny the Tree of Life, and that is what the *Zohar* means by the people of the world "hiding" from the Messiah. Moreover, this is why, as the *Zohar* says, the appearance of the Messiah will *anger* the world—because it has already been heralded in and is telling us to accept our spiritual responsibility and alter our state of consciousness.

But Kabbalah does not come to preach fire and brimstone. That would negate the necessity of free will. In fact, as Rabbi Berg says, if one can afford the luxury of retaining robotic consciousness of the physical realm, that is his prerogative. What Kabbalah does is offer us the means or the necessary tools by which each and every one of us can attain and connect to the level of the Tree of Life. There is no coercion in spirituality. Kabbalah in our Messianic Era has become available as a support system to assist us from falling prey to satanic consciousness and to the false gods and hope of the physical world.

The Light is the seed of all. It is whole and complete and unified; thus, as the Ari calls It, It is "simple." What can solve *all* of our problems is the Endless Light, or rather, our connection to It. All fulfillment is from the Light; thus, It answers all our questions and fulfills all lack. The farther we go from the seed or root of a tree, which parallels the Light, to the many branches and leaves, the more complex the tree looks. But each branch and each leaf is only an expression of that one simple seed.

Unfortunately, the tree from which most of us nourish today is the Tree of Knowledge of Good and Evil. This is why some days seem good, while others bad. But those "bad leaves" seem to be exceeding the good ones. And the good ones seem to come fewer and farther between. We can keep picking at the bad leaves of the Tree of Knowledge of Good and Evil; but (as with grey hair!) with every bad leaf that we pick many more sprout up in its place.

In fact, this is why "bad" things happen to good people. A good (sharing) person who gets caught up in the chaotic world of the Tree of Knowledge of Good and Evil is subject to the laws and forces of nature, the stars, and the predetermined universe.[21] One is subject to the laws of the level of consciousness to which he or she *chooses* to connect.

---

21. Taken from Rabbi Berg's "How to Bring *Moshiach* Into Our Lives."

Science has a good term that describes the realm of the Tree of Knowledge of Good and Evil; it is called *entropy*. Dr. Stephen Hawking defines entropy as that "which measures the degree of disorder of a system . . . disorder will tend to increase if things are left to themselves" (*A Brief History of Time*, p. 108).[22] But this is *only* true of the level of the Tree of Knowledge of Good and Evil. The Light is a constant and a unified whole. Therefore, when one connects to the realm of the Tree of Life, there is stability and certainty—no good *and* evil. At the level of the Tree of Life, one transcends the influence of the laws of nature and thus of such laws of chaos as entropy. That is, as we discussed in the Introduction, how Abraham had Isaac when he was one hundred years old, and how Sarah could conceive in her nineties.

What we have learned from our overview of metaphysics is that all doctrines of Left Column energy, the Desire to Receive for Oneself Alone, or Evil (all synonyms) have burned themselves out: Atlantis, the generation of the Tower of Babel, Egypt, and even the more recent Soviet Union. That is the power of evil: It blows its own fuses and destroys its practitioners and even its very soil.

The energy of the Desire to Receive can *give* nothing to its followers, because giving is Right Column energy; nor can it give the energy of circuitry—Central Column energy. Like a drug dealer, Left Column energy gives the illusion of giving, but only so much to where it can drain its devotees of all of their energy. That is its nature: to Receive, that is, to take. And the illusion of drugs is quite apropos, as the *Zohar* calls the Left Column system—the Impure System or the System of the Vessel—the "drug of death."

It is for this reason that it is so difficult to understand why so many today are trying to retap the energies of the Pyramids, the Egyptian gods, and Atlantis, as these are the energies that have caused the greatest short circuits in the history of the world. These are the forces of the Desire to Receive for the Self Alone, of Evil. They are destructive, because they are antithetical to the Thought of Creation.

---

22. Thus, when Dr. Hawking asks: "Why does disorder increase in the same direction of time as that in which the universe expands?" (p. 153), it is because time and this question are connected to the illusionary world of the Tree of Knowledge of Good and Evil.

As he notes in his book on Nazism, Joseph Carr points out:

Hitler's occultic involvement was nurtured by the occultic revival that swept over Europe and America in the late 19th century . . . the same philosophies and theories [are] still in vogue today, and indeed some of the same groups and personalities that fueled Hitler's occultism are still popular . . . this movement has a name . . . and has essentially the same philosophy and program as Naziism: it is called the "New Age Movement" (*The Twisted Cross*, p. 274).

It is the System of the Vessel.
Dennis Prager, while really speaking for all, expresses:

The lesson for Jews is as clear as it is painful. Moral disaster is inevitable when religious Jews forget the primacy of ethics and abandon the Jews' ethical monotheist mission, and when secular Jews think that ethics can survive the death of religion and monotheism ("The Case for Ethical Monotheism," p. 23).

Kabbalah, though, would rename Prager's objective to the "Tree of Life." However, Prager does acknowledge:

Ethical monotheism is not natural. Nature worship is natural, not the worship of an invisible Creator of nature. Feeling no moral accountability is more natural, and certainly more pleasant, than being taught that you are morally accountable and judged for every one of your deeds (ibid., p. 29).

As this twentieth century draws to a close, have we not learned the most obvious lesson of this century, that all attempts to change the world that do not place God and goodness at their center will make a worse world? (ibid., p. 26).

The energy of Satan is that of the vacuum. Darkness, which is synonymous with the energy of Satan, is merely a lack of Light. Satan is an illusion and a nonentity. It is like when one walks into a dark room. The only way to get rid of the physical darkness is to turn on the light. Per the physical (and metaphysical) law of the conservation of energy, if darkness were an entity, then it could not just disappear. That is why Kabbalah flatly calls darkness an illusion.[23]

One might also note that the energy of the light—electricity—is already in the room. To illuminate the room, one merely needs to complete the closing of the circuit, by flipping the switch. Metaphysical darkness works the same way: the way to rid the world of darkness is by revealing the Light.

The Light is everywhere and in all things. But in this physical world, like in the dark room, It must be concealed. It is our job to close the metaphysical circuit of energy to reveal this Light, and when we do, darkness will inevitably disappear. And, as we have already said, this illumination from darkness is called Messiah.

Despair is an effect of metaphysical darkness. The fact that there is so much darkness in the world has left many of us with a sense of despair. Darkness is a vicious, self-perpetuating cycle. But just like in a room, one does not battle the darkness. Again, to get rid of darkness, one simply needs to turn on the Light.

God tells us that He has set before us "life and death . . . therefore choose life, that thou mayest live, both thou and thy seed" (Deuteronomy 30:19). Life comes from the Tree of Life. And only at the level of the Tree of Life is there peace on earth and goodwill towards our fellow human beings. Let us, therefore, help one another attain this and *choose life*. Amen.

---

23. Refer to Rabbi Berg's "How To Bring *Moshiach* Into Our Lives."

References

Aranoff, Stanford. "The Age of the World." In Carmell, *Challenge*. First published in *Intercom* (August 1962): 150–163.

Ashlag, Rabbi Yehuda. *Kabbalah: A Gift of the Bible*. Trans. Dr. Samuel R. Anteby. Jerusalem: Research Centre of Kabbalah, 1984.

Bach, Richard. *The Bridge Across Forever: A Lovestory*. New York: William Morrow and Company, 1984.

———. *Illusions: The Adventures of a Reluctant Messiah*. New York: Dell, 1977.

———. *One: A Novel*. New York: Dell, 1988.

Ben Isaiah, Rabbi Abraham, and Rabbi Benjamin Sharfman in collaboration with Dr. Harry M. Orlinsky and Rabbi Dr. Morris Charner. *The Pentateuch and Rashi's Commentary: A Linear Translation into English—Genesis*. Brooklyn: S.S.& R. Publishing Co., 1949.

Berg, Philip S., "*Brit Milah*." Nos. 1–2. New York: The Kabbalah Centre.

———. "How to Bring *Moshiach* into Our Lives." New York: The Kabbalah Centre.

———. *Reincarnation: The Wheels of a Soul*. Jerusalem: Research Centre of Kabbalah, 1984.

————. *Kabbalah for the Layman: A Guide to Cosmic Consciousness*. Jerusalem: Research Centre of Kabbalah Press, 1981.

————. *Kabbalah for the Layman: A Guide to Cosmic Consciousness*, Vol. II. Jerusalem: Research Centre of Kabbalah Press, 1988.

————. "Passover." Nos. 1–5. New York: The Kabbalah Centre.

————. *Power of Aleph Beth*. Vol. I. New York: Research Centre of Kabbalah, 1988.

————. *Power of Aleph Beth*. Vol. II. New York: Research Centre of Kabbalah, 1988.

————. "*Shoftim*: Four Kinds of Judgement; Witnessing in Court." New York: The Kabbalah Centre.

————. "Soulmates and Relationships." New York: The Kabbalah Centre.

————. "Spiritual Insights Into the Rise of Neo-Nazism." New York: The Kabbalah Centre.

————. *The Star Connection: The Science of Judaic Astrology*. New York: Research Centre of Kabbalah, 1986.

————. "Talmud–Baba Metzia." New York: The Kabbalah Centre.

————. "Ten Luminous Emanation—No. 466." New York: The Kabbalah Centre, 1993.

—. *Time Zones: Your Key to Control*. New York: Research Centre of Kabbalah, 1990.

————. *To The Power of One*. New York: Research Centre of Kabbalah, 1991.

————. *The Zohar: Parashat Pinhas*. Vol. I. Ed. and trans. Berg. Jerusalem: Research Center of Kabbalah Press, 1986.

————. "*Zohar: Bereshit*." Nos. 1–6. New York: The Kabbalah Centre.

————. "*Zohar: Ekev-Vaetchnan*." No. 1. New York: The Kabbalah Centre.

————. "*Zohar: Korach-Chukat*." Nos. 1–2. New York: The Kabbalah Centre.

————. "*Zohar: Vayakhel-Pinhas*." Nos. 1–2. New York: The Kabbalah Centre.

Bettelheim, Bruno. *The Uses of Enchantment: The Meaning and Importance of Fairy Tales*. London: Penguin, 1988.

Brontë, Charlotte. *Jane Eyre*. New York: Signet, 1960.

Brontë, Emily. *Wuthering Heights*. Harmondsworth: Penguin, 1965.

Carmell, Aryeh, and Domb, Cyril, eds. *Challenge: Torah Views on Science and Its Problems*. 2nd, rev. ed. New York: Feldheim, 1978.

Carr, Joseph J. *The Twisted Cross*. Lafayette, Louisiana: Huntington House, 1985.

Dessler, Rabbi E. "The Inner Meaning of the Creation." In Carmell, *Challenge*. First published in *Michtav Me-Eliyahu*, Vol. II: 138–140.

Dostoyevsky, Fyodor. *The Brothers Karamazov*. Trans. Constance Garnett. New York: Random, 1950.

———. *Crime and Punishment*. New York: Random House, 1950.

Gershom, Rabbi Yonassan. *Beyond the Ashes: Cases of Reincarnation from the Holocaust*. Virginia Beach: A.R.E. Press, 1992.

Glazerson, Rabbi Matityahu. *From Hinduism To Judaism*. Jerusalem: Yerid Hasfarim, 1990.

Hawking, Dr. Stephen W. *A Brief History of Time: From the Big Bang to Black Holes*. New York: Bantam, 1989.

Hildebrand, Joel H. and Richard E. Powell, PhDs. *Principles of Chemistry*. 6th ed. New York: Macmillan Co., 1952.

Hodges, John C. and Mary E. Whitten. *Harbrace College Handbook*. 10th ed. Orlando: Harcourt Brace Jovanovich, 1986.

Isaac of Akko, Rabbi. "Selections from Ozar ha-Hayyim." In *Immortality, Resurrection, and the Age of the Universe* by Rabbi Aryeh Kaplan. Hoboken, NJ: KTAV Publishing House: 1993.

Jung, C.G. *Four Archtypes: Mother, Rebirth, Spirit, Trickster*. Trans. R.F.C. Hull. Princeton: Princeton University Press, 1973.

"Kabbalah and Medicine." New York: The Kabbalah Centre, 1994.

Kahaner, Larry. *Cults That Kill: Probing the Underworld of Occult Crime*. New York: Warner, 1988.

Kamert, Yuval, ed. *Yudaica Lexicon*. Jerusalem: Keter, 1976.

Kaplan, Rabbi Aryeh (Moshe Eliyahu ben Shmuel). *Immortality, Resurrection, and the Age of The Universe: A Kabbalistic View*. Hoboken, NJ: KTAV Publishing House, 1993.

———. *Innerspace: Introduction to Kabbalah, Meditation and Prophecy*. Ed. Abraham Sutton. Jerusalem: Moznaim, 1990.

———. *Jewish Meditation: A Practical Guide*. New York: Schocken, 1985.

———. *Waters of Eden: An Exploration of the Concept of Mikvah Renewal and Rebirth*. New York: NCSY, 1982.

Klahr, Carl N. "Science versus Scientism." *Carmell*: 288–295.

Kushi, Michio. *An Introduction to Oriental Diagnosis: Your Face Never Lies*. Ed. William Tara and David Lasocki. Wayne, NJ: Avery Publishing, 1983.

Kushner, Lawrence. *God was in this Place and I, i did not know: Finding Self, Spirituality and Ultimate Meaning*. Woodstock, VT: Jewish Lights Publishing, 1991.

Larson, Bob. *Satanism: The Seduction of America's Youth*. Nashville: Thomas Nelson Publishers, 1989.

Lemonick, Michael D. "Hawking Gets Personal." *Time* Sept. 27, 1993: 80.

Levi, Leo. "The Uncertainty Principle and the Wisdom of the Creator." In Carmell, *Challenge*. First published (in Hebrew) in *Hamma 'Yan* (Tammuz 5731) [1971]: 296–304.

Lipschitz, Rabbi Israel. "*Derush Or ha-Hayyim*: A Theological Reflection on Death, Resurrection, and the Age of the Universe." From a sermon delivered in 1842, trans. and ann. Yaakov Elman. Danzig (Gdansk), 1842. In Kaplan, *Immortality*.

Litvin, Baruch, ed. *The Sanctity of the Synagogue: the Case For Mechitzah—Separation Between Men and Women in the Synagogue—Based on Jewish Law, History and Philosophy, From Sources Old and New*. Mount Clemens, Michigan: Baruch and Ida Litvin, 1959.

Luria, Rabbi Isaac. *The Kabbalah: A Study of the Ten Luminous Emanations*. Trans. Rabbi Levi I. Krakovsky (z"l) vol. I. Jerusalem: Research Centre of Kabbalah Press, 1969.

———. *Gates of Reincarnation* (Hebrew). Tel Aviv: Yeshivat Ohr Khozer, 1986.

———. *The Kabbalah: A Study of the Ten Luminous Emanations: Circles and Straightness*. Vol. II. Comp. and ed. Rabbi Dr. Philip S. Berg. Jerusalem: Research Centre of Kabbalah Press, 1973.

Man, Myth & Magic: The Illustrated Encyclopedia of Mythology, Religion and the Unknown. Vol. 9, ed. Richard Cavendish. New York: Marshall Cavendish, 1983.

Marsh, Jeffrey. "Physics vs. Metaphysics." *Commentary* 96: 5 (1993).

Melville, Herman. *Moby Dick: Or the Whale*. New York: Random House, 1930.

Milton, John. "Paradise Lost," in *Paradise Lost, Samson Agonistes, Lycidas*. New York: New American Library, 1961.

Moody, Raymond A., Jr. *Life After Life: The Investigation of a Phe-*

nomenon—Survival of Bodily Death. New York: Bantam, 1990.

Nigal, Gedalyah. *Magic, Mysticism, and Hasidism: The Supernatural in Jewish Thought*. Trans. Edward Levin. Northvale, NJ: Jason Aronson, 1994.

Orwell, George. *1984*. New York: Signet, 1949.

Pirsig, Robert M. *Zen and the Art of Motocycle Maintenance: An Inquiry Into Values*. New York: Morrow Quill, 1974.

Prager, Dennis. "The Case For Ethical Monotheism," *Ultimate Issues* 7:3 (1991).

Rinpoche, Sogyal. *The Tibetan Book of Living and Dying*. Ed. Patrick Gaffney and Andrew Harvey. San Francisco: Harper, 1992.

Rosenberg, Moshe. "Kabbalah For Beginners—English." Nos. 1–12, 18–19 (audio cassettes). New York: The Kabbalah Centre.

Schroeder, Gerald L., Ph.D. *Genesis and the Big Bang: The Discovery of Harmony Between Modern Science and the Bible*. New York: Bantam, 1990.

Schwab, Rabbi Simon. "How Old is the Universe?" in Carmell, *Challenge*. First published in *Mitteilungen* (April/May 1962): 164–174.

Shelley, Mary. *Frankenstein: Or the Modern Prometheus*. Ed. M.K. Joseph. Oxford: Oxford University Press, 1985.

Skelton, Robin. *The Practice of Witchcraft Today: An Introduction to Beliefs and Rituals of the Old Religion*. London: Hale, 1988.

Sklar, Dusty. *Gods and Beasts: The Nazis and the Occult*. New York: Thomas Y. Crowell Company, 1977.

Steinsaltz, Rabbi Adin. *The Essential Talmud*. Trans. Chaya Galai. New York: Basic Books, 1976.

Vainstein, Yaacov. *The Cycle of the Jewish Year: A Study of the Festivals and of Selections From the Liturgy*. Jerusalem: World Zionist Organization, 1976.

Weiss, Brian L. *Many Lives, Many Masters*. New York: Simon & Schuster, 1988.

Walker, Alice. *The Color Purple*. New York: Pocket Books, 1982.

Webster's II New Riverside University Dictionary. 1984.

Wright, Ronald. *Stolen Continents: The Americas Through Indian Eyes Since 1492*. New York: Houghton Mifflin, 1992.

Youdkevich, Shaul. "Kabbalah and UFOs." New York: The Kabbalah Centre, 1994.

Index

About the Author

Nekhama Schoenburg has taught, researched and studied Kabbalah in Israel and North America (classes taught in the U.S. in coordination with Rabbi Philip Berg's Kabbalah Centre). She currently studies Kabbalah at the Sulam Raphael Center, headed by Rabbi Daniel Stawsky HaCohen (student of Rabbi Mordechai Shineberger), and is preparing a number of articles about the Jewish holidays from the perspective of Kabbalah, under the tutelage of her rabbi.

A graduate of Tel Aviv University, Ms. Schoenburg has published a number of articles in English and American Literature. She is employed at Israel Aircraft Industries and lives on Moshav Tzafria in Israel.

DATE DUE